IMAGES
of America

HARRISON TOWNSHIP
MICHIGAN

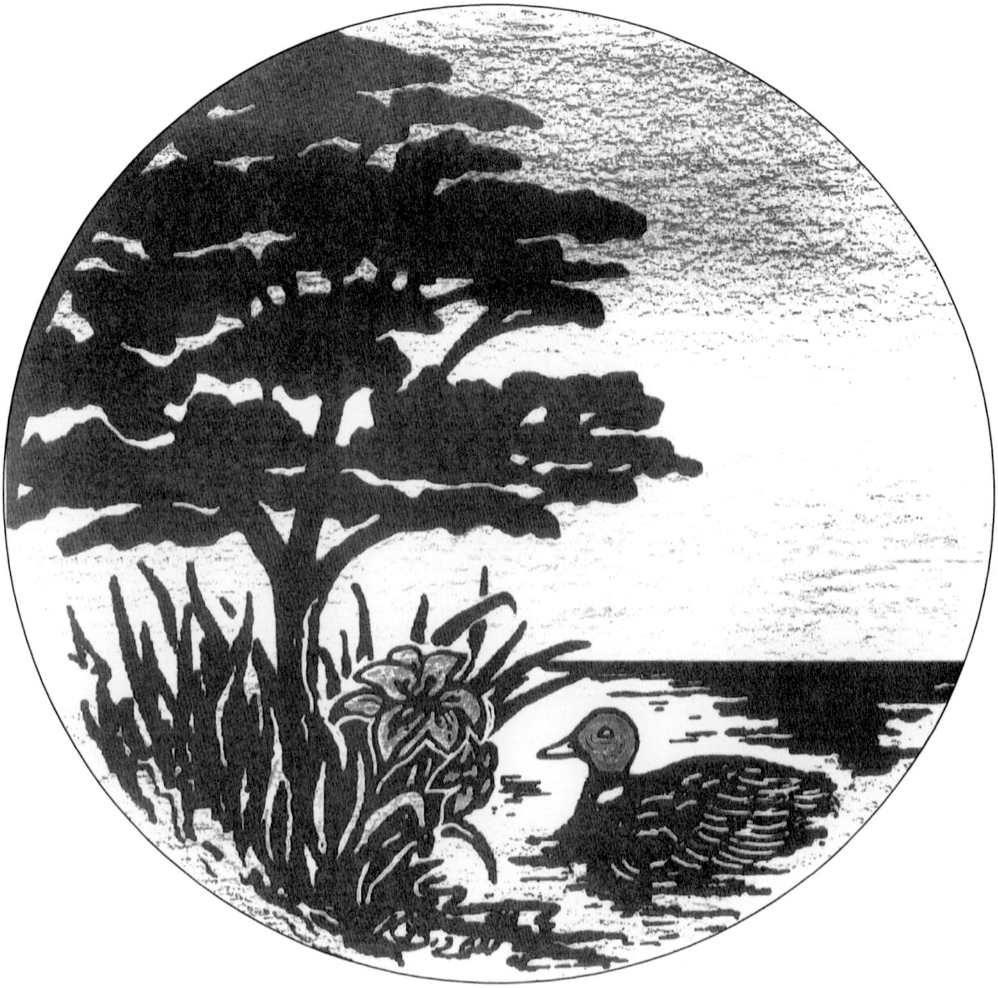

In September of 1988, the Harrison Township Beautification Commission presented their choices for township symbols to the Board of Trustees. After unanimously accepting the suggestion that the tiger lily, mallard duck, and sunburst locust tree be adopted, the board created a contest for the best logo design that incorporated the new symbols. The logo seen here, designed by Kaye Bizon, is a tribute to the beauty of this waterfront community.

IMAGES
of America

HARRISON TOWNSHIP
MICHIGAN

Marie Ling McDougal

ARCADIA
PUBLISHING

ISBN 978-0-7385-1925-8

Published by Arcadia Publishing
Charleston, South Carolina

Printed in the United States of America

Library of Congress Catalog Card Number: 2001093324

For all general information contact Arcadia Publishing at:
Telephone 843-853-2070
Fax 843-853-0044
E-mail sales@arcadiapublishing.com
For customer service and orders:
Toll-Free 1-888-313-2665

Visit us on the Internet at www.arcadiapublishing.com

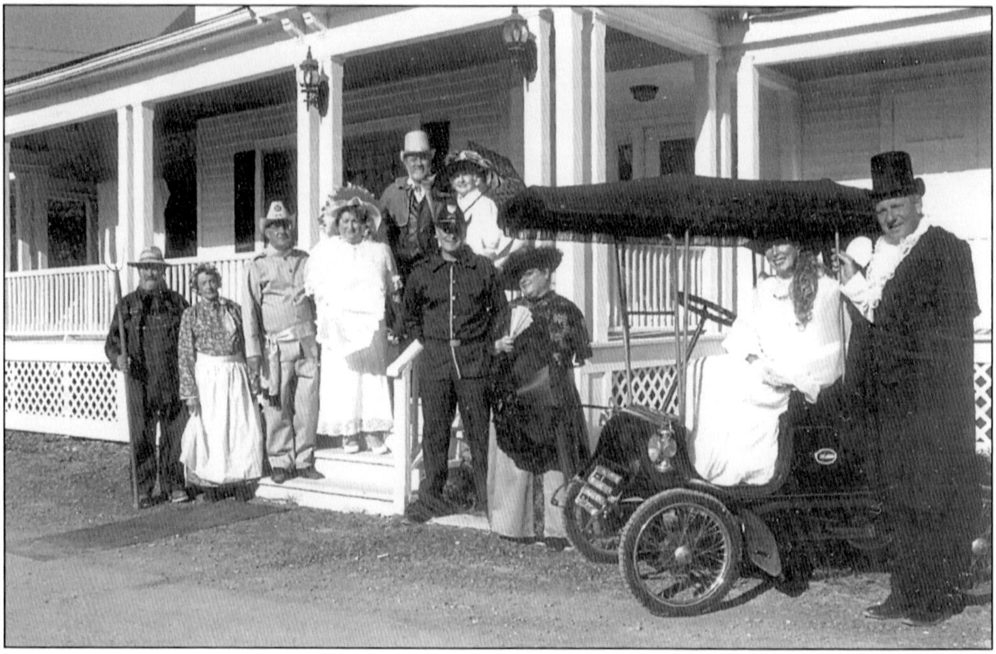

This book is dedicated to the hard work and persistence of the Harrison Township Historical Commission. Since 1993 commissioners and members have devoted their time and talents to collecting and preserving township history in pictures and anecdotes. Here Bob Ballard, Shirley Hosler, Tom Gregor, Linda Karczewski, Jeff Minch, Ruthee Cowan, Chuck Pierce, Marie McDougal, Jack and Ann Peeler's 1902 Cadillac, Peggy Kennard, and Dave Scott pose in vintage dress beside what has been known for decades as the Verschaeve farmhouse. The 131-year-old house is being renovated as part of the new Brigantine Estates. Members Beverly and Randy Tromley, Allene Clemons, and Barbara Urban are not pictured but are equally important to commission efforts. This book is also in memory of Eleanor Buchman and Margaret MacLeod.

Contents

ACKNOWLEDGMENTS

The Harrison Township Historical Commission would like to thank all of the people, businesses, and organizations who supplied us with the pictures used here and the information that made this book a unique tribute to the first 175 years of the township. Thanks to Steve Aston, Bob Ballard, Sue Balow, Jack Beaber, Boca Grande Marina, Donna Bolster, Eleanor Buchman, Jane Buchman, Julie Buchman, Henry and Rita Callewaert, Perry Calisi, Linda Claeys, Clinton River Cruise Line, Ruthee Cowan, the Crook family, Joe Duggan, Clarence Gentz, Mr. and Mrs. Howard Harder, Harrison at Metro Church, Harrison Twp. Fire Department, Jack Hart, Tom Havey, Ron Heck, Shirley Hosler, Island Cove Marina, Rick Jantz (Eagles), Hazel Jarvis, Ronald Keine, Knox Presbyterian Church, Cal and Diane LaForest, Allene Lee, Nelly Longstaff, Bert Lozen, Macomb County Historical Society, Markley Marine, Don and Dolores Marlowe, James Pershing (Metropolitan Beach), Don Moore, New Apostolic Church, North Star Sail Club, Ann Nowicki, Chuck Pierce, Ken MacCarroll (The Old Crowd), Ron Parker, Larry Peplin, Paul Remillard, Minnie Rickert, Beverly Rivard, Jack and Arlene Rood, Betty Rumble, St. Hubert Catholic Church, St. John Hospital—Macomb Center, Claude Saum, Sandy Schwab, Selfridge Military Air Museum, Sheila Streu, Shirley Thomas, Beverly Tromley, Barb Urban, Brian Wegner, Phyllis Wellman, the Wollborg family, Don Worrell (Mt. Clemens Public Library), and Magdalen Ziolkowski. Since mistakes are bound to happen in a project like this, special thanks to those who have unintentionally been omitted from this list and to all who provided the funds to keep the commission functioning for eight years. I would like to thank our photographer, Mike Robinson (Robinson Photography), and above all, graphic artist Pete Williams (PAW Graphics), whose unwavering patience made this book possible.

This book is not a definitive history of the township. The families, businesses, organizations, and events pictured here are representative of all people, places, and great times that have made Harrison Township what it is. Hopefully those same families can make it even better in the decades to come.

The cover photo, which formerly hung on the wall in the township home of Mr. and Mrs. Howard Harder, is an excellent example of the importance of the preservation of family history. Although the Harders could not identify the relative in the picture, the Denmarsh Hotel is easily identified. The hotel was once the end of the road for travelers on North River. It was, according to an early *Cutter's Guide*, "an ideal place to spend a week hunting and fishing."

INTRODUCTION

Strangely enough, Harrison Township's history can be traced to a Virginia homestead in 1754. While working on the family farm, 11-year-old William Tucker and his younger brother, Joseph, watched as their father was murdered and his scalp sold. The boys were taken captive by members of the Chippewa Indian tribe and brought to this area as members of the tribe. Unfortunately, Joseph became the first white man known to the Native Americans to have died when his canoe tipped or drifted away on a hunting trip. William, however, went on to become the first English speaking white settler in Macomb County.

Tucker was given his freedom when he was 18, but he still took his dual heritage seriously. He served as an interpreter for the British but with an eye toward protecting the interests of his Native-American family. During the Pontiac uprising, he helped save the fort at Detroit. He used information given to him by his Indian sister to warn the commander and stayed on to fight. He served during the Revolution as a captain in the American militia. His presence in the area was an asset to relations between the settlers and the Native Americans, and his home became a center for township activities.

In 1780 Tucker was rewarded for his loyalty to the Chippewa. He was given all the land he could walk around in one day. Reports differ on the amount of land he received, but the number most quoted is 3,300 acres. Many of those acres are today within the bounds of Selfridge Air National Guard Base, but the family home remains in its riverfront location. It is believed to be the oldest house in Michigan, but it is no longer a log cabin. Its many exterior changes over the years make it hard to distinguish from the newer homes in the area.

Tucker stories abound including a landmark lawsuit involving his slaves and their children. Since Tucker had ten children of his own, many county residents can trace their roots to the pioneer family. His descendants went on to find their own places in township and county history and politics.

Although Tucker can be considered the township founder, the beginning of local politics dates to the meeting held on May 28, 1827, in the home of Charles Peltier Jr. The executive decree of 1818 had created a Harrison Township, but it included a great deal of the territory to the north of today's township and excluded the south side of the river. In 1827, however, the county was laid off under legislative enactment, creating townships much like those that exist today.

Once the government was established, Harrison was on its way to becoming the boating center it is today and the home of Selfridge Air National Guard Base and Metropolitan Beach Metropark. This book provides a look back at the people and places of the past and the efforts that went into making this a township its residents can be proud to call home.

The pictures used in this book are representative of the many family and business photos lent to the historical commission for copying in order to preserve a time gone by but not forgotten. In Chapter One the reader looks back at the failed efforts to create cities within the township. The commission is still seeking pictures of the City of Belvidere and the logging town of Liverpool. Luckily the resort of Lakeside was well documented in postcards and family albums.

Chapter Two is a brief look at government buildings and the people who kept the township running. These include full time, part time, and volunteer workers.

The township was originally divided into strip farms. Chapter Three salutes the brave and dedicated farmers as well as the boating industry and small businesses that have provided livings for residents across the decades.

The history of a waterfront community would not be complete without Chapter Four. It looks at the sights along the river and lake. Of course, Mother Nature has created her own sights due to cycles of low and high water and ice jams.

Chapter Five takes the reader back to the days of the one and two-room schoolhouses. From the early missionaries to the fledgling congregation of Harrison at Metro Church, which is currently saving money for its own church building, religion has played a part in the lives of township residents. This chapter looks at the growth of both education and religion.

Log cabins, farmhouses, summer retreats—the houses of the township have a charm of their own. They don't become homes, however, until they are filled with people, families. Chapter Six takes a look at the changes generations of those families have made on the face of the community.

Chapter Seven is dedicated to two major attractions that have brought residents and visitors to the shores of Lake St. Clair. Selfridge Air National Guard Base and Metropolitan Beach Metropark have given the township a distinct reputation that extends far beyond the local scene.

"The Gateway to Water Fun," is the township motto, but fun can be found in many ways and places. From the early fishing, hunting, and gun clubs to fraternal organizations to Gowanie Golf Course and Total Sports, the township has always offered leisure time activities for all tastes.

The township continues to grow and change. The last chapter provides a look at some of those changes, big and small. In 2002 the township will celebrate its 175th anniversary and look to the future in hopes of preserving the past.

Sources

Building a Base: Selfridge and the Army

Cutter's Guides to Mount Clemens

History of Macomb County

Mount Clemens Library history files

Pageant of Progress

Past and Present of Macomb County, Michigan

When Eastern Michigan Rode the Rails

One

Lost Villages and Resorts

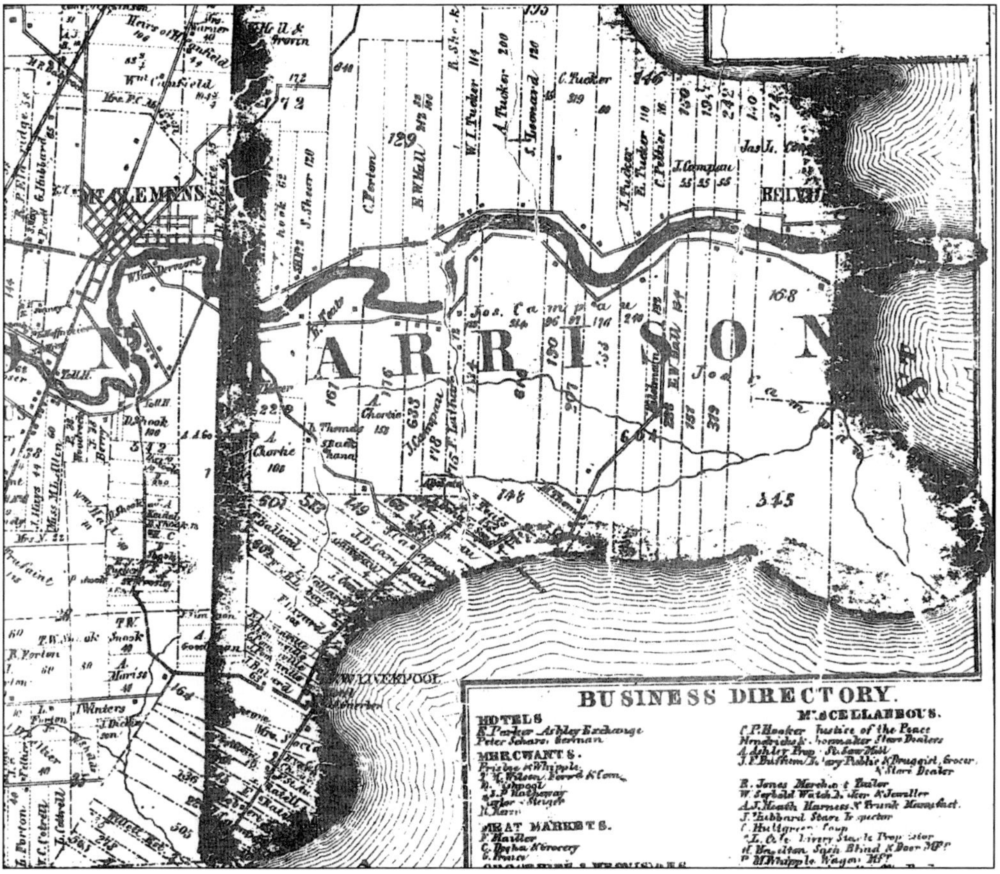

In February of 1856, David Shook acquired land at what is now Shook and Jefferson. He surveyed the property and filed a map for the city of New Liverpool. Shook declared it would be a lumbering port to rival Mount Clemens, St. Clair, and even Detroit. Lots were sold for $90–$100. Unfortunately, by the turn of the century, Liverpool had fallen victim to the devastation of pestilence, disease, fire, and flood.

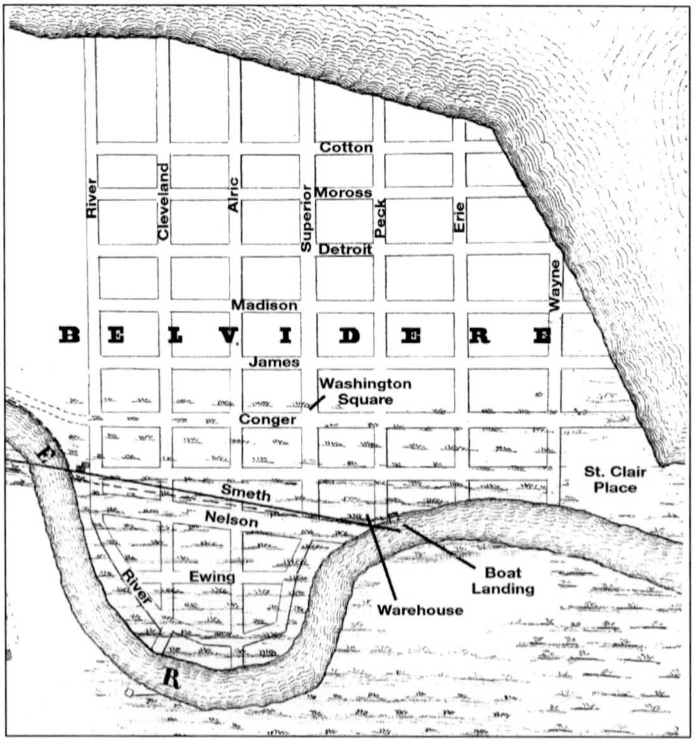

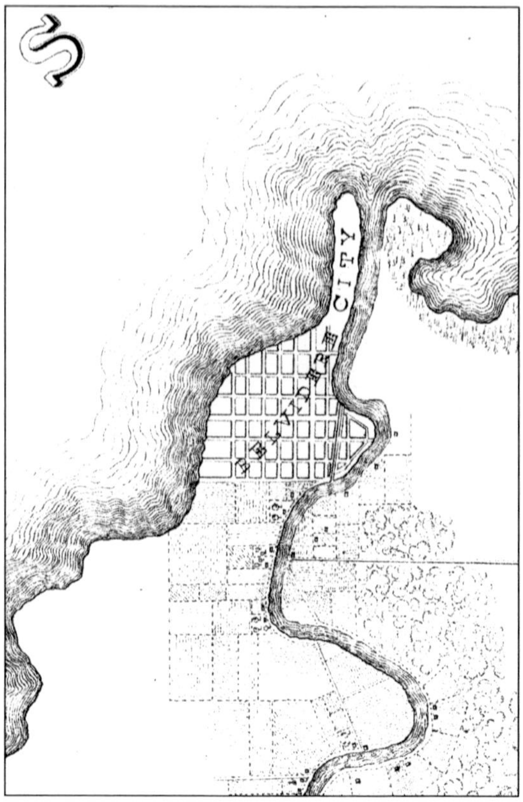

James Conger had a dream—to build "the queen city of the lower lakes." In 1835 he chose his site on the northern banks at the mouth of the Clinton River. He predicted that his Belvidere would outclass the "saw-buzzy" town of Christian Clemens. By 1838, the town was described as "a post office recently established, a sub-collector's office, a steam sawmill, a store and storehouse, a tavern, several mechanics, and some 12 or 15 dwellings." Many factors kept Conger from realizing his dream but the key was lake levels. Legend says that an old Chippewa chief predicted the downfall. He warned, "No can stay. Water come high, wash away. Almost time. Every 35 years—always come." And so it did. Perhaps Conger would be proud of today's Venice Shores subdivision, which fights back with sandbags, pumps, and hip boots.

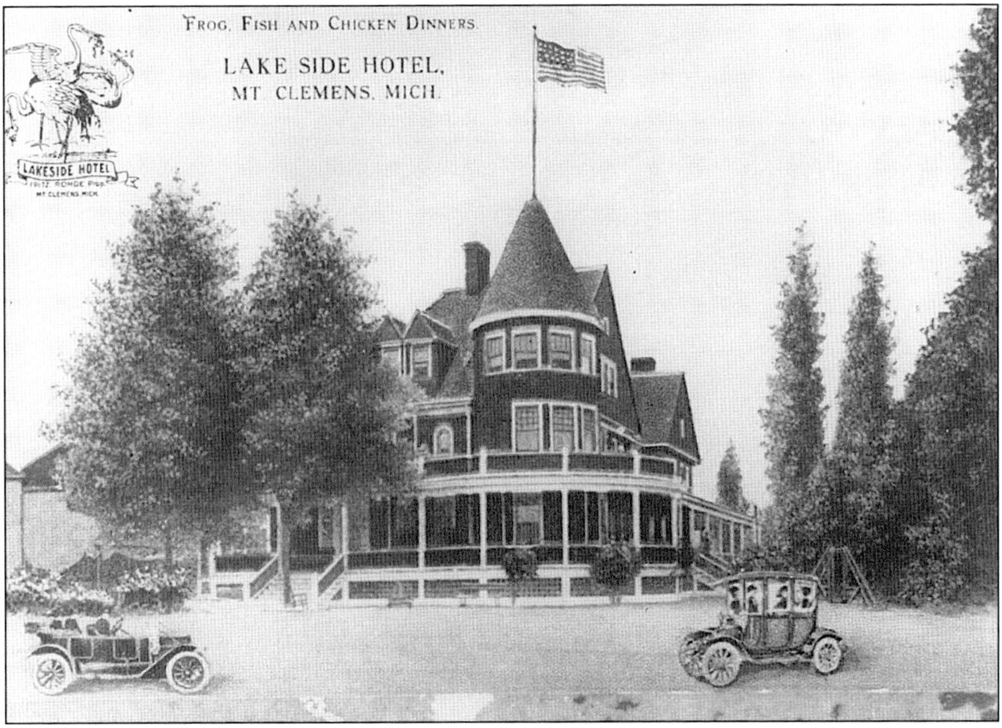

In the mid-1890s, a group of Pittsburgh capitalists, ignoring the fate of earlier township ports, founded the city of Lakeside. On Jefferson at the foot of Crocker, the resort town flourished thanks to the fame of Mount Clemens as a mineral bath spa. The Lakeside Hotel lured visitors with its promise of cool lake breezes, lively entertainment, and excellent frog legs.

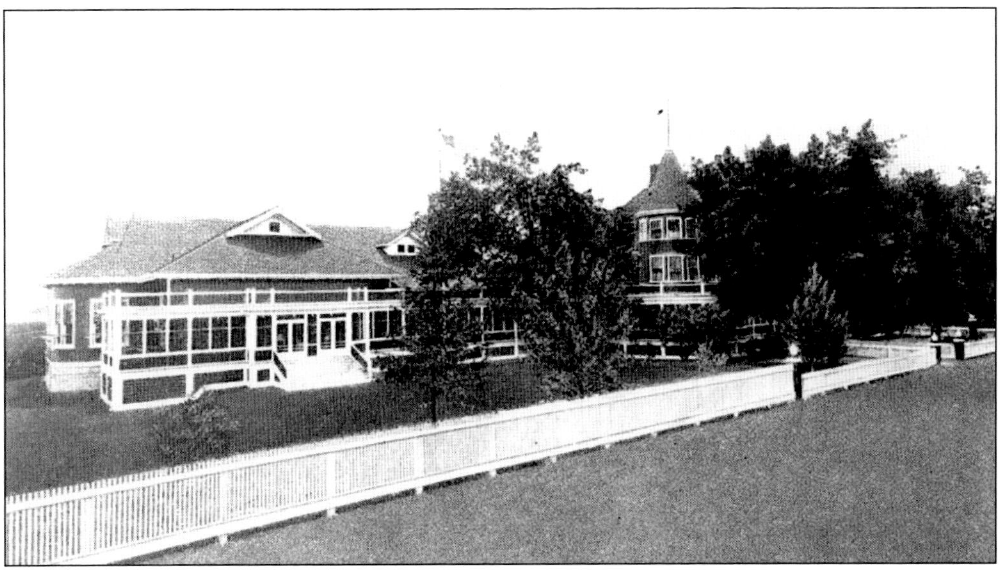

The Lakeside Inn, also known as McSweeney's, Bingham's, and the Pontchartrain-on-the-Lake, was advertised as the "place to go" for sweltering Detroiters, as well as the bath house patrons. According to an early *Cutter's Guide*, "a meal at McSweeney's is never to be forgotten, especially if you have just returned from an excursion on Lake St. Clair, a fishing trip, or a duck hunt."

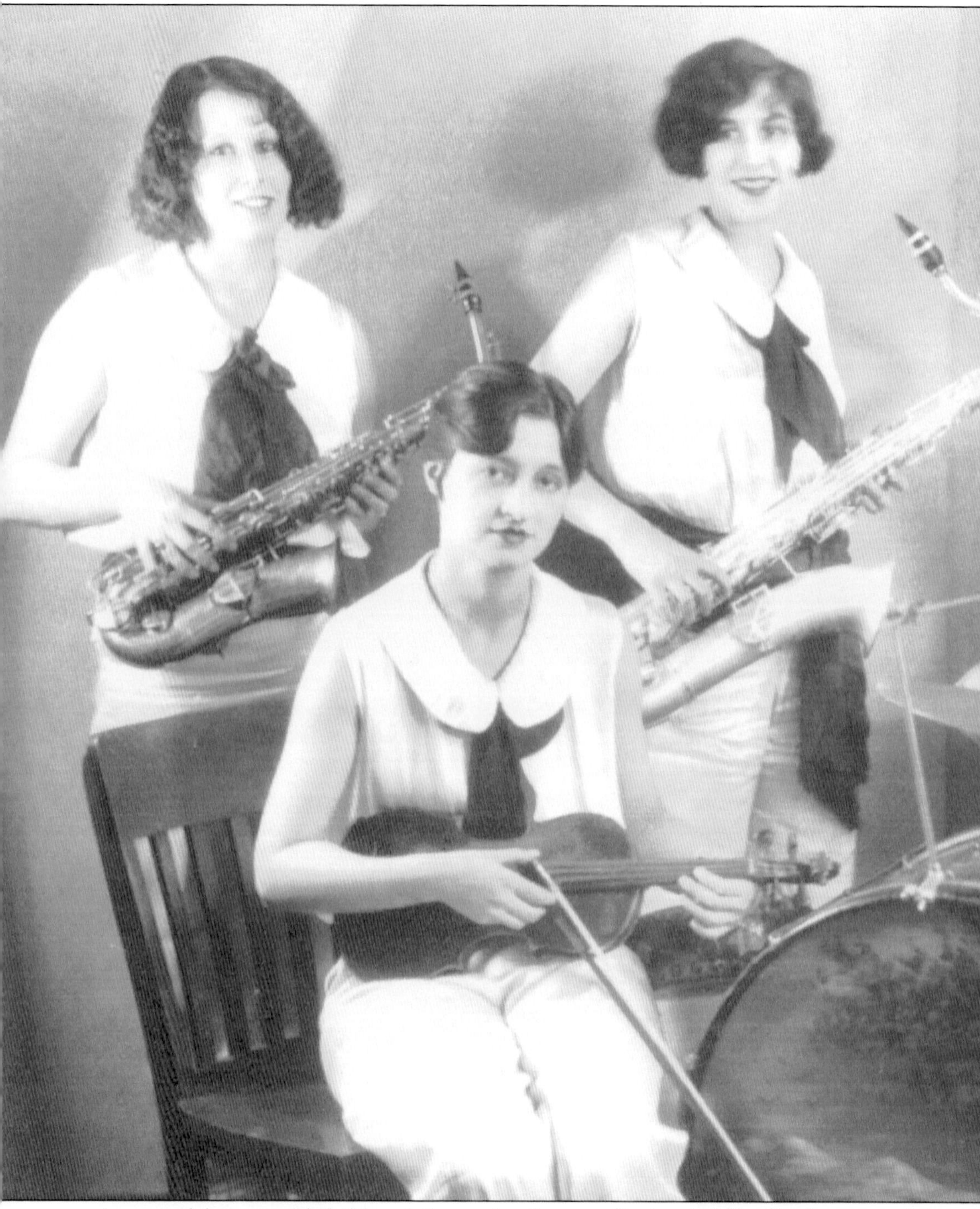

A tattered letter entitled "How I Spent the Summer During 1924" tells the story of the demise of the famous Lakeside hotel. "Nellie Jay and her 'Syncopated Jay Birds' played at the Pontchartrain-On-The-Lake, near Mount Clemens, during the summer of 1924. Being that I was the drummer of course I was there." The account, signed "from a thrill craver Eleanora C. Crafton," tells of being awakened at about 2:30 a.m. by a loud crash. "The crash was the roof of

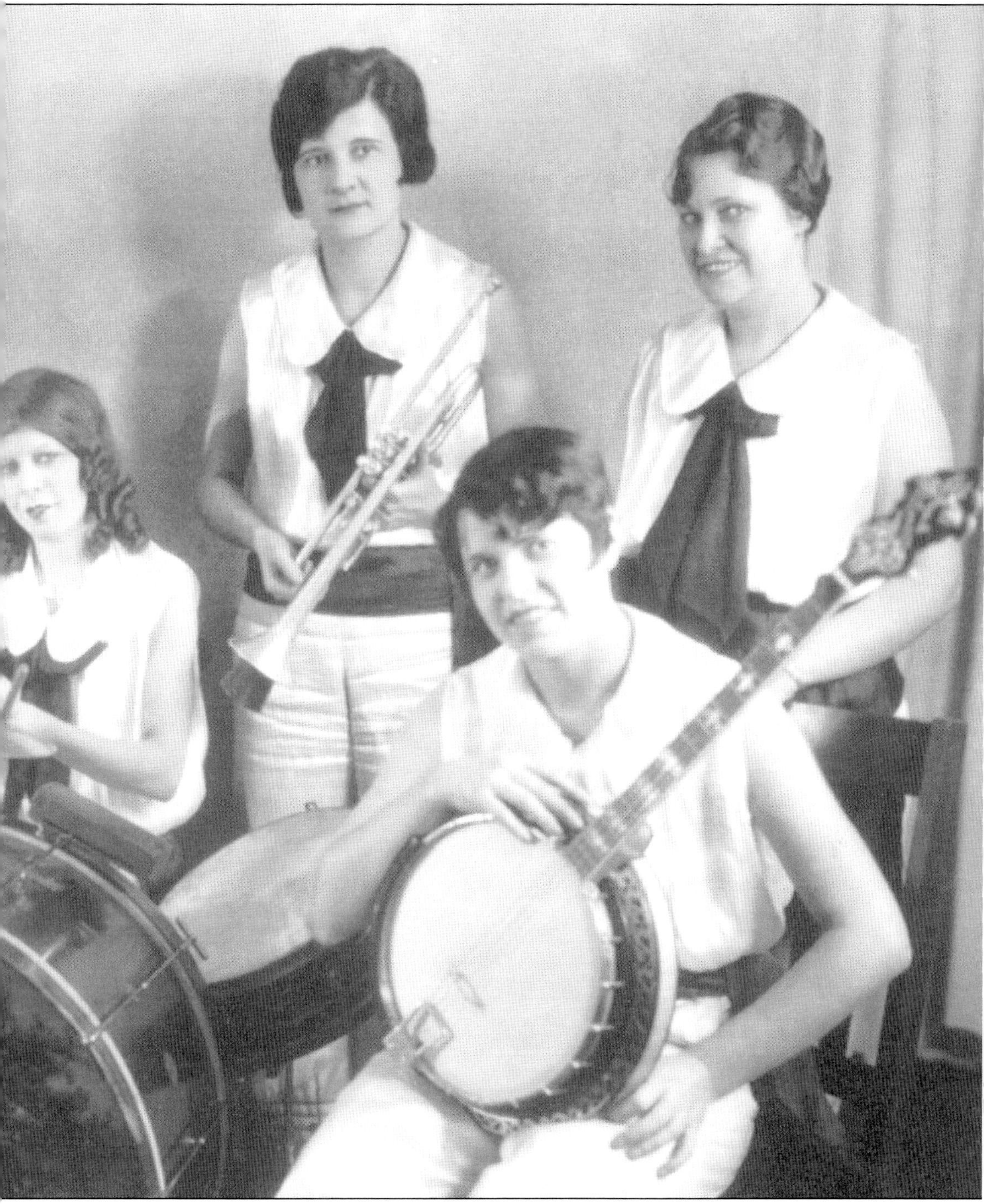

the (new) dancing pavilion that had fallen. I had time to grab my watch and get downstairs." Her mistake was in going back for her clothes and drum. Her next escape was through the window, to the top of the porch, and down onto the cinders. She admitted, "I craved excitement and I did get it at the end."

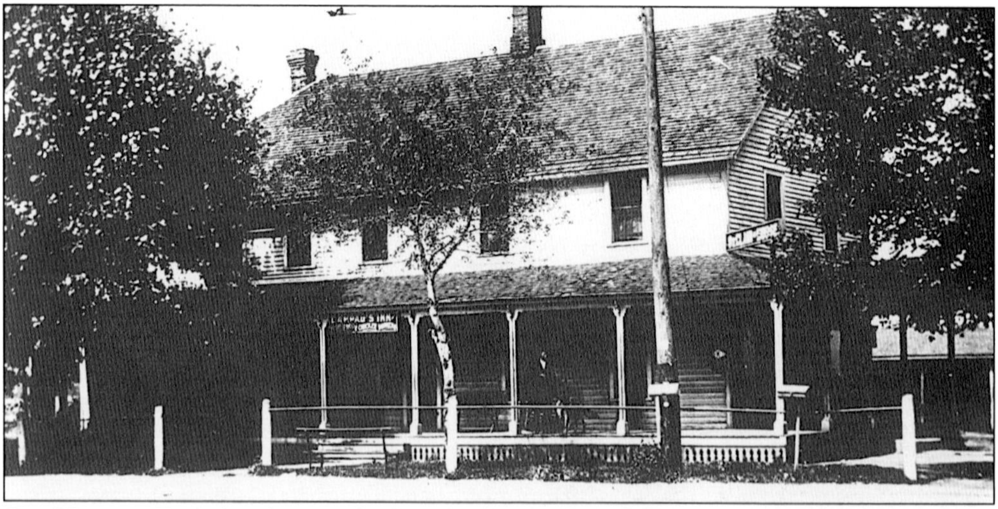

One Harrison Township farmer who benefited from the popularity of the Lakeside Resort was Frank A. Campau. In 1896, he built a hotel on his farm at the foot of Crocker and called it the St. Clair House. Campau was known as a capable manager, public-spirited citizen, politician, township official, and postmaster at Lakeside. In later years the hotel burned, and what remained was moved across Crocker to become the Sentimental Lady Saloon.

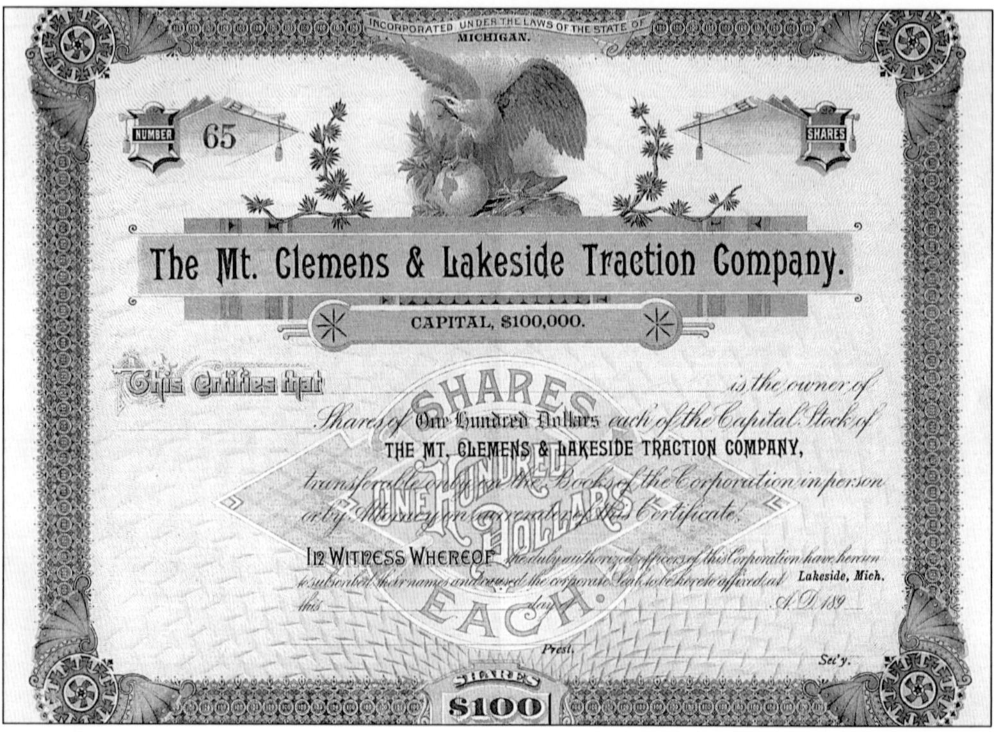

INCORPORATED UNDER THE LAWS OF THE STATE OF MICHIGAN.

NUMBER 65 SHARES

The Mt. Clemens & Lakeside Traction Company.

CAPITAL, $100,000.

This Certifies that ______ is the owner of ______ Shares of One Hundred Dollars each of the Capital Stock of THE MT. CLEMENS & LAKESIDE TRACTION COMPANY, transferable only on the Books of the Corporation in person or by Attorney on surrender of this Certificate.

In Witness Whereof the duly authorized officers of this Corporation have hereunto subscribed their names and caused the corporate Seal to be hereto affixed at Lakeside, Mich. this ______ day ______ A.D. 189

SHARES ONE HUNDRED DOLLARS EACH.

Prest. Sec'y.

SHARES $100

Travel between Lakeside and Mt. Clemens was greatly improved by the early horse-car line and later by the electric railway. The Mt. Clemens and Lakeside Traction Company was formed in 1895. When an agreement between the Traction Company and the Rapid Railway failed, a nasty dispute resulted in cut wires and cars chained to the tracks. Although an agreement was reached, by 1897 the Traction Company was out of funds and out of business.

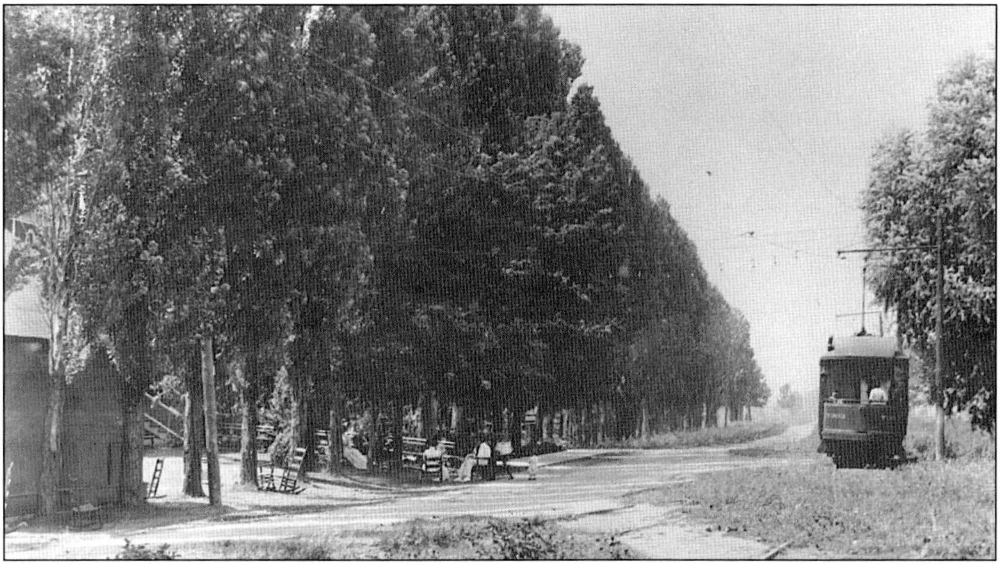

The Shore Line of the Rapid Railway brought passengers into or through Lakeside on their way to Mt. Clemens, Port Huron, or many destinations in between. Here, car 7303 is shown approaching the Lakeside Hotel. It might have paused at Grosse Pointe or St. Clair Shores stops, such as Moross Road, Verniers, Gaukler's Point, L'Anse Creuse, Erin School, Jefferson Beach, or the Maple Club.

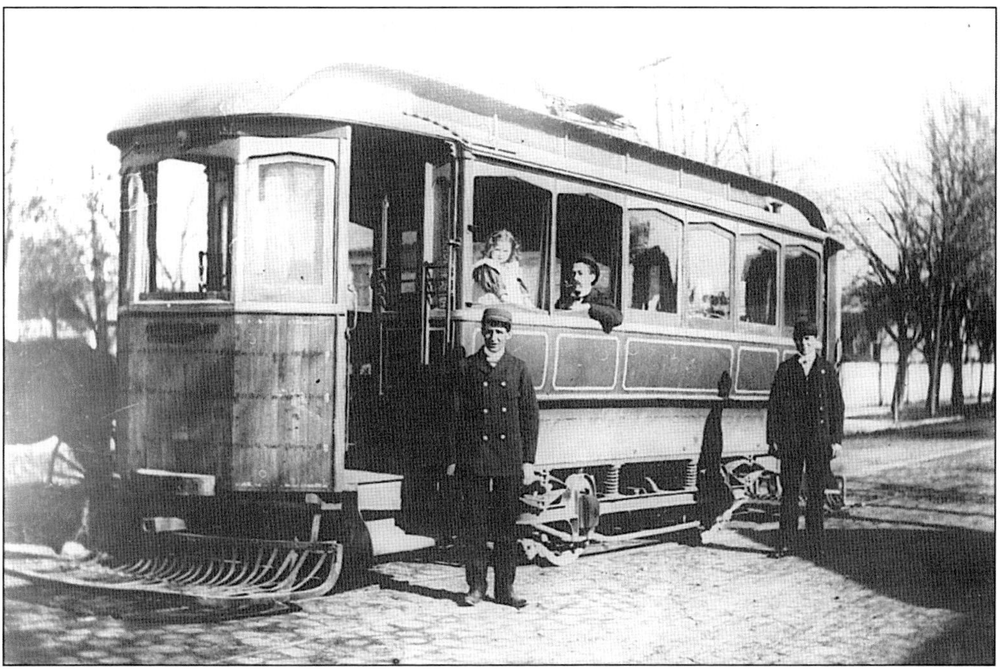

The Dinky, as the smaller electric cars were called, is shown here on September 10, 1899. The car was certainly an improvement in transportation, but the short distance from Mt. Clemens to Lakeside was said to take about 30 minutes. Since the tiny car rocked violently, it was not a good choice for those suffering from extreme pain or the faint of heart. The conductor was E.G. Boyer and Henry Scott was the motorman.

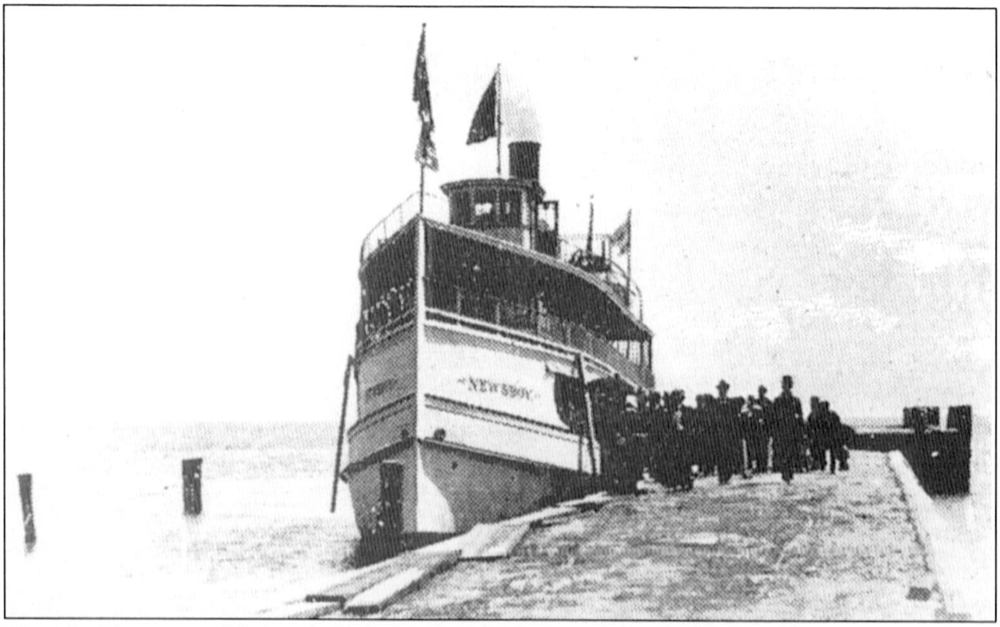

The Mt. Clemens and Lakeside Traction Company owned the property at the end of Crocker in 1896 and built a pier that extended about 1,200 feet out into the lake. The pier allowed ships like the *Newsboy* to pick up and disembark passengers to or from Detroit, the St. Clair Flats, or destinations in between. Of course, to reach Mt. Clemens, visitors would probably use the electric cars also owned by the Traction Company.

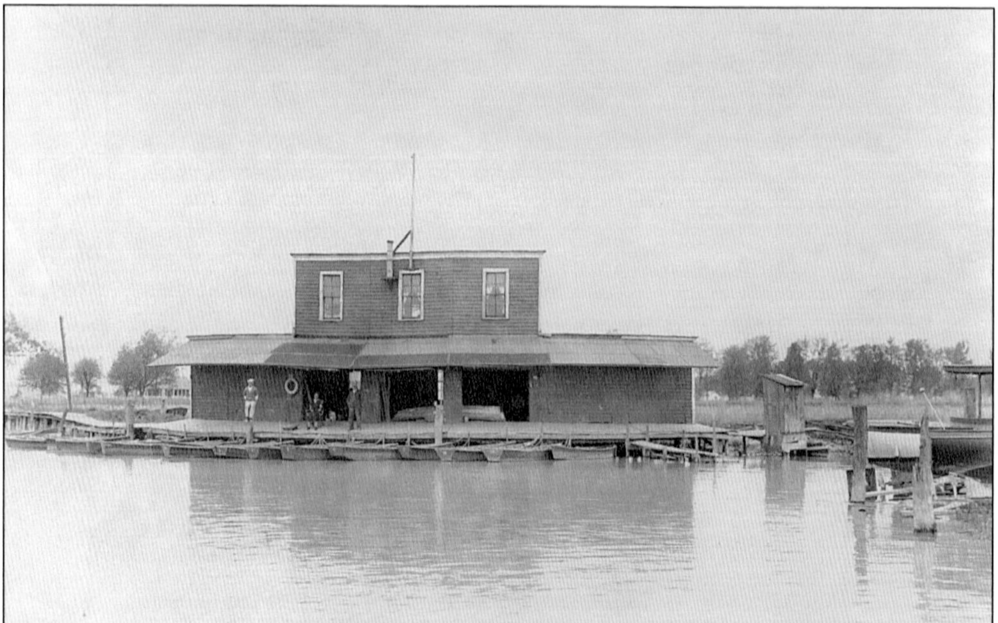

The Lakeside Boat House, owned by Peter VandenBossche, was in an excellent location. Next to the Lakeside Hotel, it was handy for visitors who wanted to hunt or fish. According to Cutter, the Lakeside Hotel owner was always happy to provide information on the best fishing spots, but, "...best of all, persuade him to go with you, and you will be sure to return with a boat load."

Two

Government and Politics

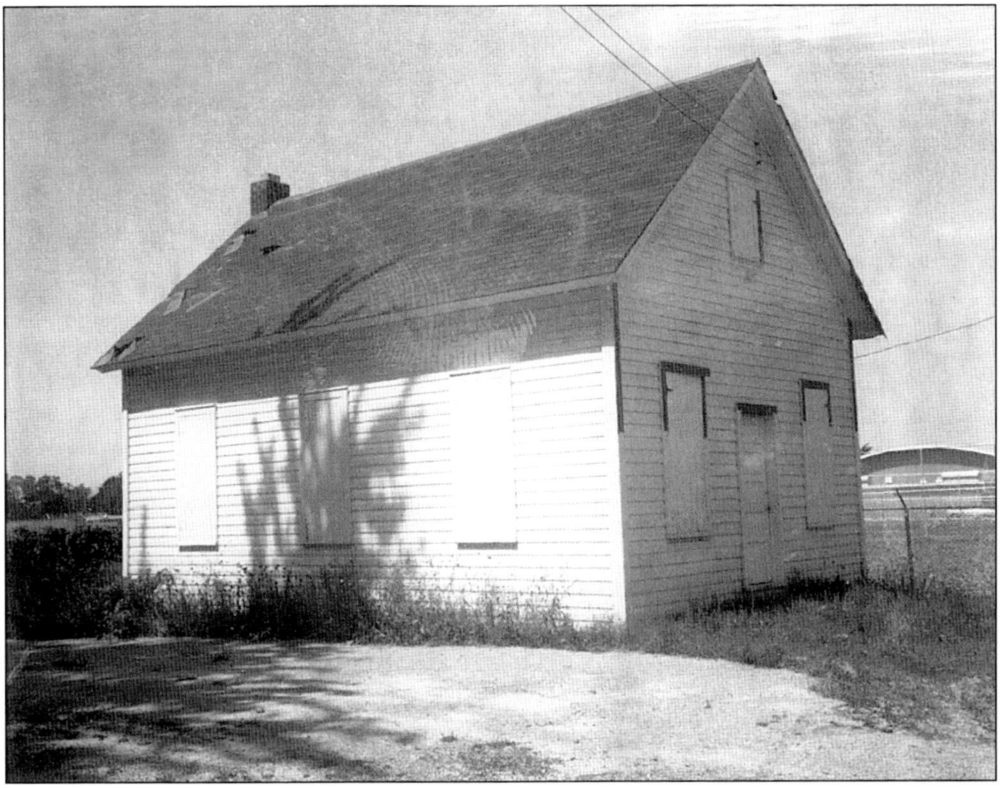

The old Township Hall, built in the early 1900s, is still a landmark on L'Anse Creuse Road, not far from the high school. According to long-time resident Alga Ballard, who remembered the night the first hall burned, the existing building was the second meeting place for local residents. Prior to the first hall, township officials gathered in private homes. This building was also used as a Boy Scout clubhouse and a library.

HARRISON TOWNSHIP

SUPERVISORS

Henry Taylor	1827-28	Floyd W. Rosso	1927-55
Jacob Tucker	1829-37	Ralph Beaufait	1956-74
David Lyon	1838	Antonio Salvatore	1975-76
George Kellogg	1839	David Mercier	1977-81
Herman Beal	1840	Candice McDonald (Miller)	1981-92
Henry J. Tucker	1841	Pamela Weeks	1992-96
Henry Teats	1842-44	John C. Hart	1996-00
William J. Tucker	1845-47	James P. Senstock	2000-
Antoine Chartier	1848		
Alonzo A. Goodman	1849		
Robert Teats	1850-54		
William J. Tucker	1855-60		
Alonzo A. Goodman	1861-62		
Edward Teats	1863		
William Tucker	1864-67		
Edward Teats	1868-72		
Frederick C. Forton	1873-74		
John Feller	1875-76		
Edward Teats	1877-82		
Henry Campau	1883-87		
Charles Mooney	1888-92		
John Irwin	1893-02		
Joseph Hatzenbuhler	1903		
John Irwin	1904-13		
Frank Campau	1913-22		
Oran Arnold	1922-24		
Frank Campau	1924-27		

The township is governed by a Board of Trustees, but the person in charge is the supervisor. From the list above, it appears that in the early years the political positions were, more or less, passed around. In a time when all residents were listed as farmers, that practice made a lot of sense. Today the consistency of having the same person in these positions is a more logical system. In 1902, the issues of importance were dredging, small pox vaccinations, road repairs, and streetlights. Today, major issues are dredging, road repairs, problems associated with residential expansion, and the possibility of again dealing with vaccinations.

HARRISON TOWNSHIP

CLERKS

Henry Taylor	1827	Arthur Teats	1902-15
James Meldrum	1827-33	Edward Lefevre	1915-16
Valorous Maynard	1834-35	Robert Hubbard	1916
Robert Medrum	1835-38	Arthur Teats	1916-17
A.C. Hatch	1839	H.A. Reimold	1917-20
A.W Flagg	1840	Carl Jobse	1920-36
Henry Teats	1841	Ralph Beaufait	1943-55
Henry Tucker	1842-43	Howard Phillips	1955-60
Robert Teats	1844-46	Hiram Stroup	1960
Alonzo A. Goodman	1847-48	Richard Munroe	1960-70
Robert Teats	1948-49	Caroline Jorgenson	1970-74
Jacob Tucker	1850	Shirley Schilk	1974-76
David Tucker	1851-53	Dorothy Garvey	1976-80
Henry VanAllen	1854-56	Laura M. Paletta	1980
Randolph Stiger	1857	Doris M. Lyon	1980-82
Robert Teats	1858-59	Laura M. Paletta	1983-86
Edward Teats	1860-62	Kathleen M. Lyon	1987-96
Simon Rackham	1863-66	Carol Brazil	1096-99
Dositee Chartier	1867-70	Charles Pierce	1999-
John Feller	1871-72		
Henry Fries	1873-74		
Lemuel Sackett	1875		
Henry Campau	1876-77		
Stephen Lawton	1878-80		
Francis Chartier	1881-83		
Charles Winkler	1884		
Frank Chartier	1885		
Fred Reimold	1886		
Jacob Hatzenbuhler	1887		
Thomas Shoemaker	1888		
Joseph Turcotte	1889-96		
Arthur Teats	1897-00		
Henry Reimold	1901		

Historically, political positions in the township have been family affairs. The same last name appears regularly on these lists. Occasionally the same person would run for different positions, but usually the siblings or descendants of officials would take on the task of helping to govern the township. Agreement on how anything should be run is often hard fought. Whenever a group of individuals have to make choices, there are bound to be differing opinions. In 1917, the decision was who to appoint as the orchard inspector. In 1918, the big problem was how best to blast ice out of the river in order to protect Selfridge Aviation Field. Today the issues are different, but it's no easier to make all of the people happy all of the time.

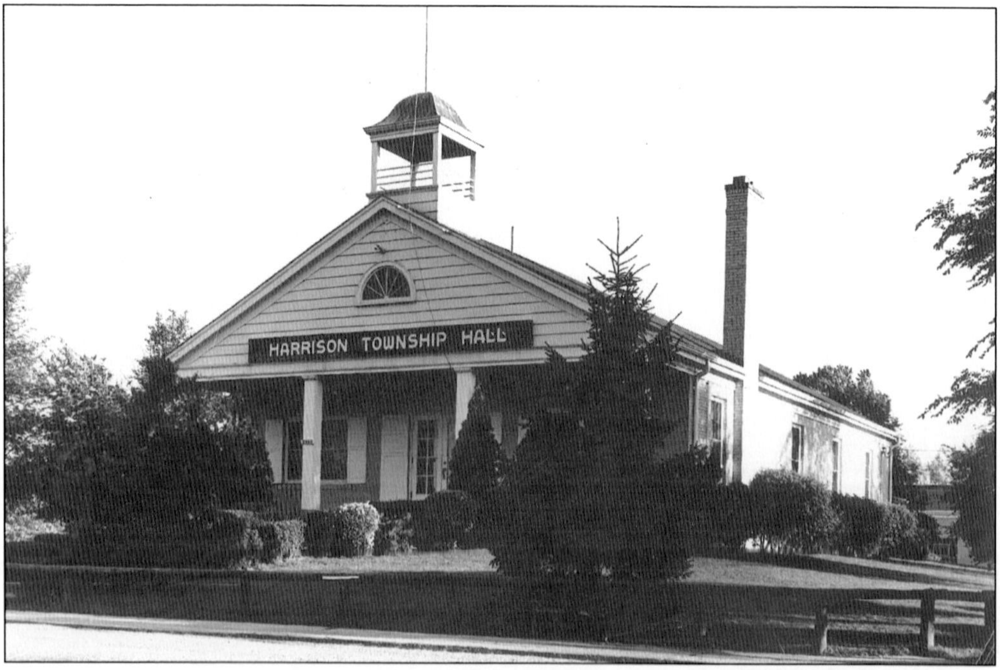

Harrison has no downtown, but the township offices act as a central meeting place. The old township hall was replaced in 1940 by the building pictured above at 39151 L'Anse Creuse. In 1956, it was renamed Rosso Memorial Hall after Floyd W. Rosso, the township supervisor from 1927 to 1955. The Beaufait Addition was added in 1978 for local meetings and social gatherings. The township offices, seen below, were built in 1955 and added on to in 1978. In this 1960s photo, Al Trombley, Ralph Beaufait, and Richard Monroe stand before the office building. In 1973, the Fire Station #1 was converted to office space for the Water and Sewer Department. In 1995, the building was completely gutted and renovated into the Engineering Building.

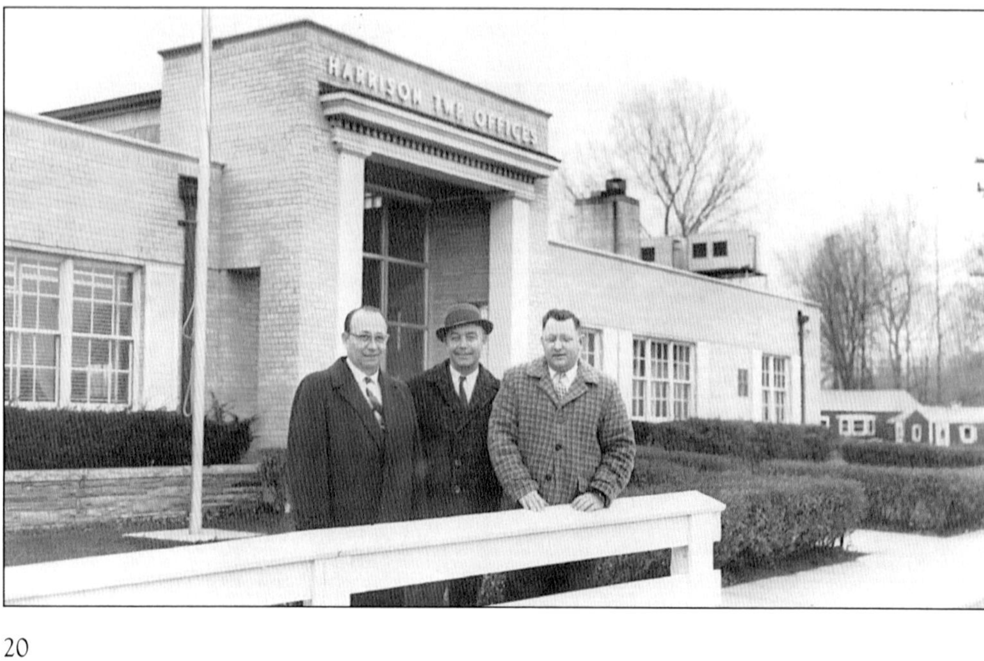

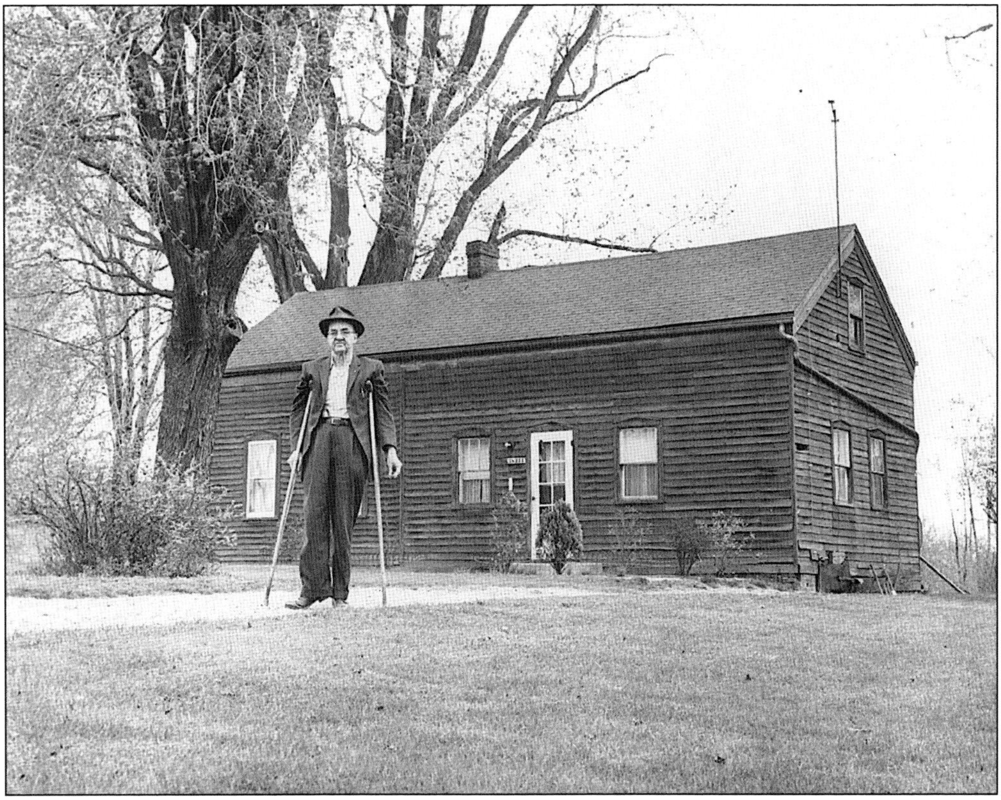

Former township treasurer William Tegeder—more commonly known as Grandpa Tegeder—is shown here near his Townhall Road home. The homestead, established in 1809, was also the home of 1860s township clerk Simon Rackham. Simon's son, Horace, was the best known of this home's residents. He invested $5,000 in his friend's idea, his friend being Henry Ford. He became a generous benefactor, and university buildings were dedicated to his memory.

In the mid-1970s, the township was tired of the word *annexation*. Too many of the neighboring communities were looking to transfer pieces of the township for their own use. When a proposal in 1966 to create a city called Harrison Shores failed, officials began looking at the idea of a Charter Township to protect Harrison's borders. The document to the right contains the "Great Seal of the State" which makes the incorporation official.

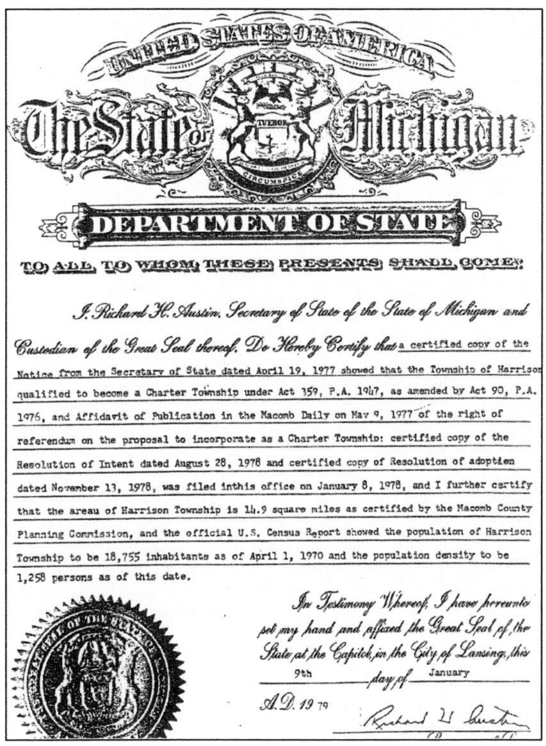

United States of America

The State of Michigan

DEPARTMENT OF STATE

TO ALL, TO WHOM THESE PRESENTS SHALL COME:

I, Richard H. Austin, Secretary of State of the State of Michigan and Custodian of the Great Seal thereof, Do Hereby Certify that a certified copy of the Notice from the Secretary of State dated April 19, 1977 showed that the Township of Harrison qualified to become a Charter Township under Act 359, P.A. 1947, as amended by Act 90, P.A. 1976, and Affidavit of Publication in the Macomb Daily on May 9, 1977 of the right of referendum on the proposal to incorporate as a Charter Township: certified copy of the Resolution of Intent dated August 28, 1978 and certified copy of Resolution of adoption dated November 13, 1978, was filed inthis office on January 8, 1978, and I further certify that the areau of Harrison Township is 14.9 square miles as certified by the Macomb County Planning Commission, and the official U.S. Census Report showed the population of Harrison Township to be 18,755 inhabitants as of April 1, 1970 and the population density to be 1,258 persons as of this date.

In Testimony Whereof, I have hereunto set my hand and affixed the Great Seal of the State at the Capitol, in the City of Lansing, this 9th day of January A.D. 1979

Richard H Austin

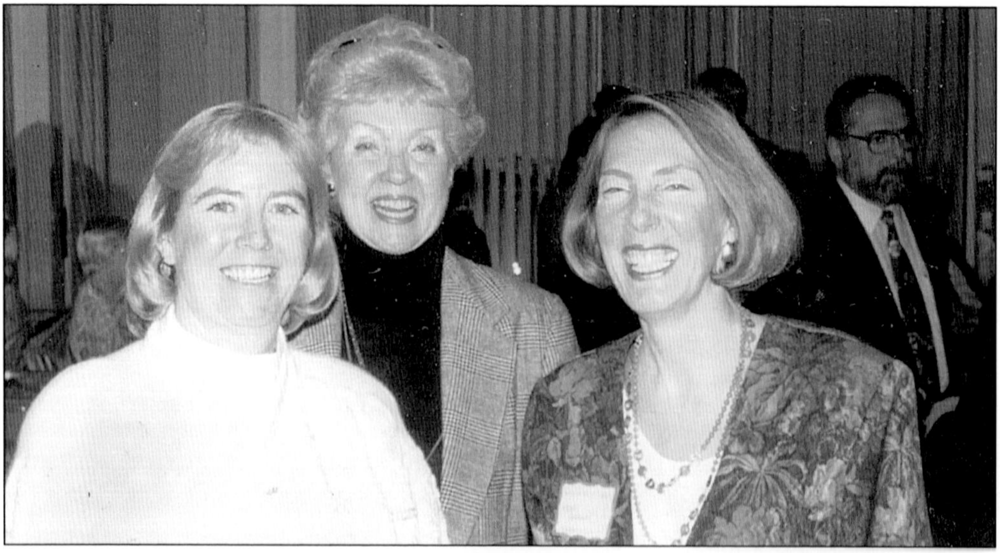

Harrison Township has had many supervisors but none that went on to make political history quite like Candice McDonald Miller did. She followed the supervisor position by becoming Macomb County treasurer. Then she took on her duties as Michigan's secretary of state. In the photo above Miller enjoys the first Harrison Township Historical Commission Champagne Reception with Evette LaBoda and then historical commission vice-chair, Peggy Kennard.

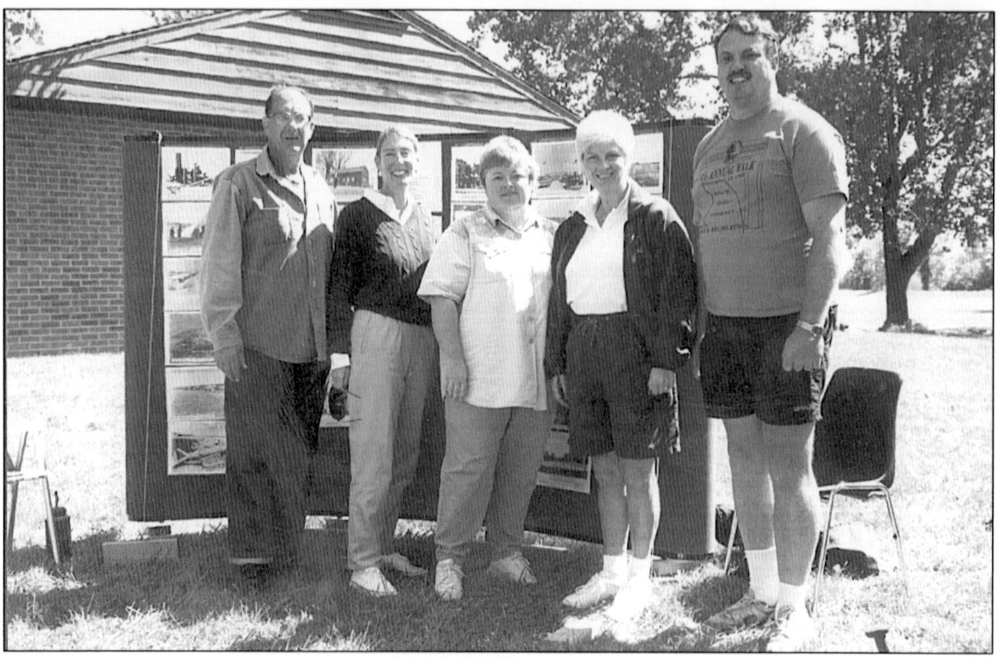

The Harrison Township Historical Commission is a volunteer group organized in 1993 as a committee of the township's beautification commission. In order to be prepared for the 175th anniversary of township government in 2002, the commission has collected and displayed vintage photos and anecdotes from earlier years. Here, commissioners Tom Gregor, Peggy Kennard, and Marie McDougal join then-supervisor Pam Weeks and current supervisor Jim Senstock in front of their display at one of the last township walks.

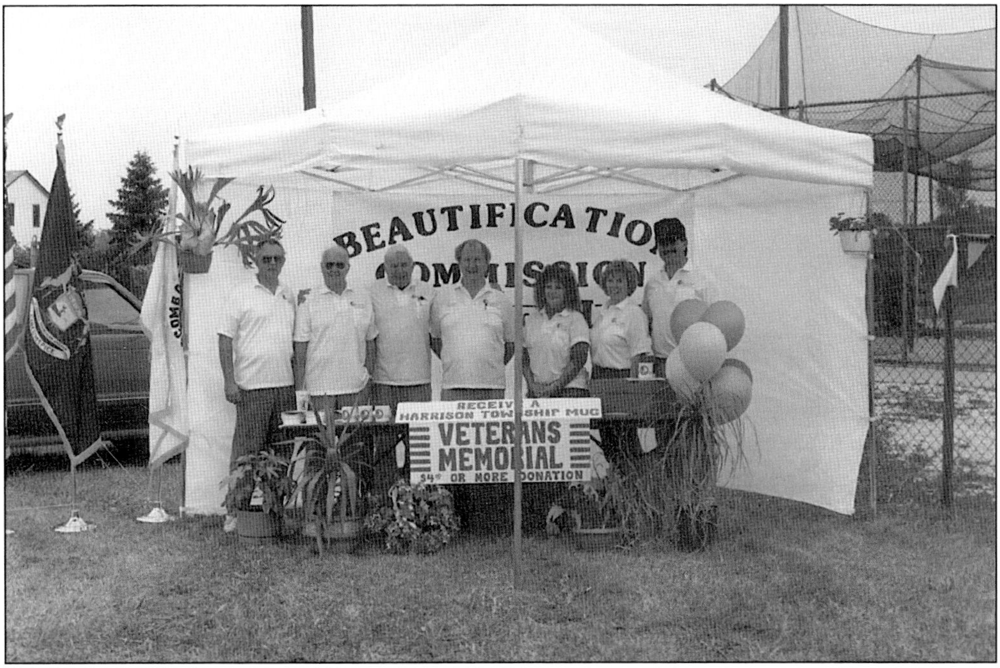

The Harrison Township Beautification Commission is a volunteer group dedicated to keeping the township clean and beautiful. Organized in 1988 by Ron Parker, the commission spearheaded many projects like the annual clean-up week, planting of flowers in public areas, and the expanded Veterans' Memorial. Here, commission members Herb Lorentz, Bill Shellman, Rodney Damm, Ron Parker, Virginia Kukuk, and Laura Cauley raise funds for the memorial.

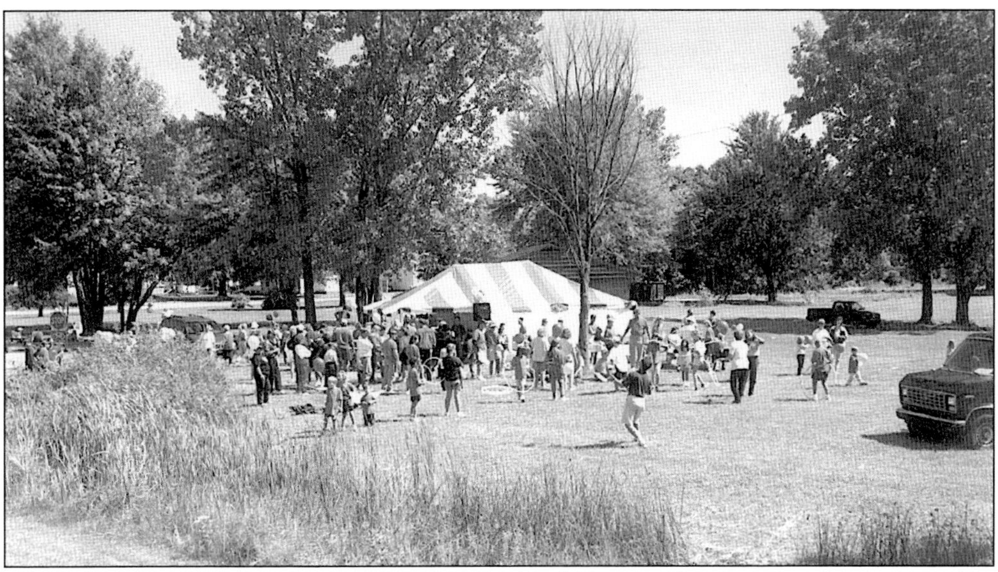

The Parks and Recreation Department, under the direction of Marge Gatlif, was created in 1995. Offering a wide variety of recreational opportunities for all ages, Parks and Rec is busy all year long. From the summer Concerts in the Park to the very popular Daddy/Daughter Dance to the athletic leagues for all seasons, the programs keep Gatlif hopping, sometimes literally. Above, residents enjoy the fun after a township walk.

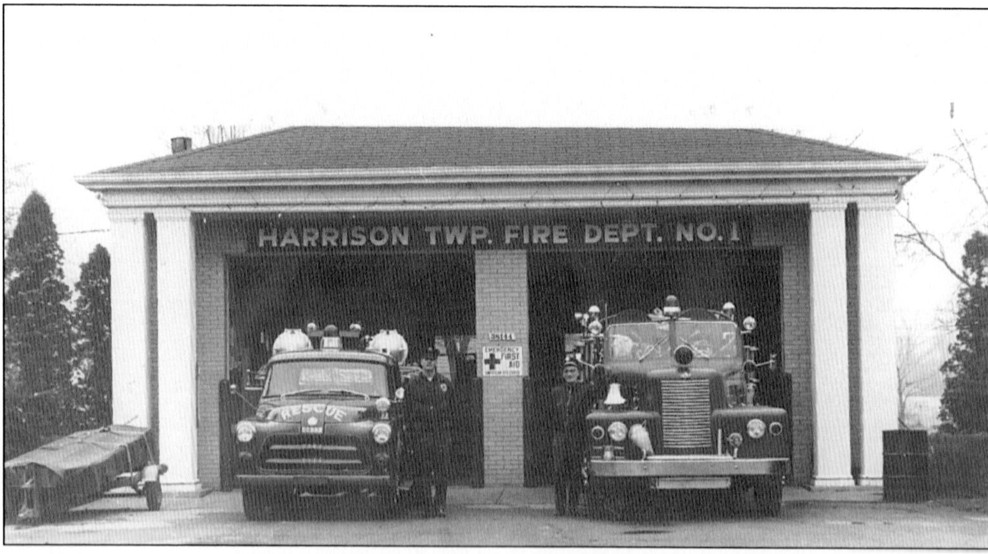

In the early days, Mount Clemens provided many of the township's services. In 1929, however, the township was notified that it would no longer receive fire protection from the city. Many special meetings and discussions later, the fire equipment and truck were purchased but no hall. Mount Clemens agreed to store the new purchases and continue to answer calls in the township. In 1946, 18 men responded to the call for a volunteer fire department. They elected Charles Ruddish as the first fire chief. Firefighters received $1.50 for each call answered. In 1948, Mount Clemens needed space and asked the township to house its own engine and equipment. Fire Hall #1, seen here, was completed in 1949, and the firefighters were ready to roll. Ironically, their first fire came to them. A resident drove his vehicle to the station, back seat ablaze.

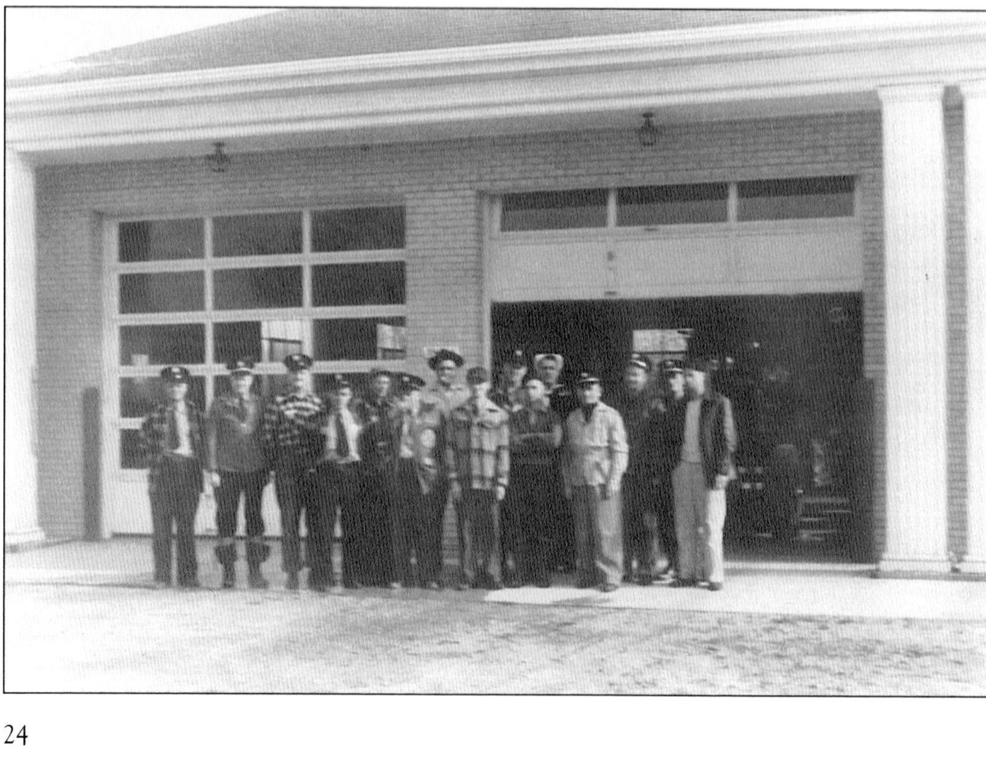

Three

Business and Industry

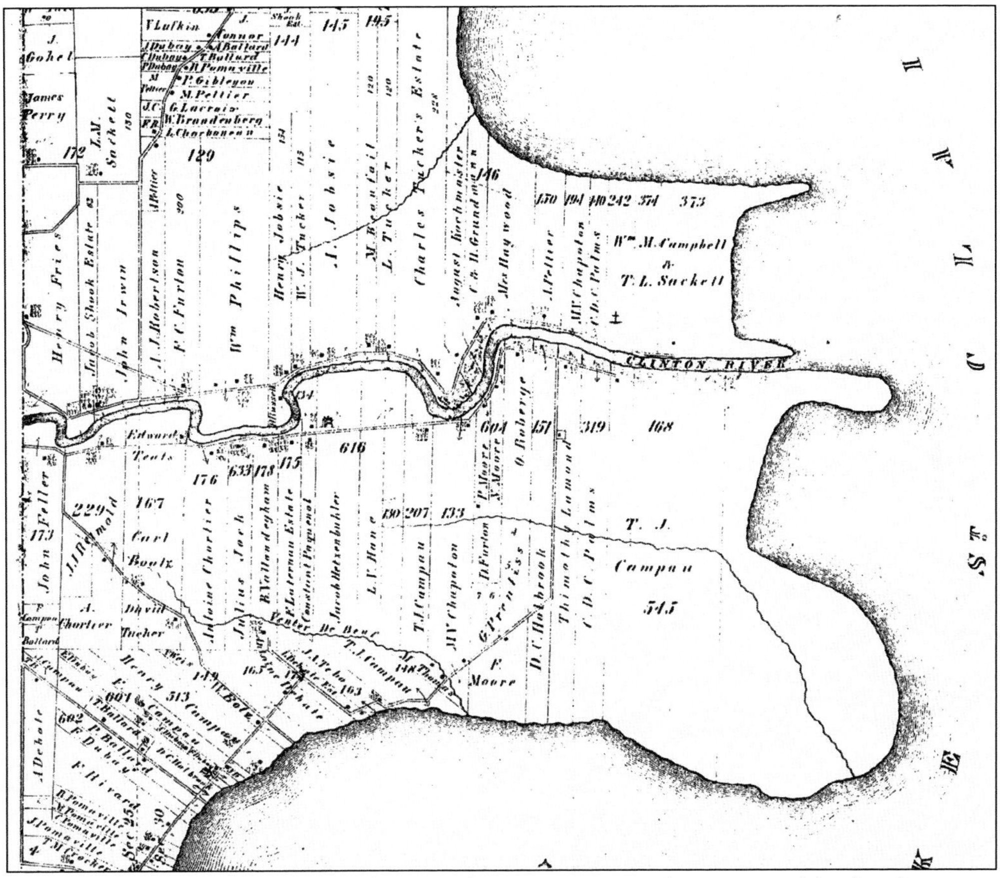

The 1875 Combined Map of Macomb County has an interesting description of the first farmers to settle the area. "The farmers are as poor as they are unfortunate in the choice of their situation." Of course, the writer also implies that the land was basically worthless, describing the obstacles that "...neither the industry nor the perseverance of the agriculturist will be able to surmount." Luckily, he was wrong.

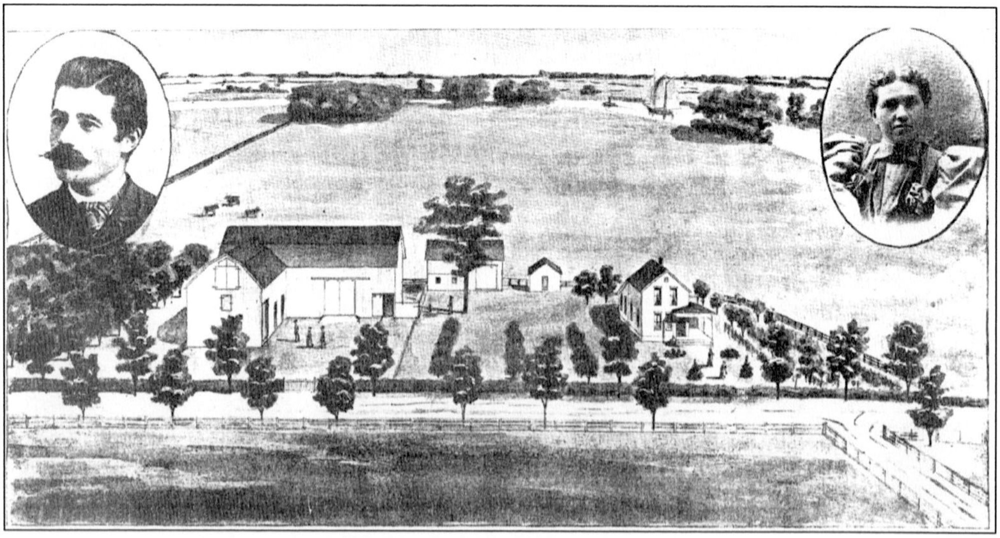

Tracing family history has become increasingly popular in recent years. Often the family Bible handed down from generation to generation lists ancestors and relationships. For the Hatzenbuhler family, however, it is the family atlas. A copy of *The 1875 Historical Atlas of Macomb County* lists the names of fathers and mothers who handed the atlas down, starting with Jacob Hatzenbuhler Sr. and ending in 1972 when Donald J. gave the book to his son, Mark. Unfortunately, it wasn't the *1895 Atlas* which contains the pictures shown here of the Joseph Hatzenbuhler farm above and the Constant Pequignot farm below. The *1875 Atlas* also includes a list of 33 farmers and lists J. Hatzenbuhler from Germany having settled on Claim 616 in 1874. Constant Pequignot from France settled on Claim 134 in 1865. The meeting to establish Harrison School District No. 3 was held in the Pequignot home.

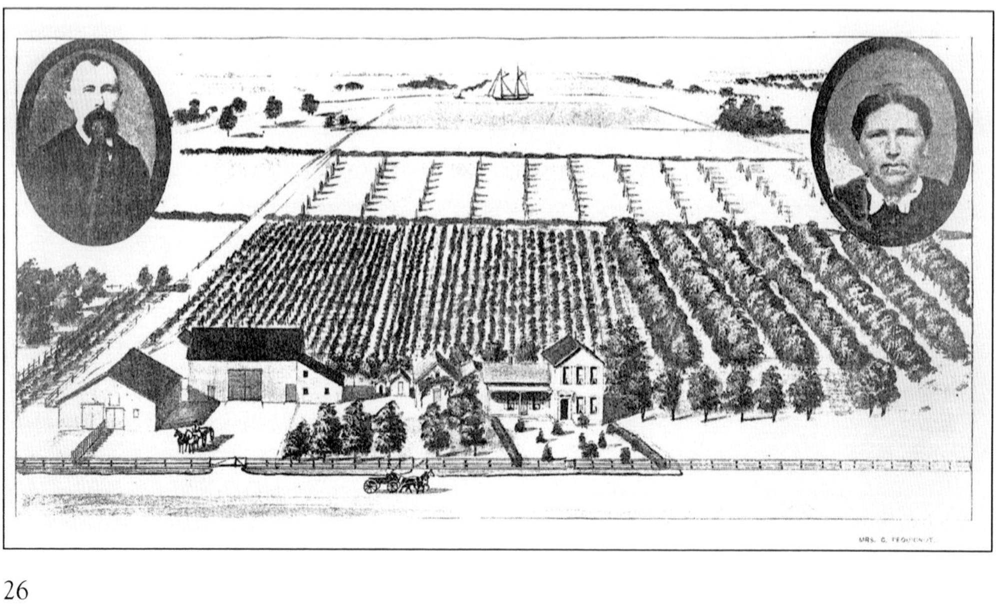

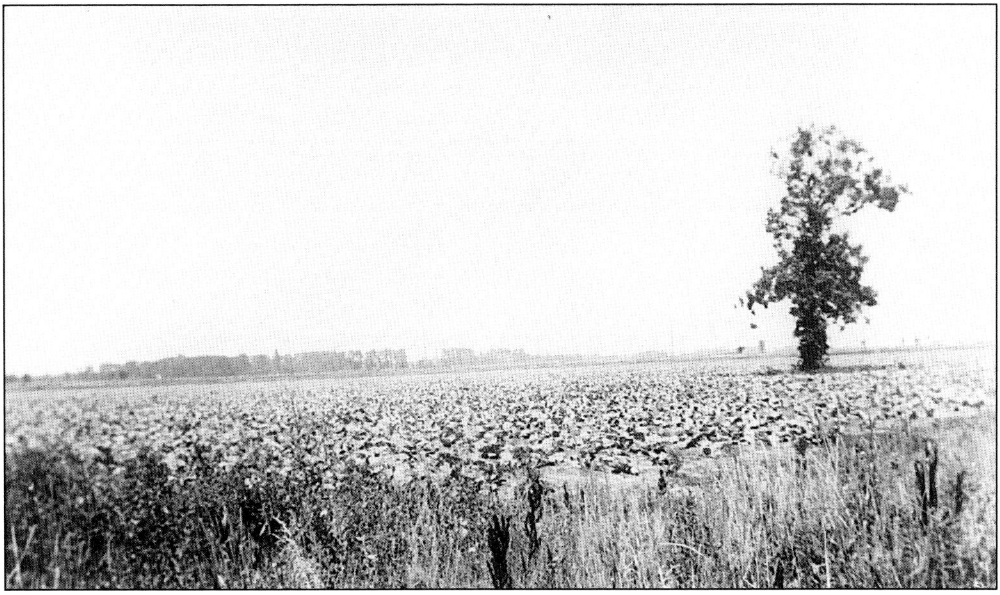

The last working farm in the township was the Callewaert farm. Although the farm was best known for its pumpkins, the photo above shows the cabbage field on Jefferson near Metropolitan Parkway. According to the *1875 Atlas*, farmers in 1873 produced 4,335 bushels of winter wheat, 8,695 bushels of corn, 13,082 bushels of oats, 526 bushels of barley, 410 bushels of buckwheat, and 2,876 bushels of potatoes, along with 22,270 pounds of marketed pork.

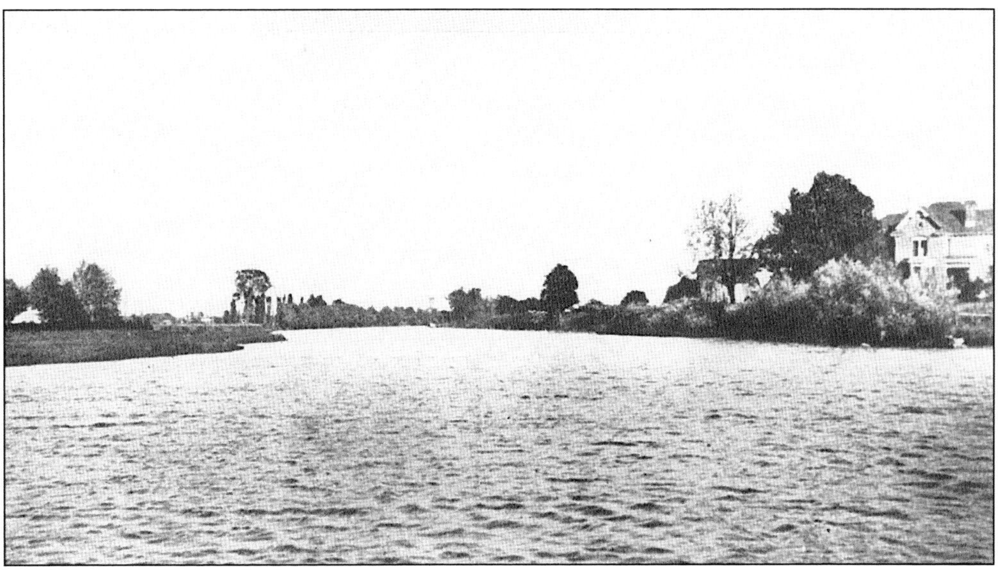

The Buttermilk Farm featured on this early postcard was perhaps better known as the Reimold Farm. Located at South River Road and L'Anse Creuse, the farmhouse has had many uses over the years. The most flamboyant was when Billie Mills converted it to a house of ill repute. Since the 1950s, it has been used by the township's Fraternal Order of Eagles as their clubhouse.

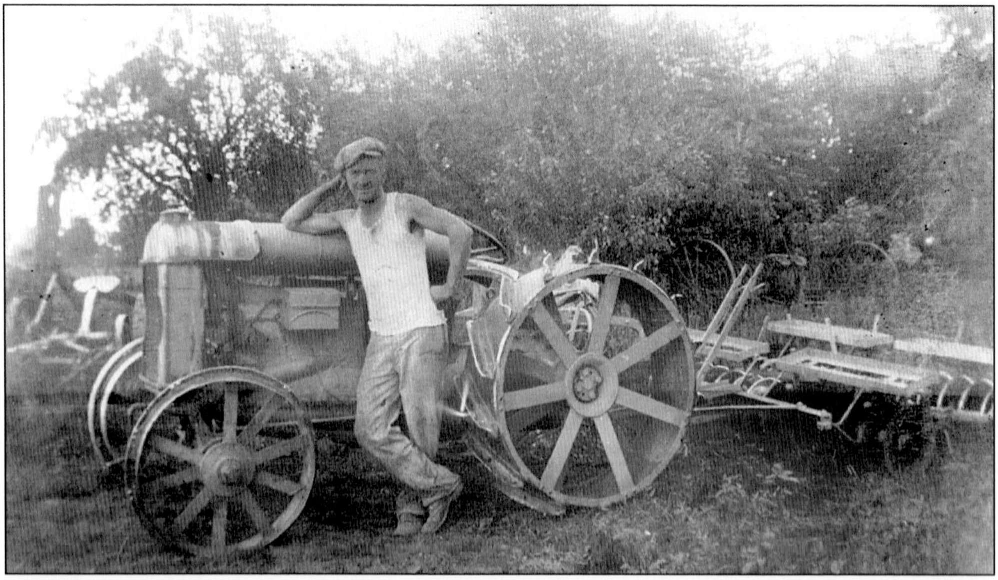

When Jim Battishill's father died, his mother was left with three young sons and six daughters to raise. She had to do something, so she farmed the boys out, a common practice in those days. That's how Jim came to be in this picture taken at the Callewaert farm. He and his brothers lived with the family and worked on the farm. His descendants still live in the township.

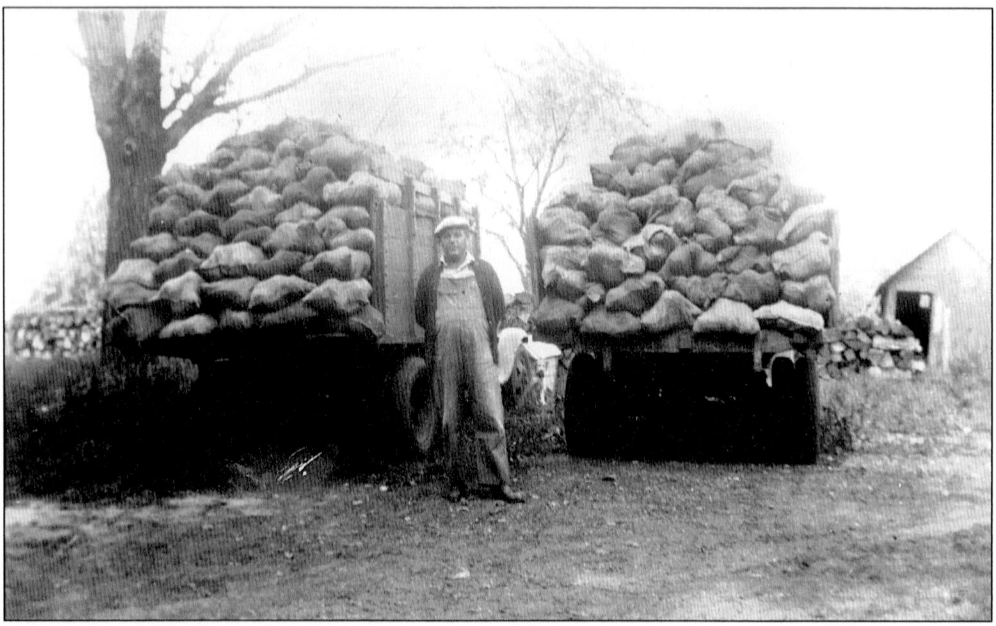

This early 1930s photo shows that some years are very good to the farmer. The Callewaerts even had to borrow a second truck from Mike Resner, another local farmer, to accommodate their 300 bushels of cabbage. Other years, of course, are not so good. Too much rain. Too little rain. Too hot. Too cold. Too many bugs. Many variables can make life on the farm a gamble, a joy, or a heartache.

The farmer's day started early, especially if it was market day. Here Gentille, better known as Chuck, Callewaert has the family and the 1929 Model A all loaded for the Eastern Market. Chuck, his wife Mary, and son Henry wanted to be at the market in time for the bell. The buyers might get there as early as 3 a.m. to get the best produce for peddling in the city.

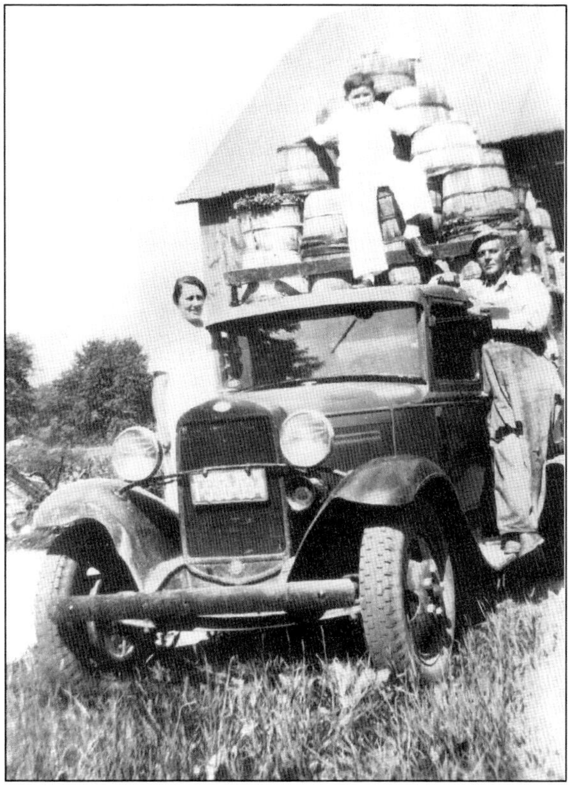

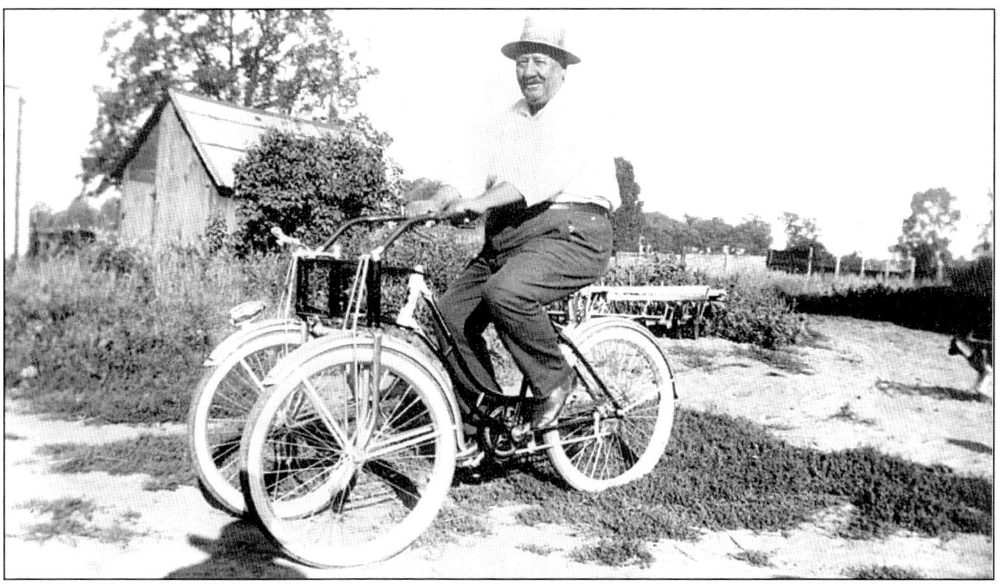

There was no bike path or even a paved road, but Fred Mallast liked to visit his neighbors on this sturdy three-wheeler. The barn and the fields in the background were typical of most of the township in the 1920s. As the farms in the township vanished, so did a very special kind of life, a hard but satisfying life.

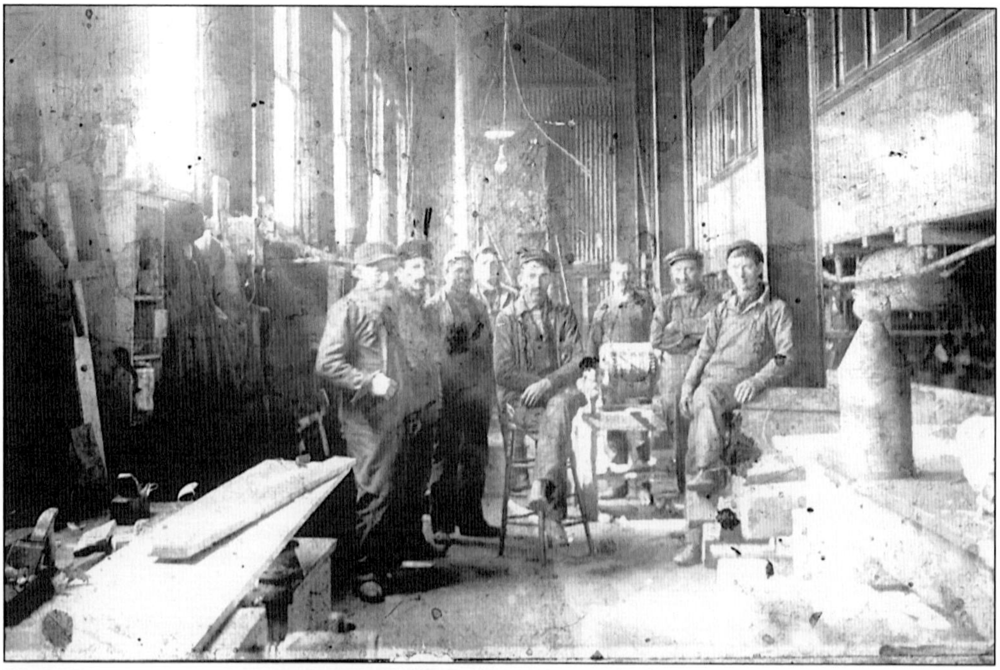

Power was an important commodity in the early 1900s. With the coming of the electric rail cars, the Mount Clemens and Lakeside Tractor Company felt a power plant on Jefferson in Lakeside was essential to their plans. These men, including historical commissioner Bob Ballard's grandfather, Robert John Campau, seated in the middle, worked hard to keep the plant running.

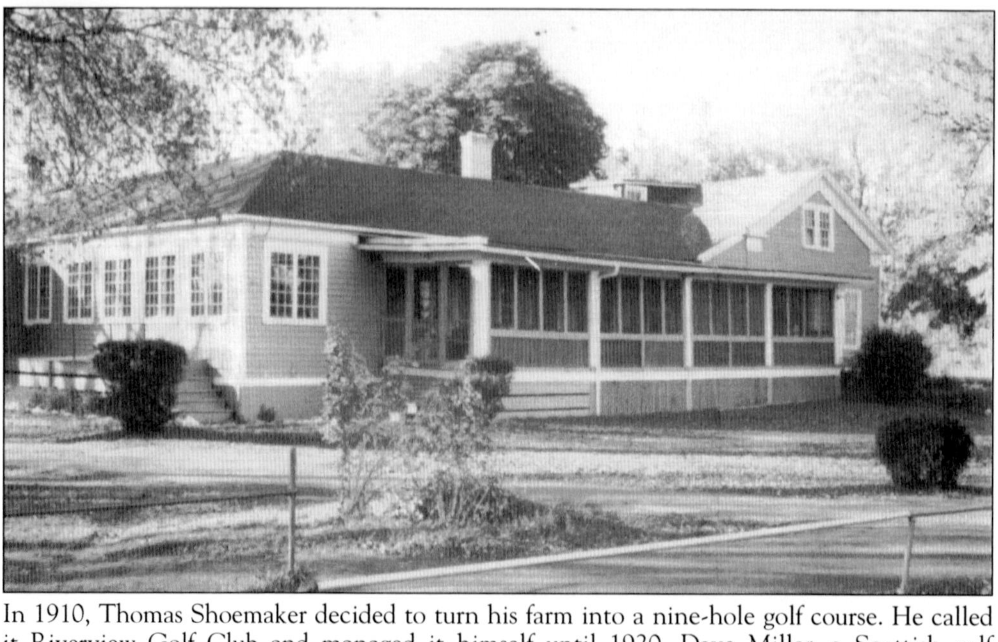

In 1910, Thomas Shoemaker decided to turn his farm into a nine-hole golf course. He called it Riverview Golf Club and managed it himself until 1920. Dave Millar, a Scottish golf professional, then leased the land and renamed it Gowanie (pronounced Gow'nee) meaning "Dell of the Daisies." Today the 18-hole course is owned by Jean Axford and leased by a non-profit corporation formed by the members.

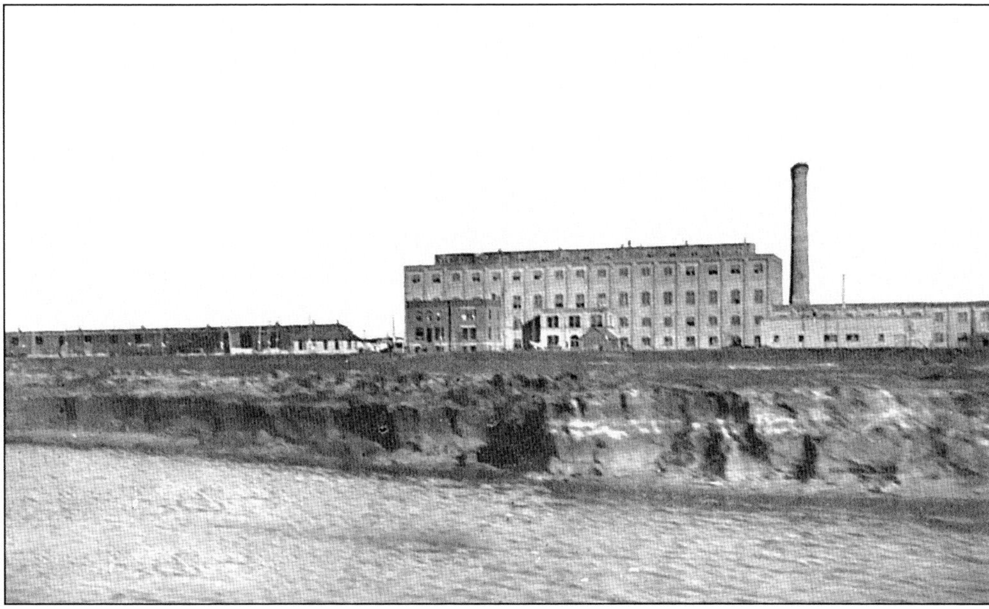

The Sugar Beet Factory property was a victim of annexation. Originally located in the township, it was near what is now the I-94 and North River Road intersection. Established in 1901 by the Macomb Sugar Company, the plant was a major employer for several decades. In 1962, however, it was torn down except for the warehouse that can still be seen today. In its heyday, the factory produced 21,000,000 pounds of sugar, 7,000,000 pounds of residue molasses, and 7,500 tons of dried pulp that was sold to the Ralston Purina Company as fodder for cattle. Many of the 80,500 tons of raw sugar beets used in the process were raised in Harrison Township. Built on a Native-American burial ground, the factory was rumored to have had several fires and mishaps of mysterious origin.

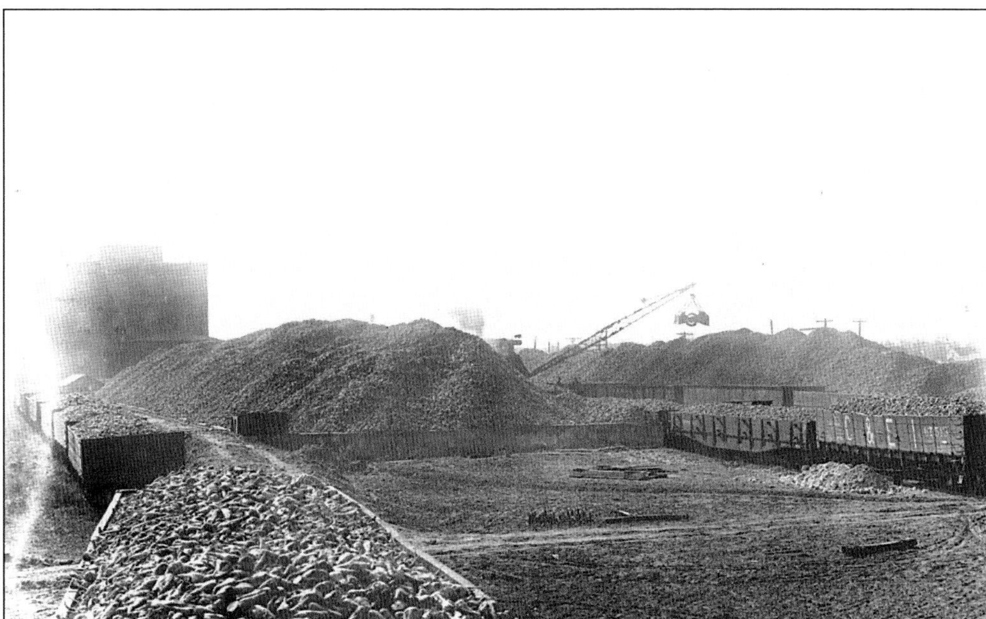

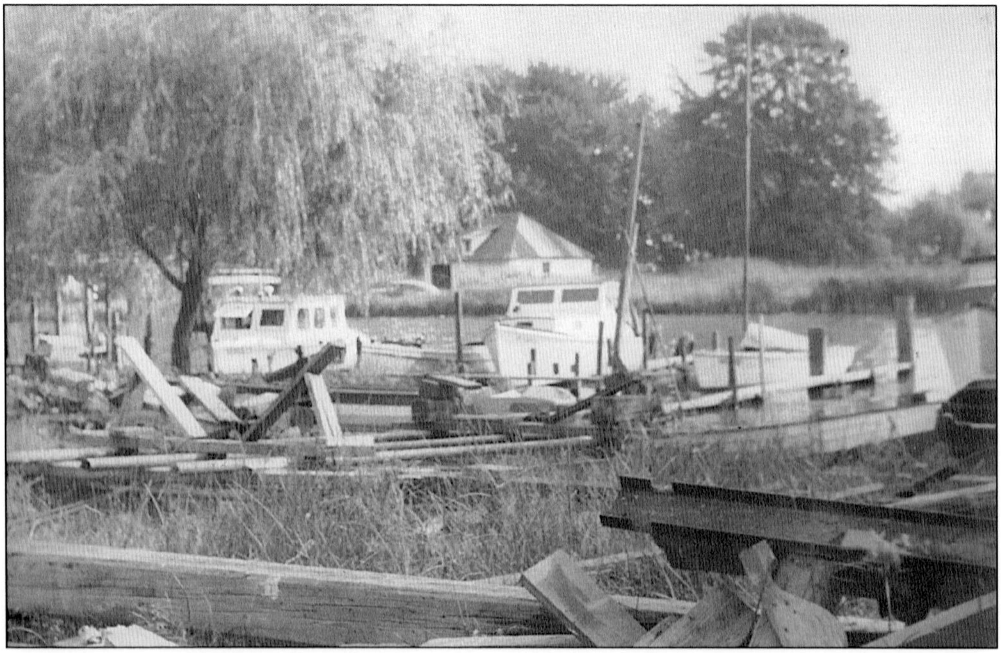

Early marinas like Rickert's, above, and the Clinton River Marina, below, used the rail system for handling boats. The boat would be slid onto a cradle atop the rail car while still in the water. The cable seen in the bottom picture would be winched up to drag the boat out of the water. The boat with cradle was then slid sideways on greased skids to the boat's winter storage place. The boat pictured here was one of the target towboats. The 34-footers were built at the Hacker Plant in Mount Clemens. They were originally radio-controlled boats used in World War II. The government rewarded the Hacker Company with the Army-Navy Production Award, similar to the Distinguished Service Medal for soldiers. Luckily, just before the War, Hacker had turned down a request from Japan to make PT boats for them.

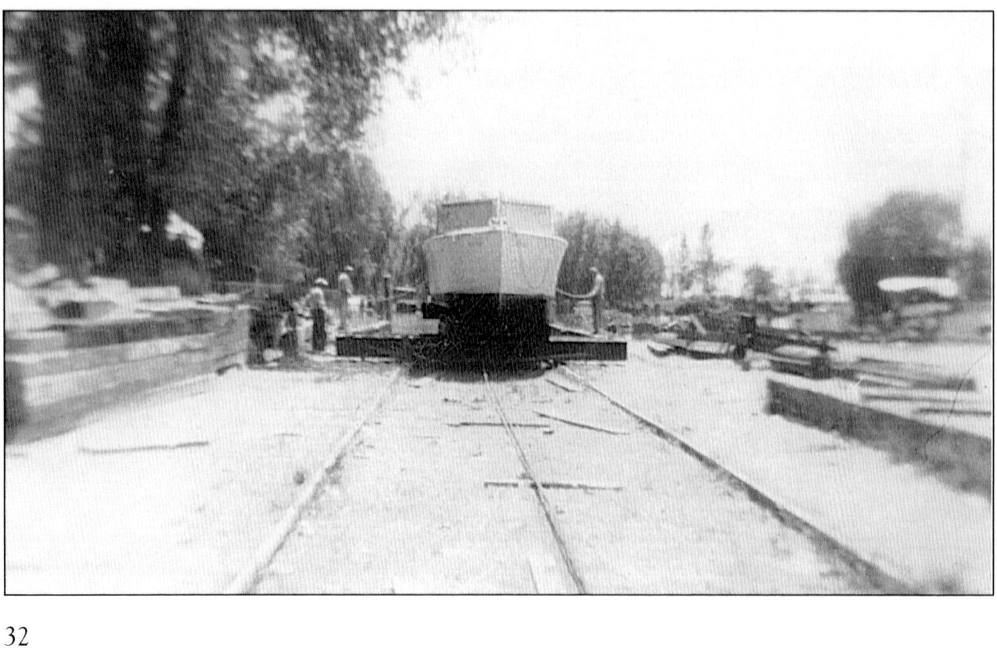

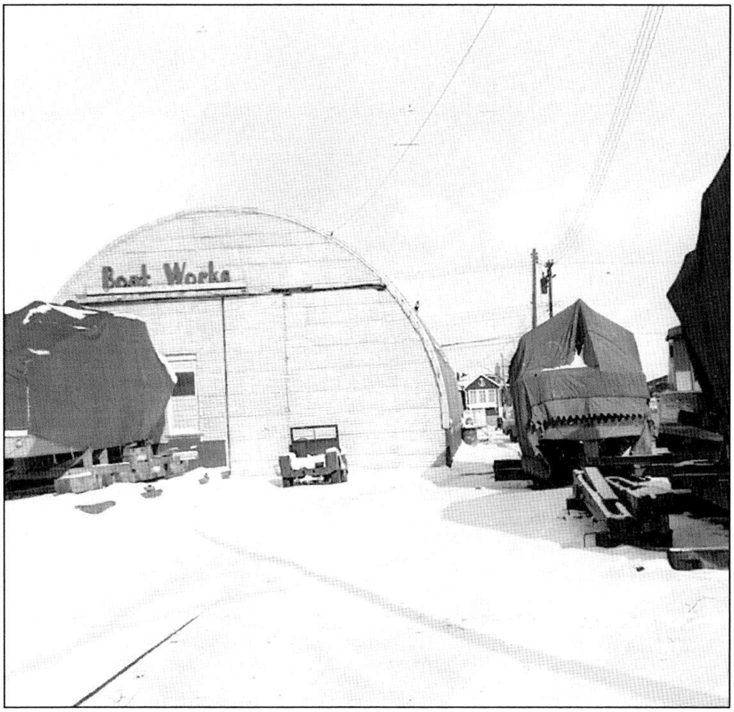

This Quonset hut, at the Clinton River Marina, was typical of the early storage and maintenance facilities on the river. Built in 1946 by Native-American laborers known for their naturally good equilibrium, the sturdy shed was where three generations of Astons repaired and rebuilt boats. It was recently dismantled and moved to Yale, Michigan. According to Steve Aston, boats were originally moved by rail from the water, directly into the hut.

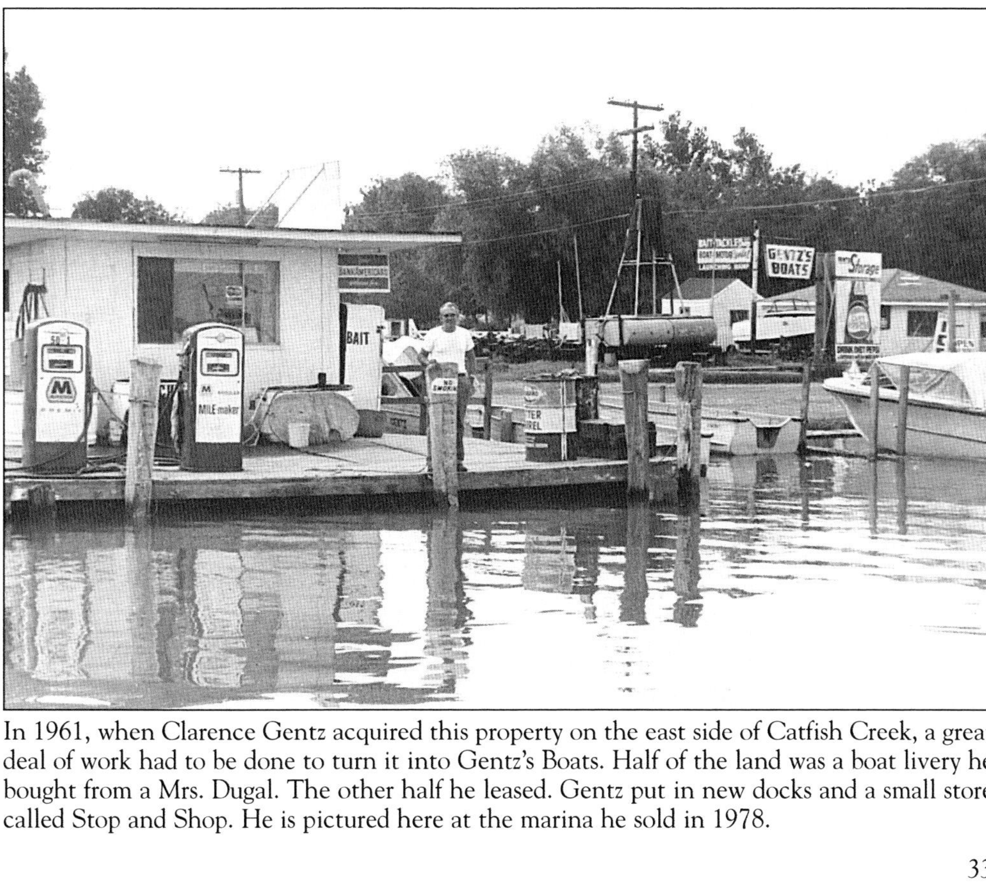

In 1961, when Clarence Gentz acquired this property on the east side of Catfish Creek, a great deal of work had to be done to turn it into Gentz's Boats. Half of the land was a boat livery he bought from a Mrs. Dugal. The other half he leased. Gentz put in new docks and a small store called Stop and Shop. He is pictured here at the marina he sold in 1978.

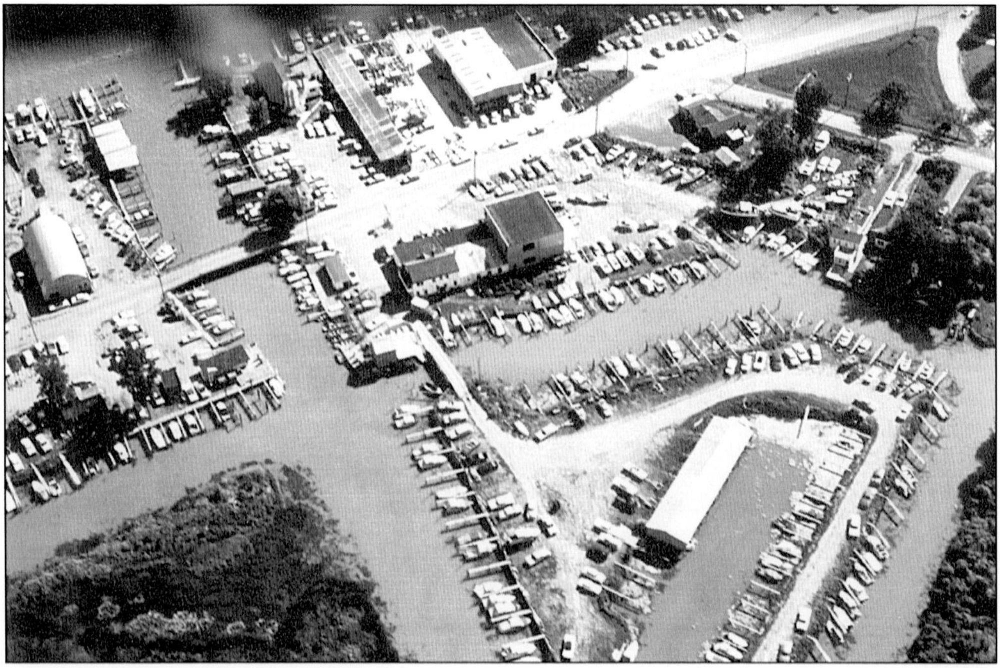

The aerial above of Romick's Marina shows that low water is nothing new. Actually, today's water levels, while they seem low to newer residents and boaters, are actually close to what the boaters of the 1960s thought of as normal. The land on Conger Bay, which once had trees and scrub brush, has been marsh for several decades. The aerial below of Island Cove in higher water shows the contrast. Work to transform Romick's into Island Cove began in 1988. Although boat owners started moving their boats to the marina in 1990, the official opening and dedication of the clubhouse was in 1991.

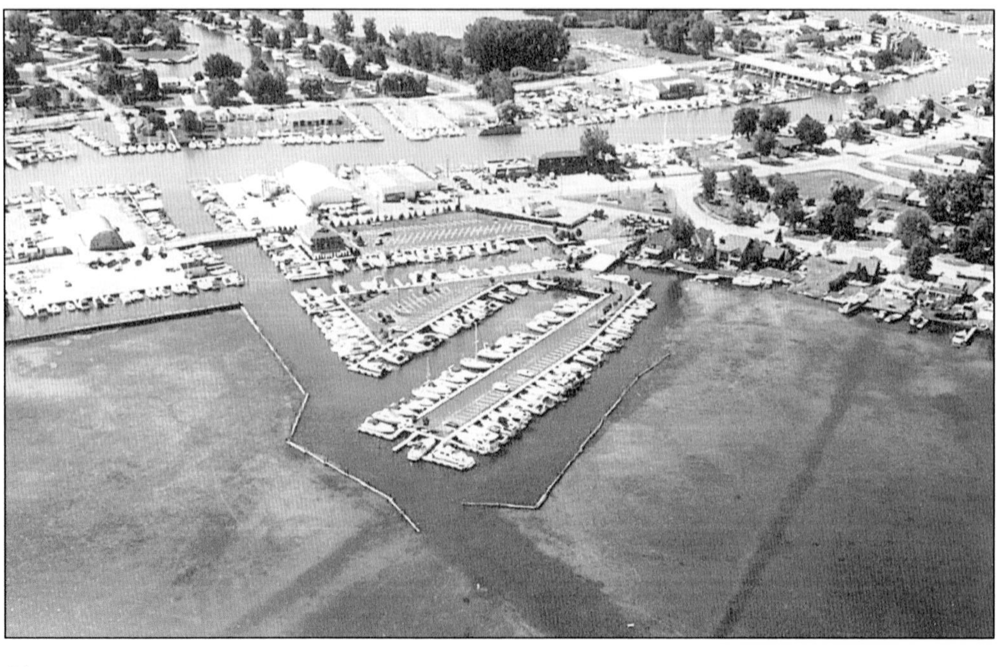

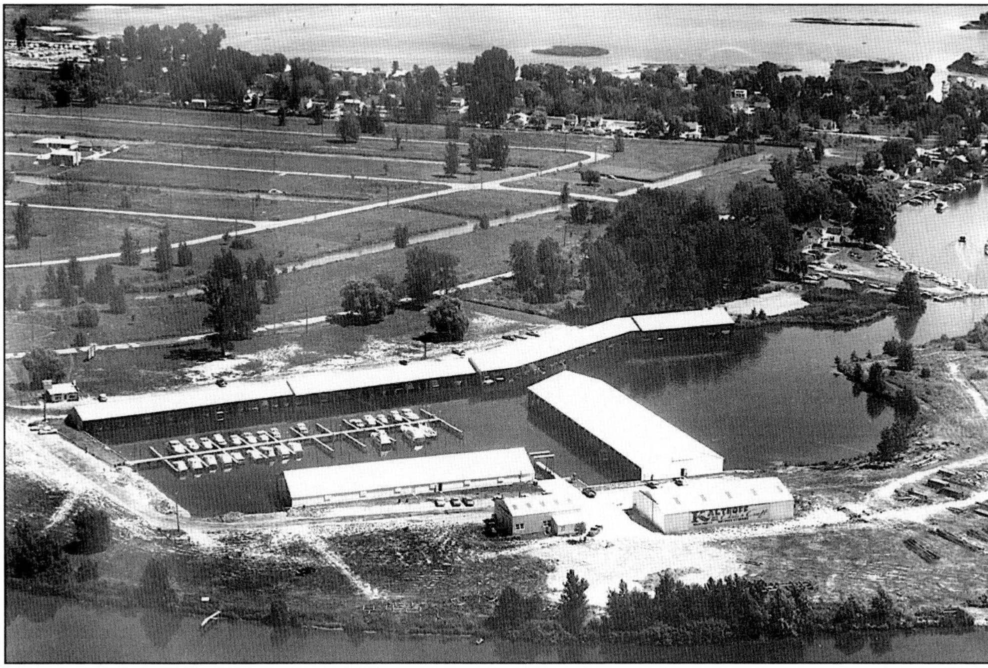

The "oxbow" that James Conger dreamed of making into the city of Belvidere became Kalthoff's Marina in the 1960s. The picture above shows the covered wells and the location in reference to a Venice Shores Subdivision that was just developing. Below is an early photo of today's Markley Marine. The popularity of the marina can be seen in the increased number of covered wells and the use of the perimeter of the property for dockage. The marina will soon be expanding to the east, land which was recently purchased for a new storage facility. This picture also shows Bryer's boat wells in the lower right.

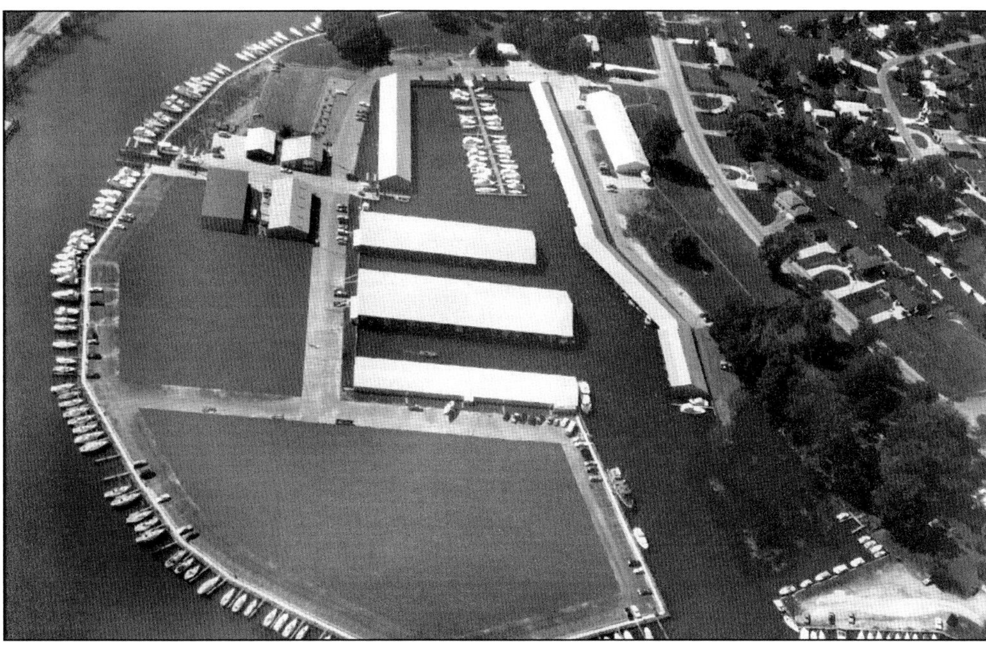

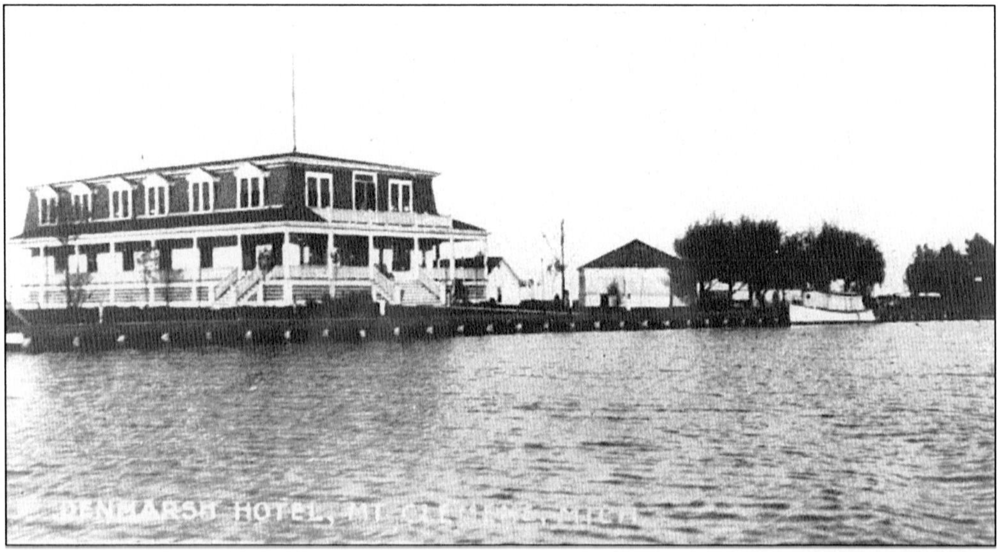

The postcard above of the Denmarsh Hotel shows its location in terms of the Round House, which was originally used for storage and later became the Lighthouse Restaurant. The Denmarsh had a reputation as a first-class inn with food that was never to be forgotten. It had another reputation, as well, during the years of Prohibition. Township seniors still tell the stories of illegal liquor, gambling, and prostitution and how the lack of trees on North River made it easy for the lookout to tell when a police raid was impending.

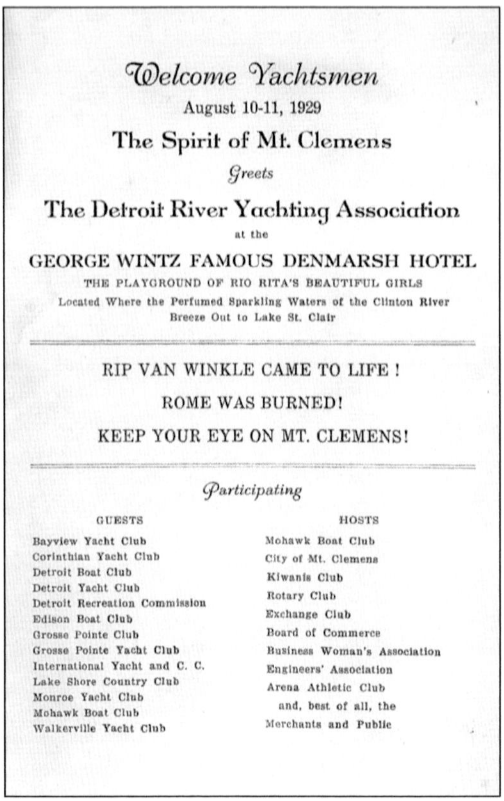

Welcome Yachtsmen

August 10-11, 1929

The Spirit of Mt. Clemens

Greets

The Detroit River Yachting Association

at the

GEORGE WINTZ FAMOUS DENMARSH HOTEL

THE PLAYGROUND OF RIO RITA'S BEAUTIFUL GIRLS

Located Where the Perfumed Sparkling Waters of the Clinton River Breeze Out to Lake St. Clair

RIP VAN WINKLE CAME TO LIFE !

ROME WAS BURNED!

KEEP YOUR EYE ON MT. CLEMENS!

Participating

GUESTS	HOSTS
Bayview Yacht Club	Mohawk Boat Club
Corinthian Yacht Club	City of Mt. Clemens
Detroit Boat Club	Kiwanis Club
Detroit Yacht Club	Rotary Club
Detroit Recreation Commission	Exchange Club
Edison Boat Club	Board of Commerce
Grosse Pointe Club	Business Woman's Association
Grosse Pointe Yacht Club	Engineers' Association
International Yacht and C. C.	Arena Athletic Club
Lake Shore Country Club	and, best of all, the
Monroe Yacht Club	Merchants and Public
Mohawk Boat Club	
Walkerville Yacht Club	

The Denmarsh was also the scene of many legal events, like the 1929 Detroit River Yacht Association Regatta. The program mentions "Rio Rita's Beautiful Girls" and the perfumed sparkling waters of the Clinton River. A lot has changed or someone had an interesting sense of smell.

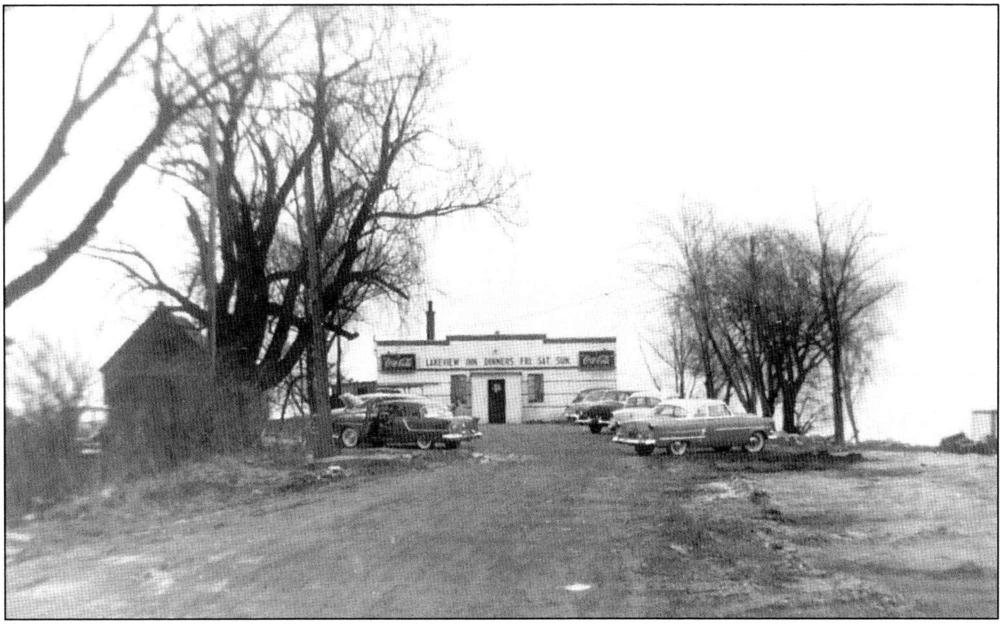

The Lakeview Inn, above, was located on Jefferson Avenue. It is better known as Gino's Surf Lounge. The Lakeview was a favorite stop for ice fishermen and hunters. Long-time residents laugh when they talk about eating at the restaurant. The floor had such big gaps in it that the diners could watch the fish swim under foot as they ate. Rumor has it that a decent breeze could set the porch to swaying. In 1971, Gino Calisi took over and made some dramatic changes, seen below. The bar is still the same, but the rest of the old inn has been incorporated into the building that served for decades as a first-class restaurant and lounge. Today Gino's son, Perry, primarily "caters" to large groups, but the Sunday Brunch is still a special feature.

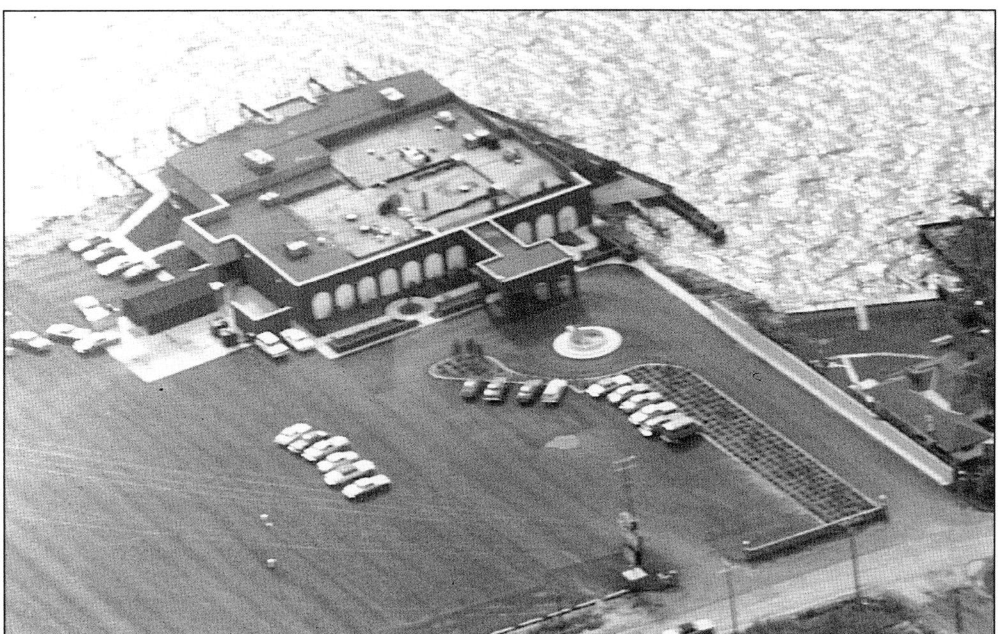

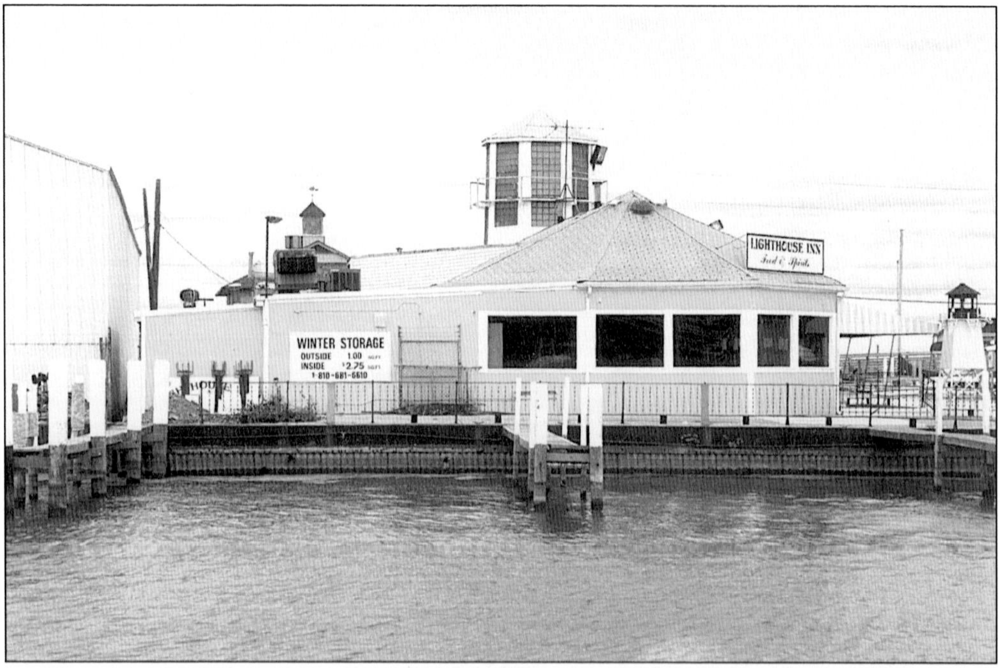

An ad in the 1944 phone directory reads, "Lighthouse Inn or Roundhouse for fine liquors, beer, wine, and lunches, telephone 9397 for reservations, 'Boat Harbor, Tel.7275' W.J.R. Young, prop. 6512 N. River Road, RFD 3." The Lighthouse Inn was originally associated with the Denmarsh Hotel. In more recent years, it was a historic restaurant that often served stories of the good old days along with its food and drink. It burned to the ground on July 29, 1998.

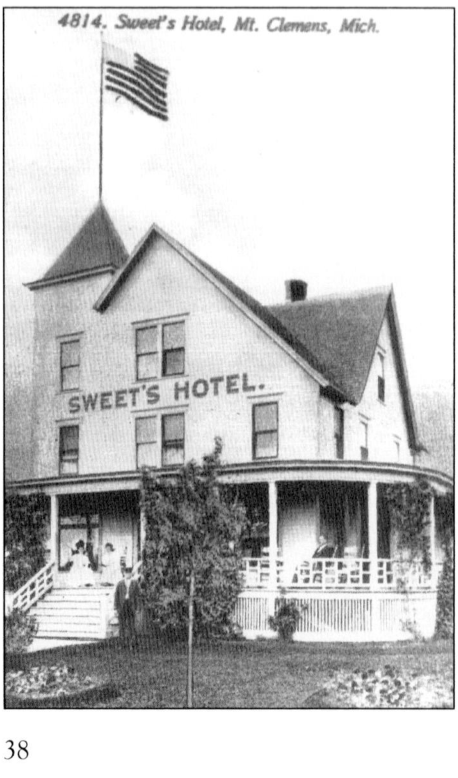

Originally owned by William Sweet, who died in 1906, the Sweet's Hotel was a hideaway for hunters, fishermen, Bath City visitors, and celebrities alike. The address in early directories was simply "the mouth of the Clinton River," but later phone books listed it as 32425 South River Road. In 1959, five boys, aged 5 to 12, were smoking in the old building. Luckily they escaped before the fire they set destroyed the hotel.

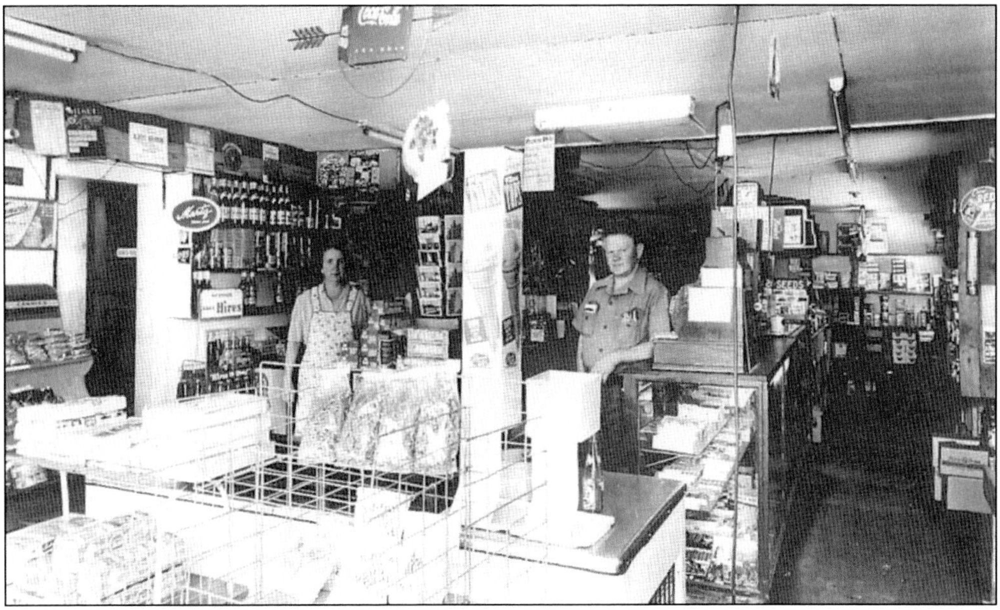

As the population grew in the township, the neighborhood "corner store" became a common sight. Above, Wilfred and Gertrude Lowe wait for customers in the 1920s. They made it convenient for the neighbors on Jefferson to get the essentials without driving into town. Shirley Streu and her mother, Laura, with their Clinton River Grocery, provided the same friendly service at the end of South River Road. They endeared themselves to their customers because they lived above the store and would open up at odd hours for that emergency loaf of bread or bottle of milk. Luckily for the township, local "party stores" have not gone out of style.

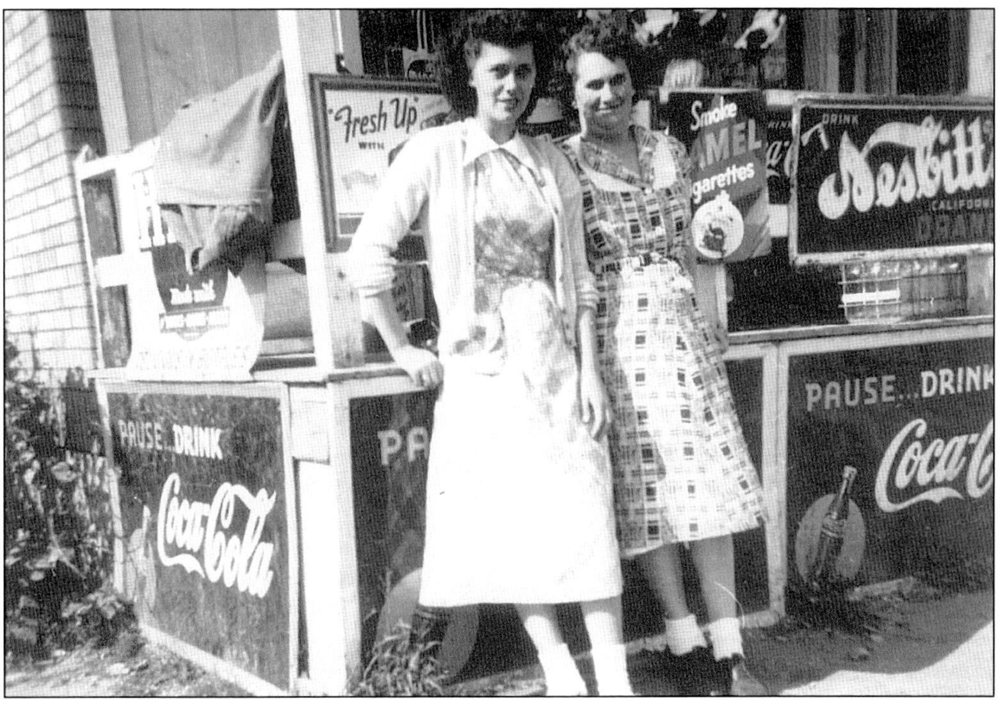

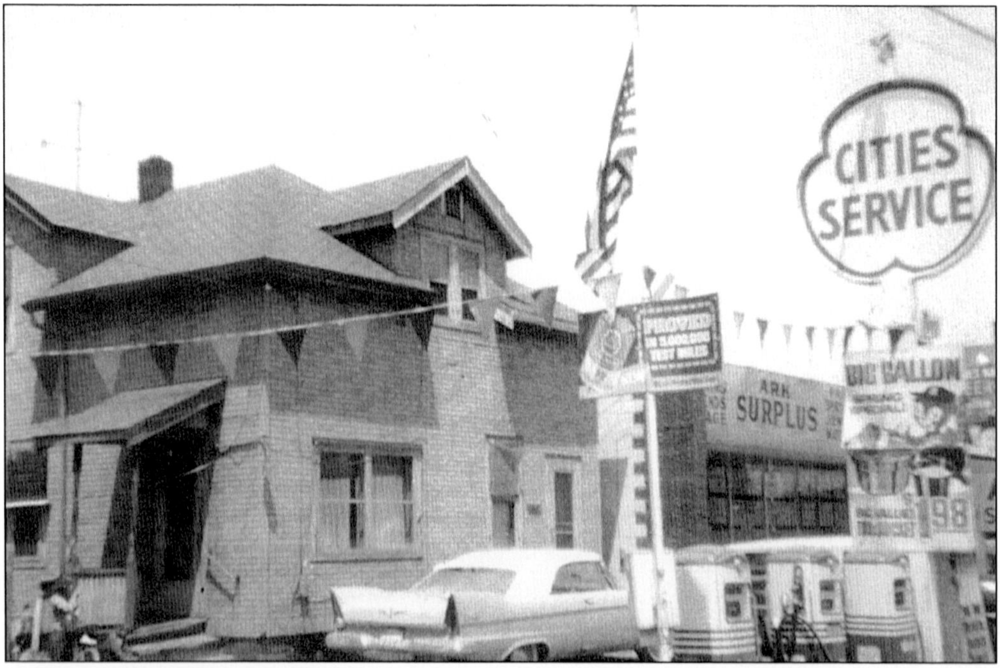

The Lowe's Service Station in 1955 is seen here adjacent to Ark Surplus, which was originally the Lowe's Bake Stand and then their grocery store. Ark Surplus carried military surplus items, along with hunting, fishing, and boating supplies. It was run by Sanford W. Feig. Linda Marlow is the young lady on the left.

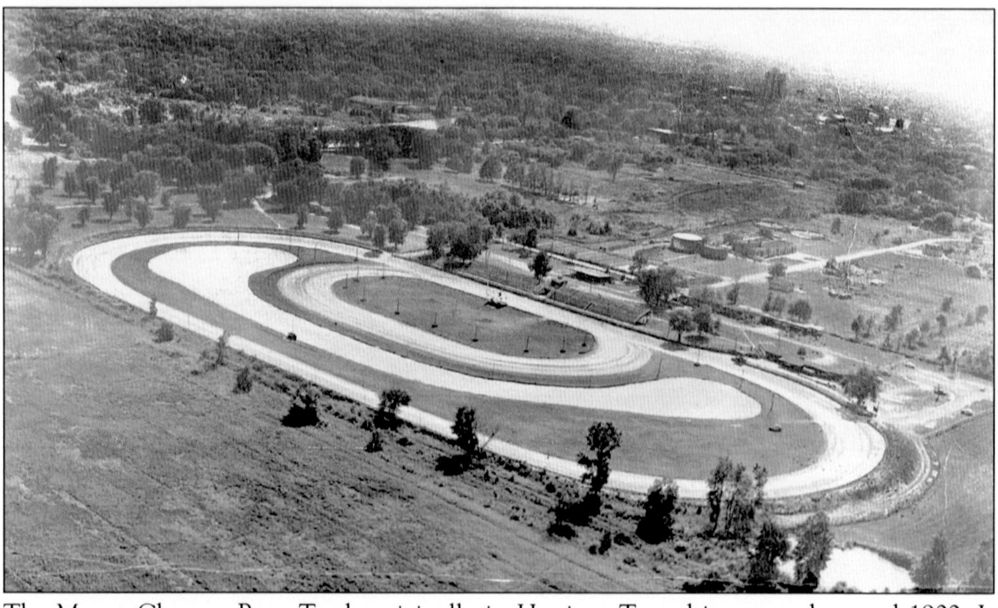
The Mount Clemens Race Track, originally in Harrison Township, opened around 1900. It featured year-round horse racing and paramutual betting. After horse racing on ice and betting were banned, the track turned to auto racing. In the 1950s, it was the only auto-boat racetrack, with a quarter mile long lagoon in the center. Today the property is part of Mount Clemens and is home to the Gibraltar Trade Center.

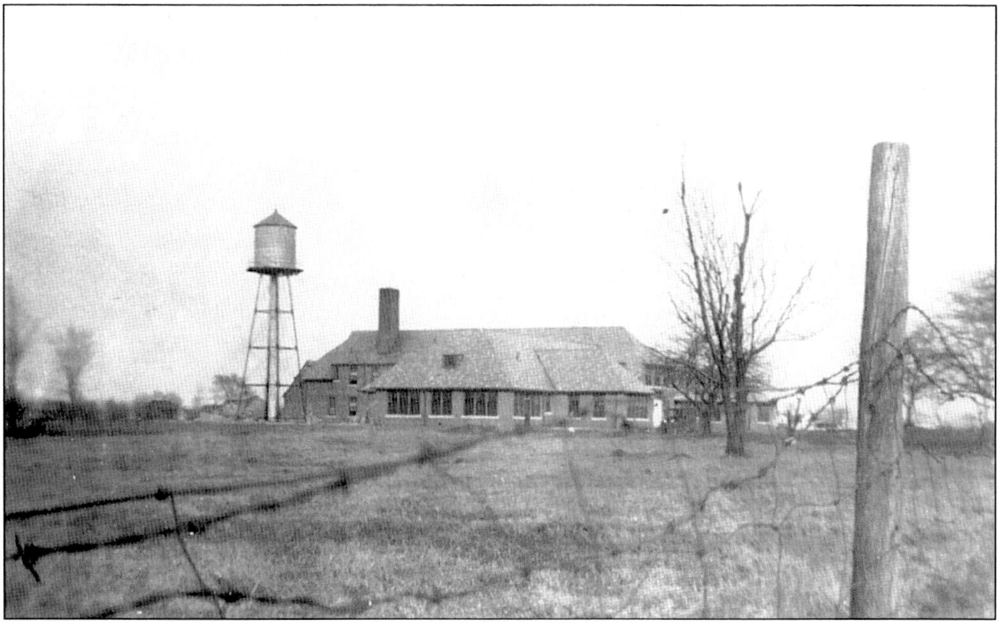

In the early 1920s, polio was rampant in the Detroit area, and a long-term care facility was needed. The photo above, taken on May 2, 1926, shows the original building on Ballard Road that was designed by distinguished architect Albert Kahn. It was known as Memorial Orthopedic Hospital, Sigma Gamma Convalescent Home, or simply Sigma Gamma after the sorority that created it. The polio center was very popular until the mid-1950s. It closed, but was opened again in 1963 as Anderson Memorial Hospital. In 1966 it was renamed Clinton Valley Hospital. It closed again in 1968 and reopened in 1969 as Harrison Community Hospital. The renovations and additions seen below made the hospital attractive to major health corporations, and in 1988 it became St. John Hospital—Macomb Center. In 1999 the name was changed to St. John North Shores Hospital.

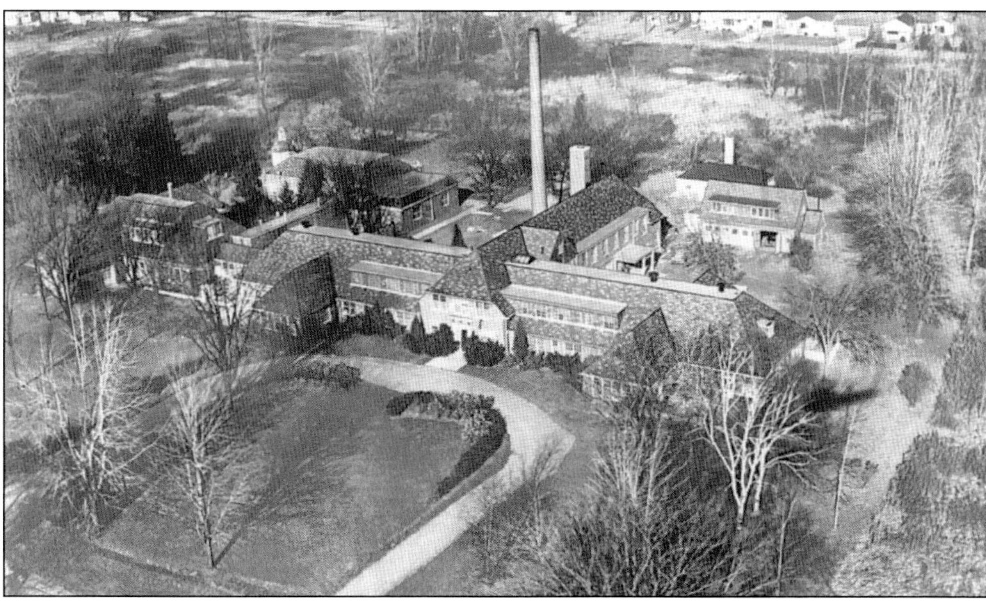

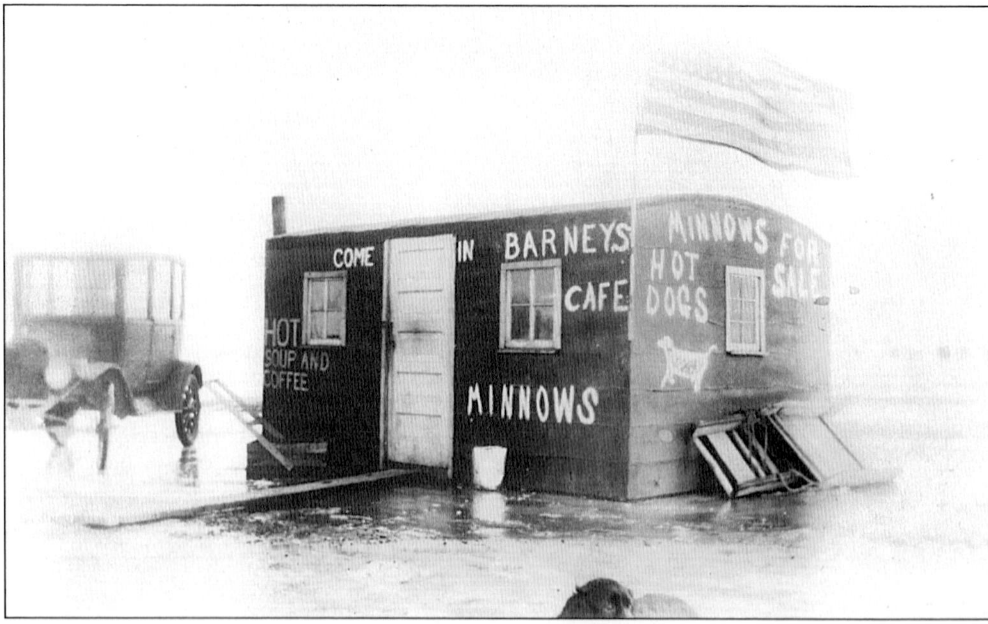

The Barney's Café was a regular sight at the mouth of the river in the early days. Mrs. Barney not only provided ice fishermen with the essentials like minnows, hot coffee, and hot dogs, she also got up early to make fresh donuts, a real treat on a freezing morning. The Barneys were among the first residents at the river's mouth when no bridges connected their property to the mainland.

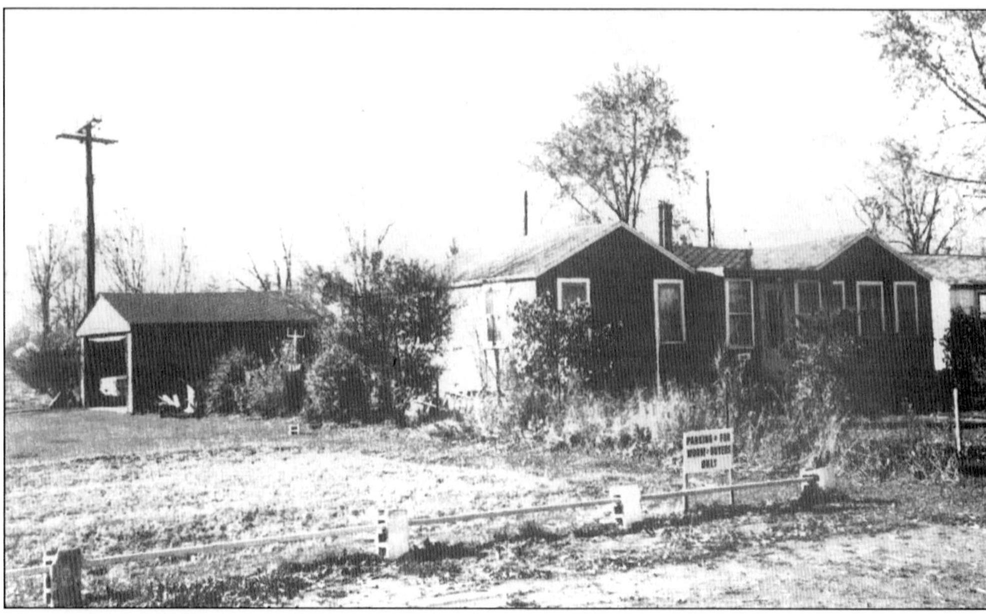

She was lovingly known as the "worm lady," but Beuna (Bea) Linderman was also one of those characters that spark fascinating legends. Her home on South River Road, near the fire station, was where the locals stopped for a dozen worms, a good story, or both. She was reputed to know "everything" that was going on in the township. The sign in front of her house read, "Parking for worm buyers only."

Four

The River and the Lake

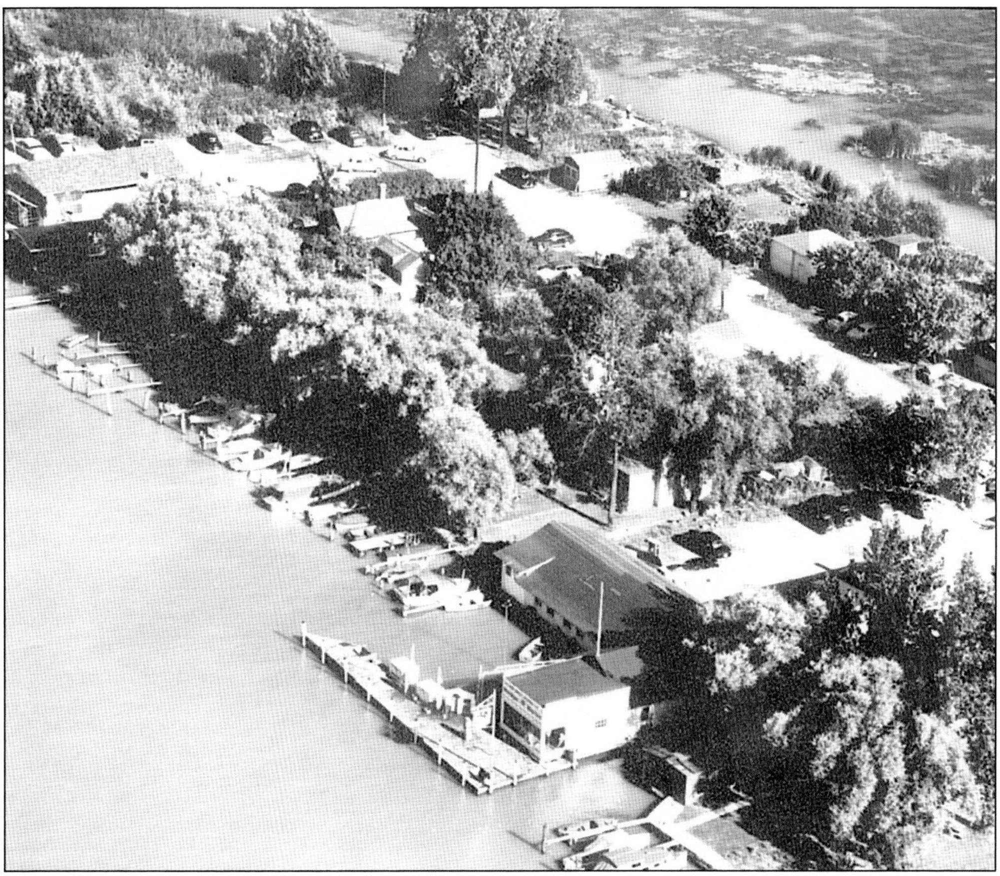

This aerial shows the end of South River Road when Zinner's (now Land's End) and Gasow's (now Boca Grande) were the marinas at the mouth of the river. Today, the marsh on the south side of the road is part of the bay. A lot of things were different when the Zinners moved to their new home. Edith was looking forward to using her electric coffeepot and was disappointed when she waited five years for electricity.

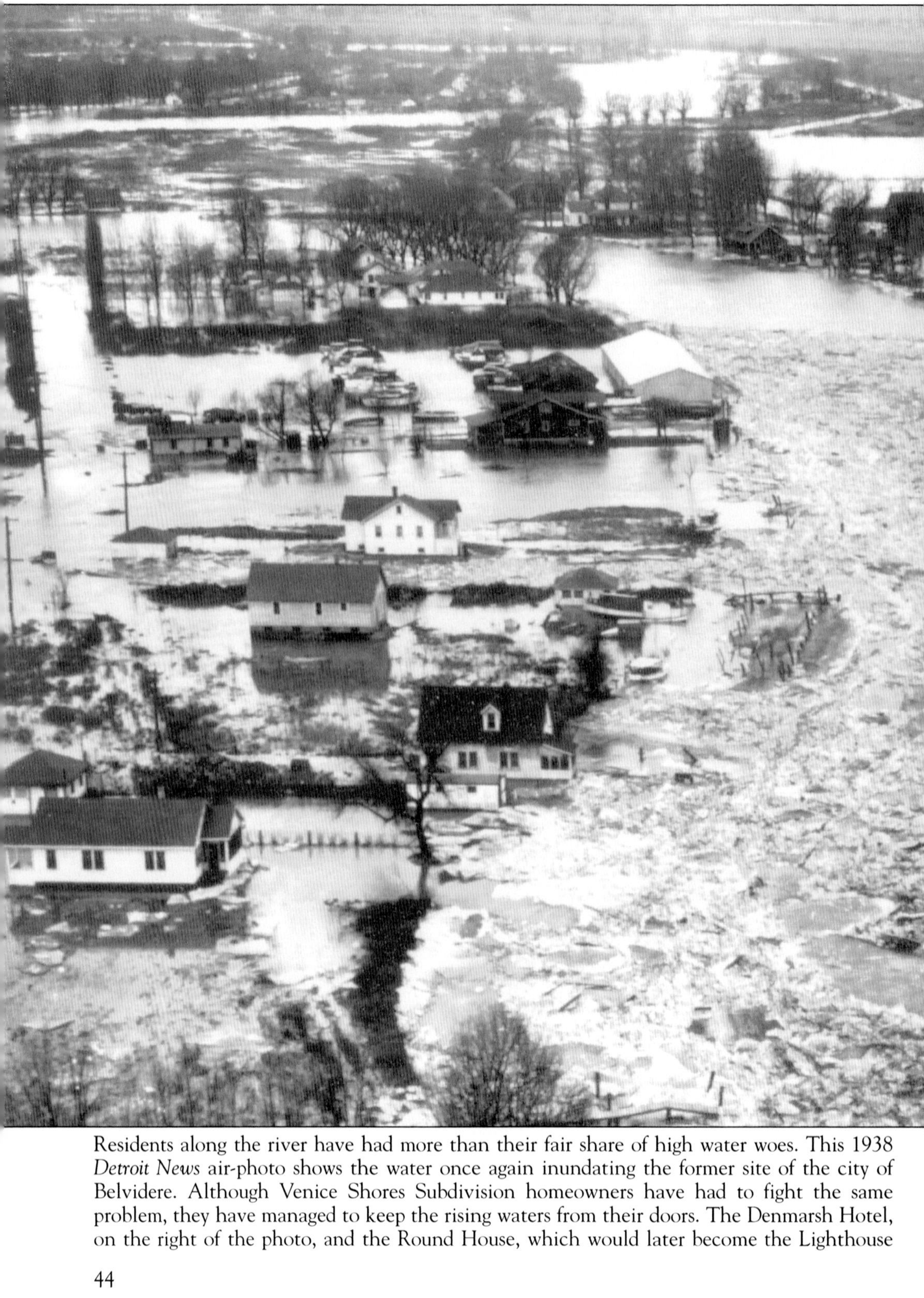

Residents along the river have had more than their fair share of high water woes. This 1938 *Detroit News* air-photo shows the water once again inundating the former site of the city of Belvidere. Although Venice Shores Subdivision homeowners have had to fight the same problem, they have managed to keep the rising waters from their doors. The Denmarsh Hotel, on the right of the photo, and the Round House, which would later become the Lighthouse

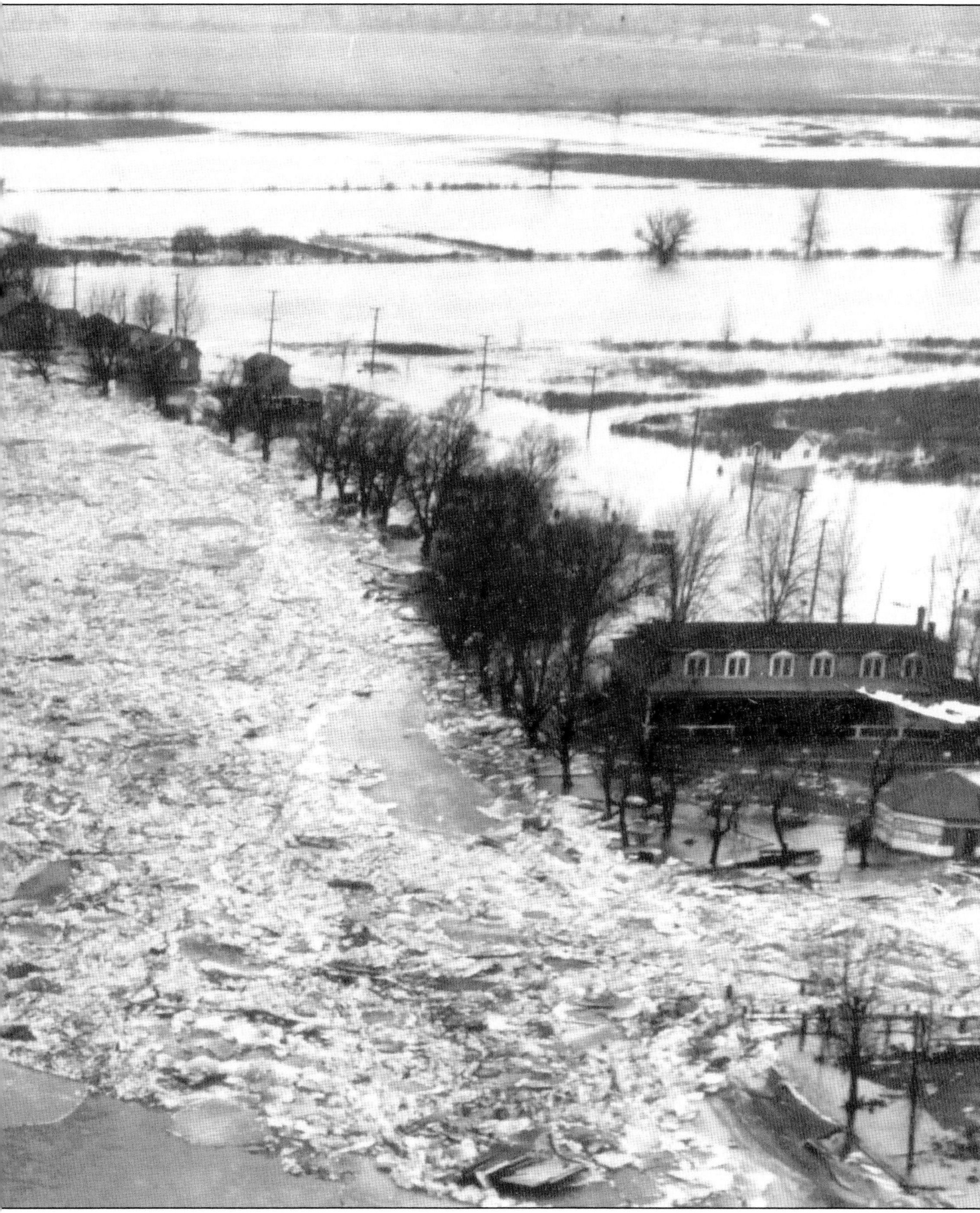

Restaurant, were obviously in need of sandbags and dikes. On the south side of the river, boats in winter storage were in danger of going for an unscheduled cruise. The lack of cars would indicate that the river roads were impassable, and residents had most likely evacuated the area to escape the frigid water.

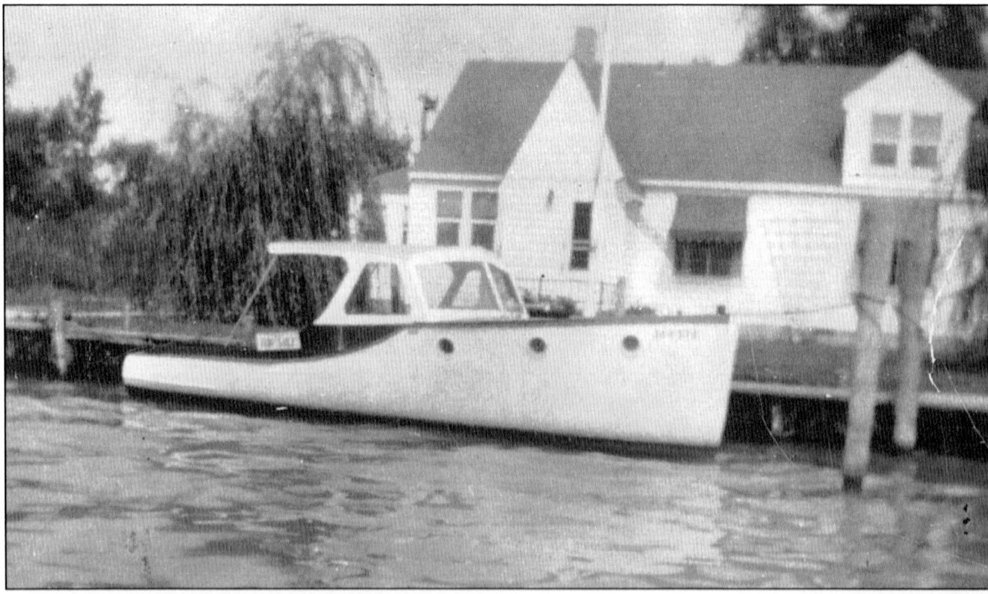

The river has always been a good place to spot all makes, models, and sizes of boats. This 26-footer behind the home of George and Marie Spear, however, was an unusual sight. Beverly (Spear) Tromley remembers that it was a Quagel, which was made locally in the builder's backyard. He made hulls only, so the buyer had to find someone to add the little extras, like portholes.

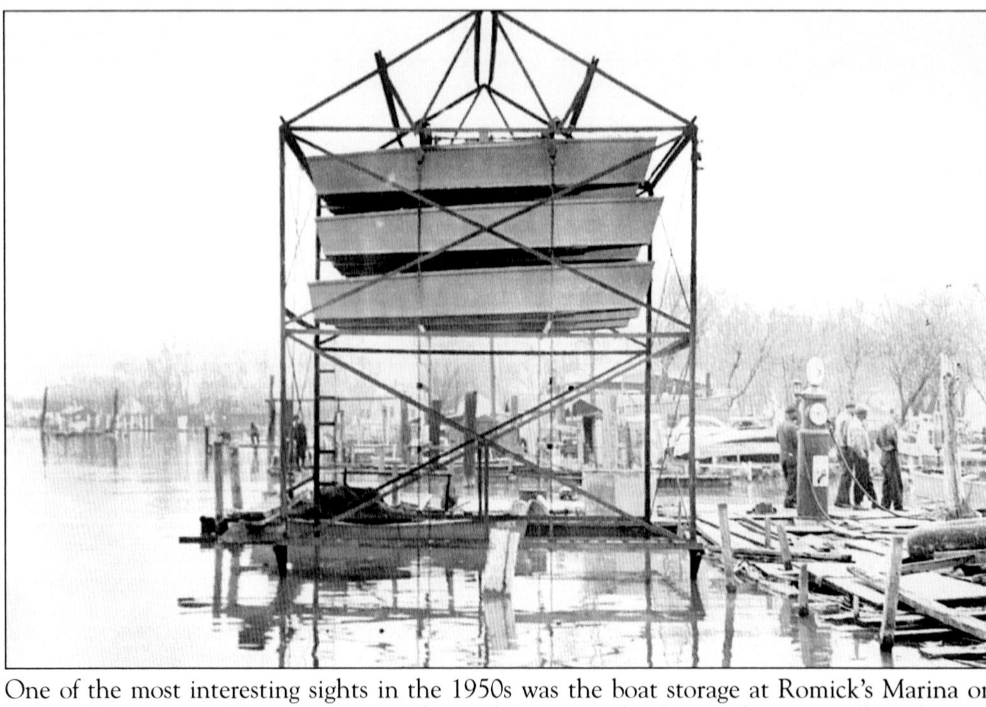

One of the most interesting sights in the 1950s was the boat storage at Romick's Marina on a foggy day. Designed by Milton Leitz, this early version of today's rack storage allowed rental boats to be stored without taking up much dock space. Leitz's son, Ray, remembers fondly working at Romick's and moving the boats up and down. The rack was later enclosed.

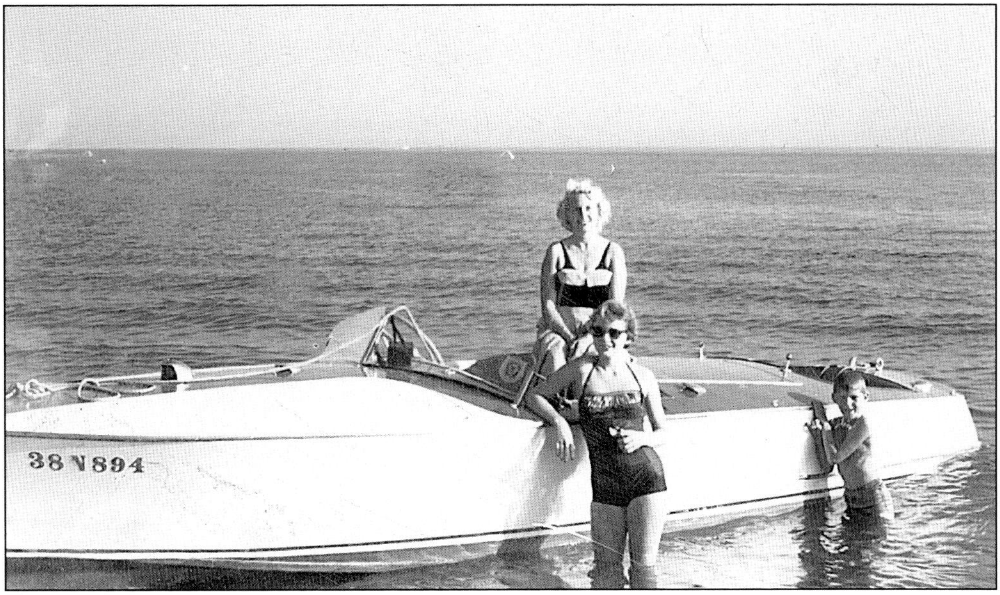

Not every 33-year-old woman with two children who had just lost her husband would take the time to study for a year to get a captain's license. Obviously R. Bright was not the ordinary woman. She was smart enough to not use her full name and deal with the possible prejudice against a woman driver. She was caring enough to be both a Girl Scout and Cub Scout leader. She was energetic enough to raise two children and then three more with her second husband. Dedication made her an active member of the Kiwanis, Soroptomists, VFW Auxiliary, Mount Clemens Art Association, Salvation Army, numerous historical organizations, the Women's National Farm and Garden Association, the Ski Club, and she still had time for church activities. Like many township seniors, Ruthee Bright Cowan gives of herself in so many ways.

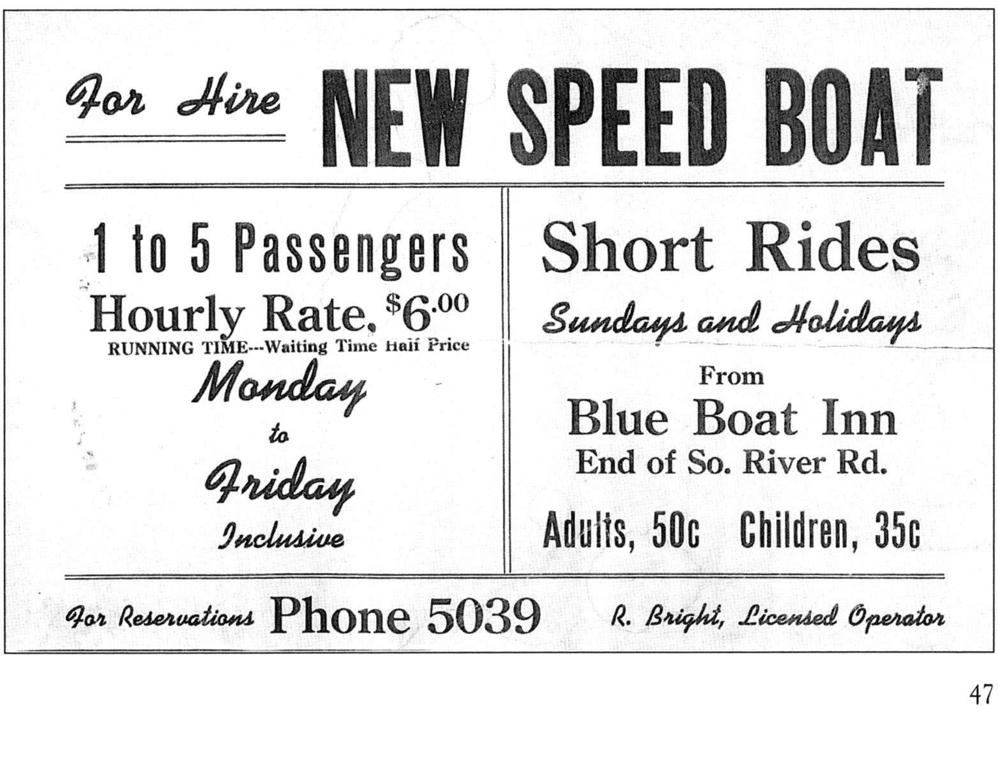

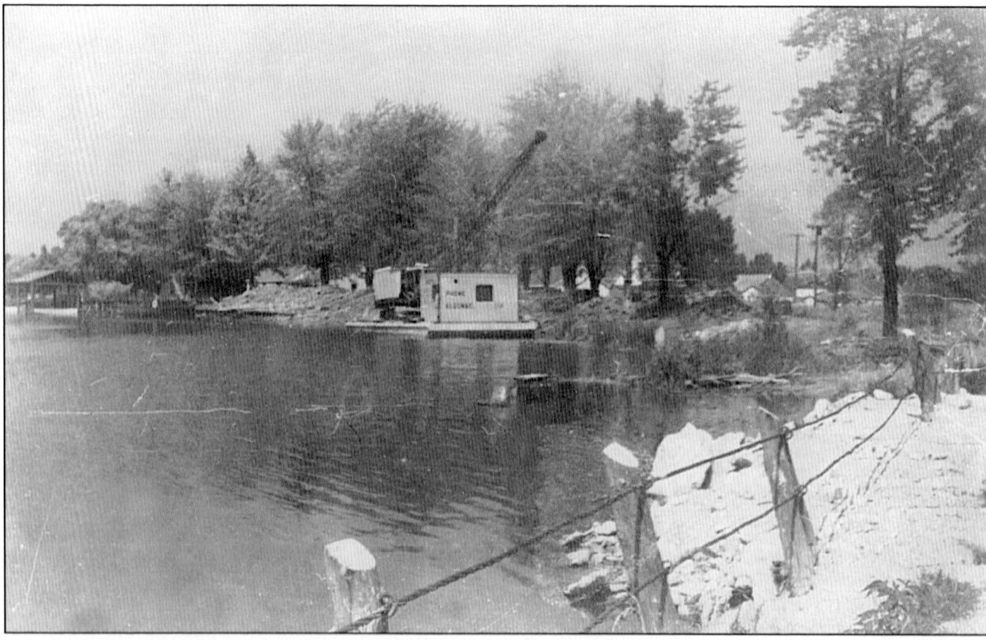

In 1944, this dredge was employing the most common form of dredging known as a dragline. In 1964, the Army Corp of Engineers DePoe Bay used the suction method to create the DNR site at the mouth of the river. Less common for larger dredging projects is the clam-shell scoop. Today, because of toxins, dredgings are usually taken by truck or barge to a contained landfill.

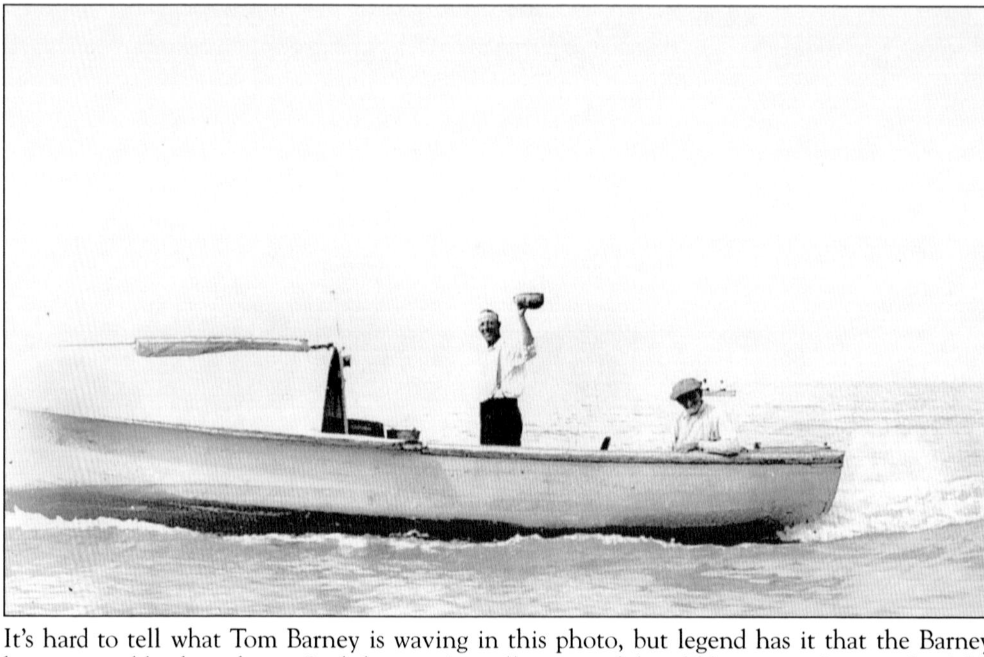

It's hard to tell what Tom Barney is waving in this photo, but legend has it that the Barney house was a blind pig during Prohibition. Actually, most of the old houses at the mouth of the river had secret panels that hid holes just big enough to conceal bottles of illegal alcohol. Jim Kelson, who like Barney was a hunting and fishing guide, bragged that the "Feds" couldn't catch him, because he was their "favorite guide." That's Tom's father in the back of the boat.

The fish shown on the right was not a prize catch. It was a model. In the hands of Alton Buchman, this fish could turn into $1,000. Buchman carved decoys—duck, geese, shorebirds, and fish decoys. At the 1987 sporting auction at Oliver's, one of his bass carvings did sell for $1,000. Chub, as he was called by his friends, caught muskrats when he was young but went on to be an avid hunter and fisherman.

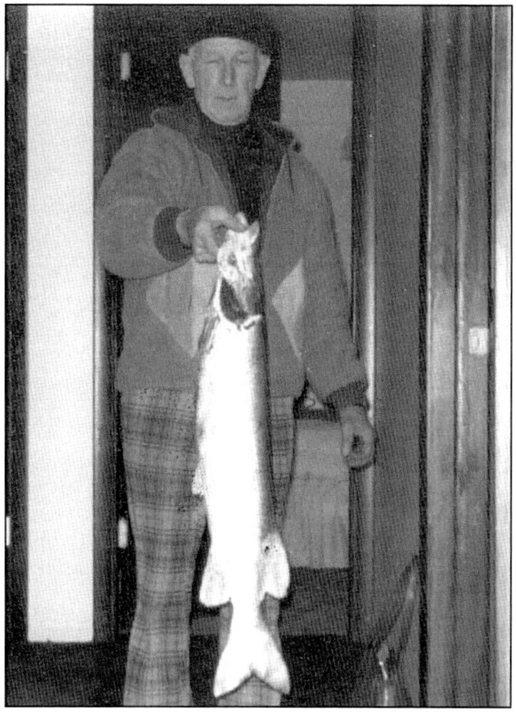

When the Historical Commission first discussed the idea of creating a Historical Hall of Fame, a worthy candidate was not hard to find. This award was created to honor those community members, past and present who have established themselves as leaders and innovators. Ray Trombley, shown here in his favorite place, was chosen because of "his tireless fight to preserve our environment for the future."

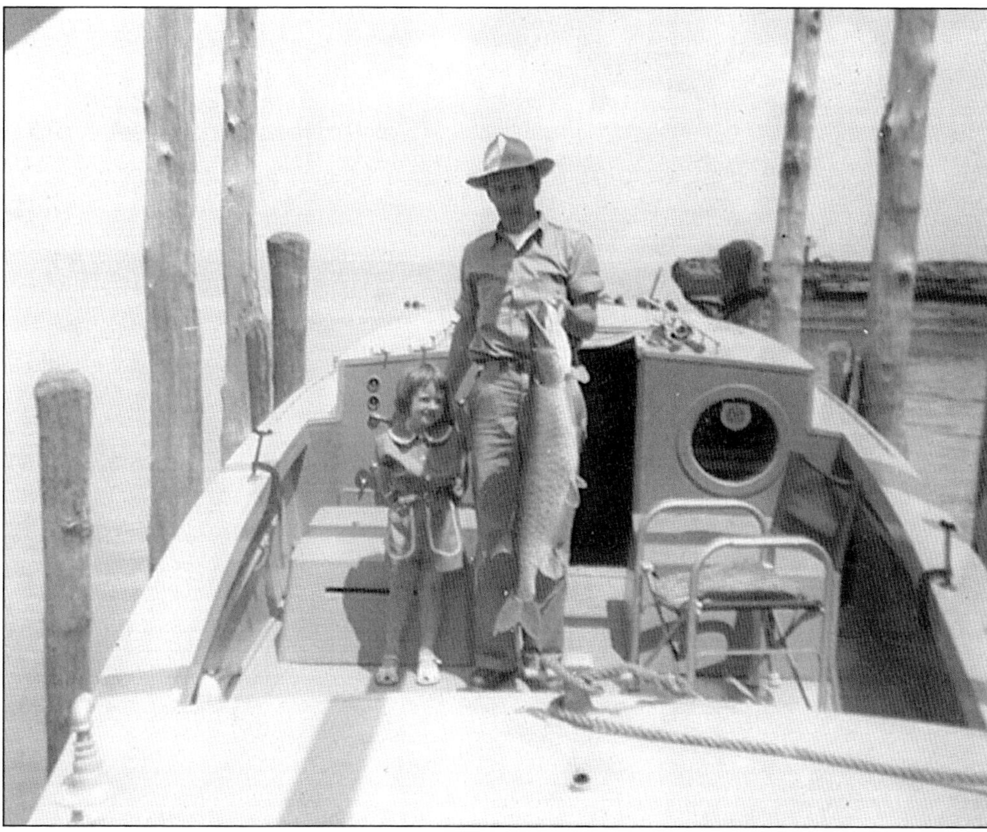

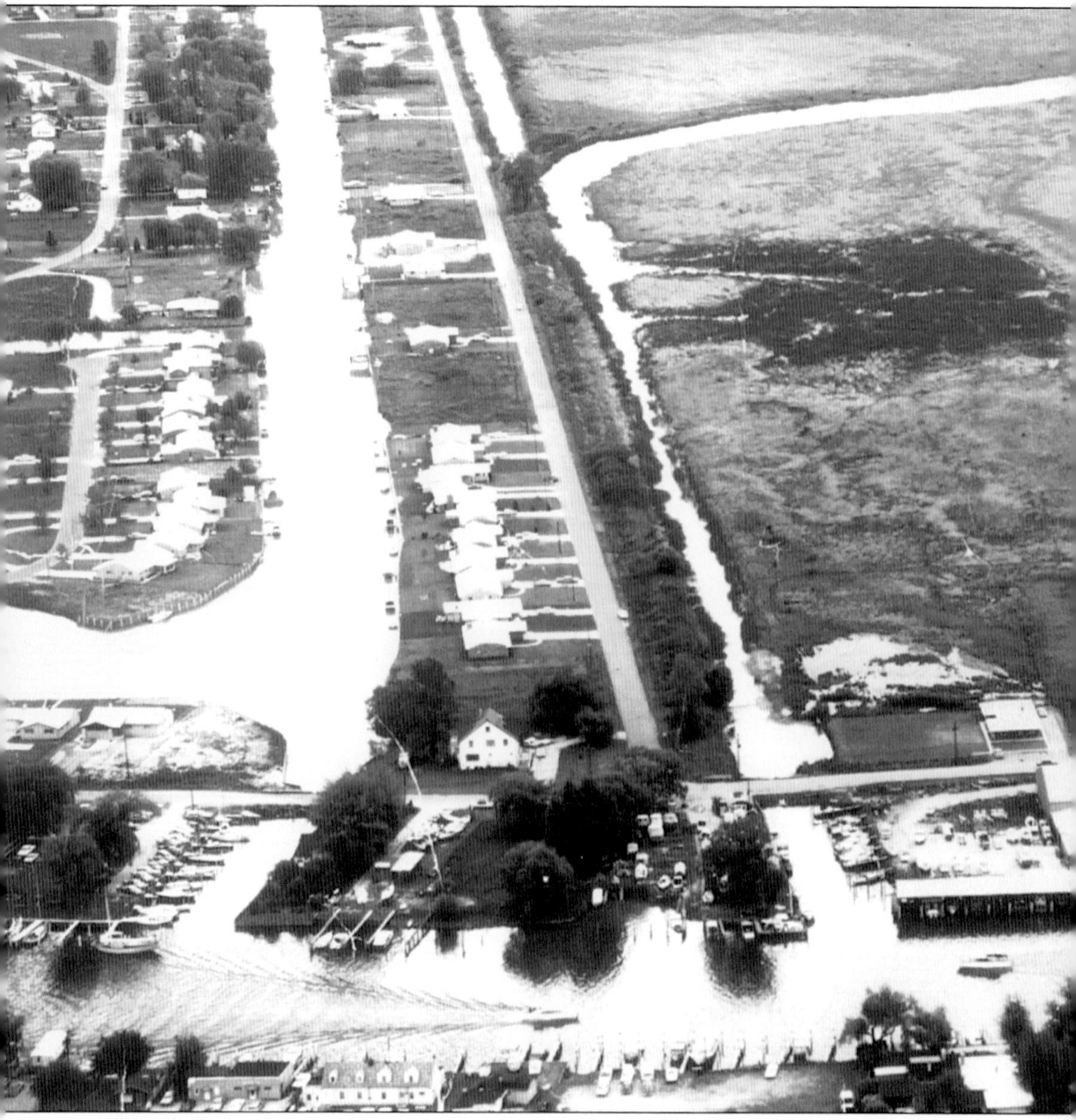

This 1960s aerial shows the marsh near South River Road and Venetian, which hasn't changed all that much. It has been the scene of several spectacular and frightening blazes over the decades, but it grows back and flourishes as a breeding ground for area wildlife. Ducks, geese, and swans have always found refuge on the river, and the occasional blue heron poses for the diners in waterfront restaurants. Bob Dickinson's Midway Marine (in the center of the photo) became Southbank Marina and is now Sundog. On the North River side those who remember

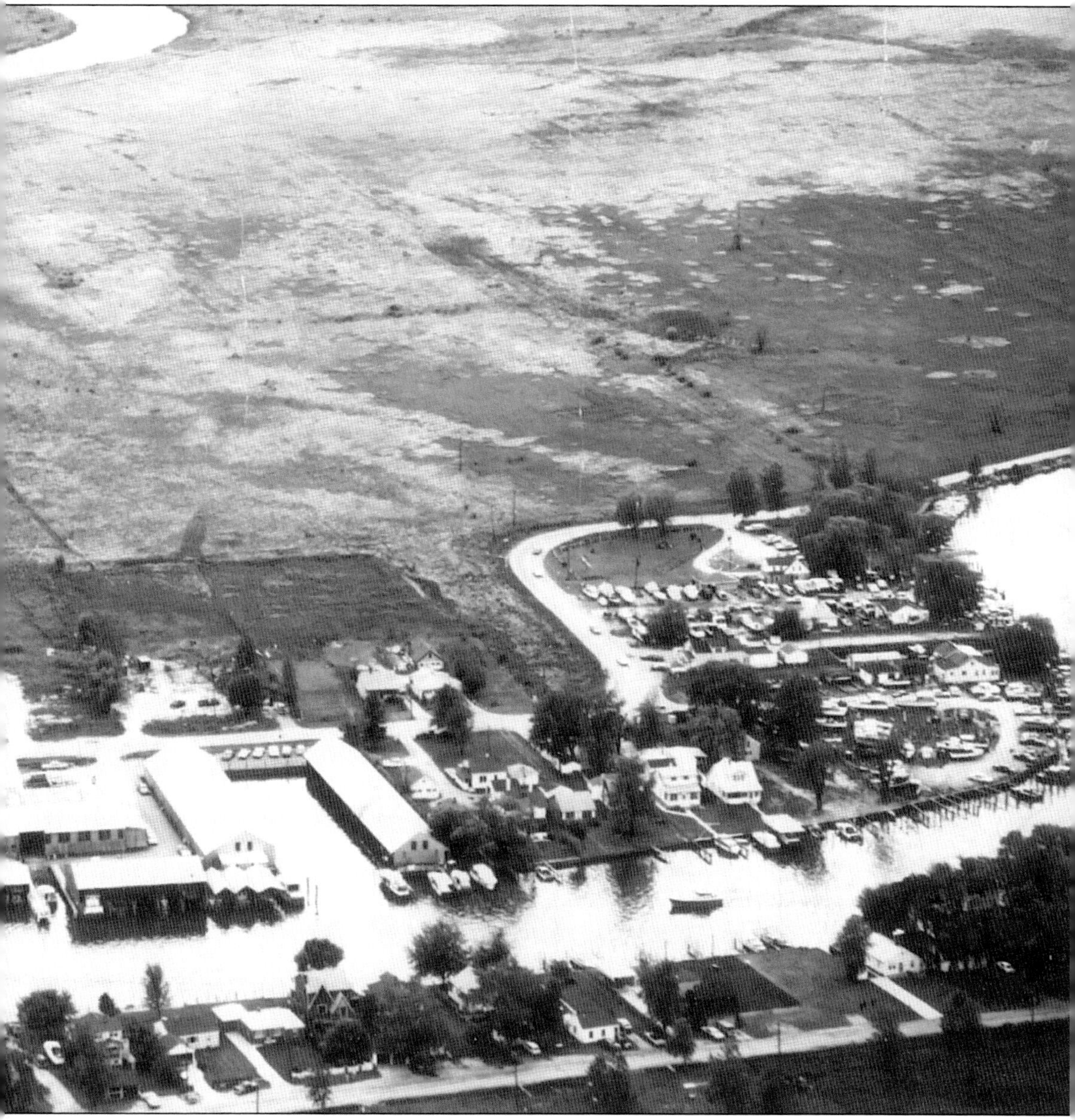

can spot Cruiser Sales and the Al-Dor Inn amid the trees, the original Crew's Inn, Mariners' Boat Club, and Koss's Restaurant, also known as Beachcomber and today as Bumpers. The river today might be very different if the Corp of Engineers had been able to carry out their plans in the 1970s. They proposed to cement the sides of the river to prevent flooding. The possible $400 million idea was abandoned in 1983 after $3.28 million had already been spent.

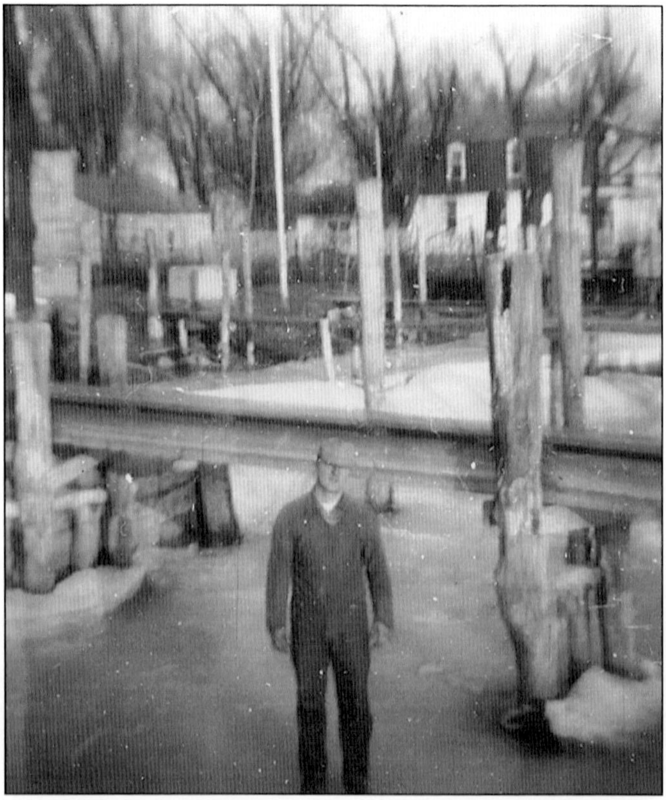

In times of low water, it's hard to remember how miserable high water is, but both ends of the cycle pose their own problems. Here Jack Aston shows just how high the ice in the river was. In 1996, residents of Wall Street, below, had no water in their canal, but that was a temporary situation caused by an ice jam in the St. Clair River. Later that same year they had a different problem. They had brought their boats home, under a very low bridge, but the water had risen before they could get the boats back out to the lake. Living on the water means learning to play a waiting game. If it went up, it will go back down, eventually.

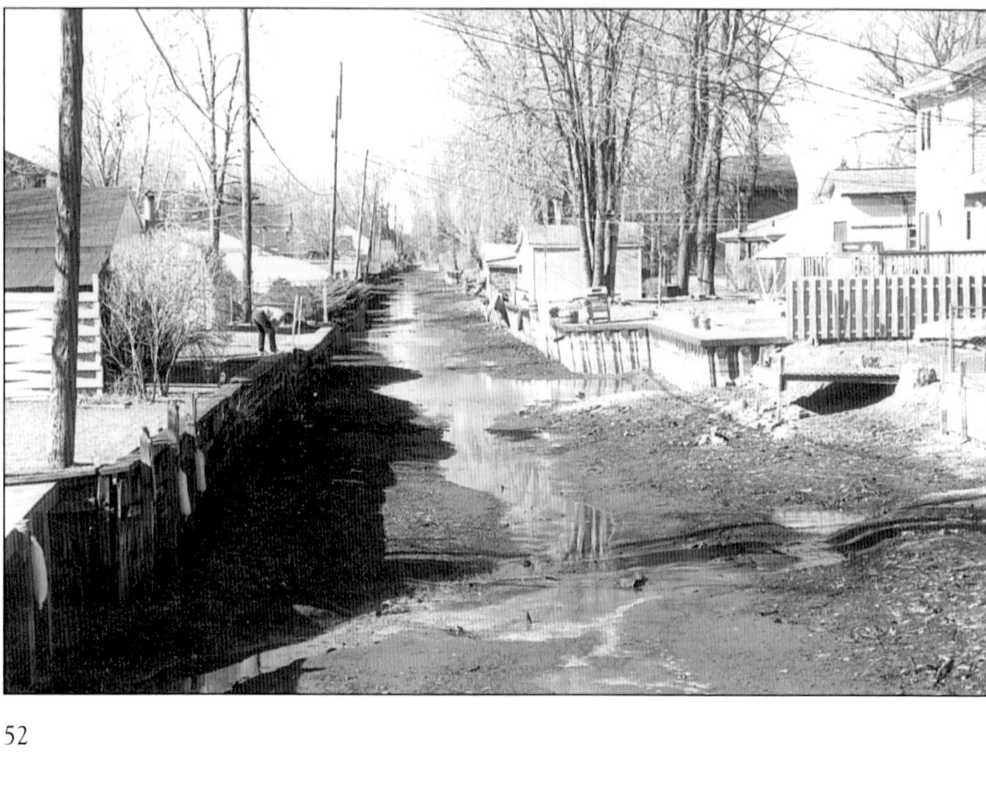

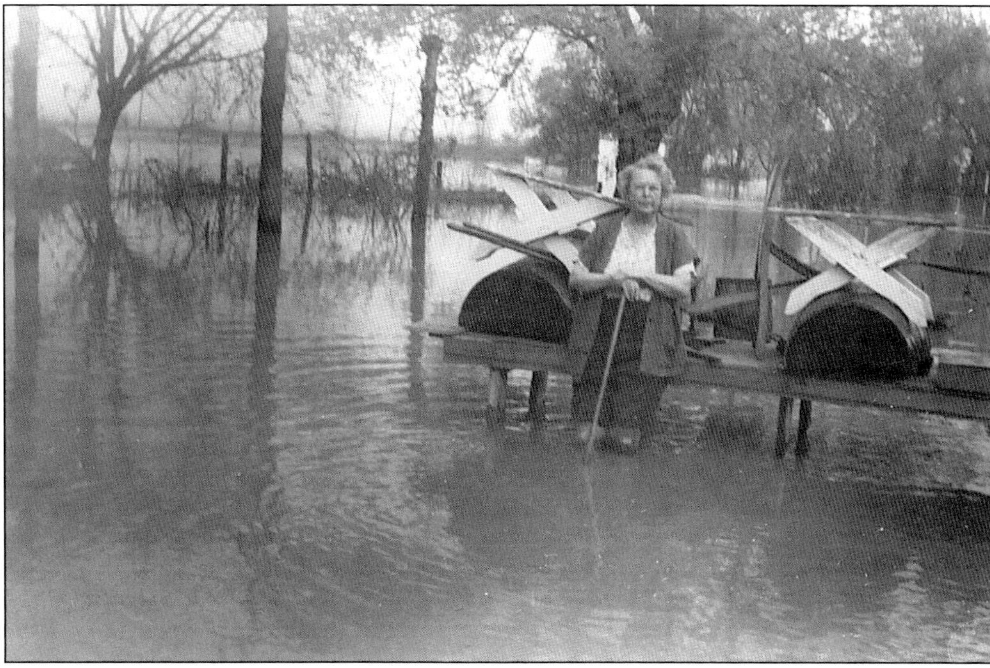

High water can hide many things but not this landmark on Meywood (now Manse). Houses in the neighborhood were often located by their proximity to Lucy Griffin's geraniums. In the early 1950s, Lucy posed in her yard with the oil drum and stands that would hold her flowerpots once the water went back down.

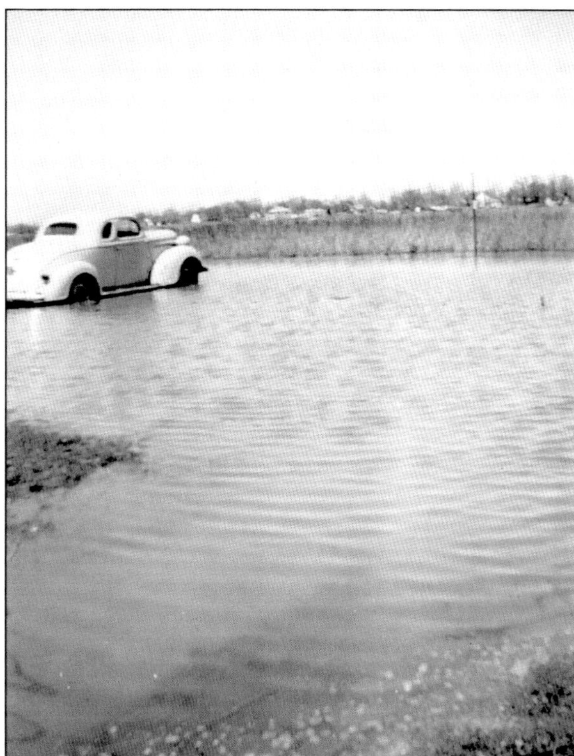

In 1952, residents were once again plagued by high water. Jack Rood recalls taking the fan belt off this 1937 Dodge Coupe and driving it to the higher ground of Streu's Market where he left his "good car." Others in the Huron Pointe neighborhood rowed across the Black River to Metropolitan Beach where they were allowed to park their cars. They were lucky. In other areas, evacuation was a common sight.

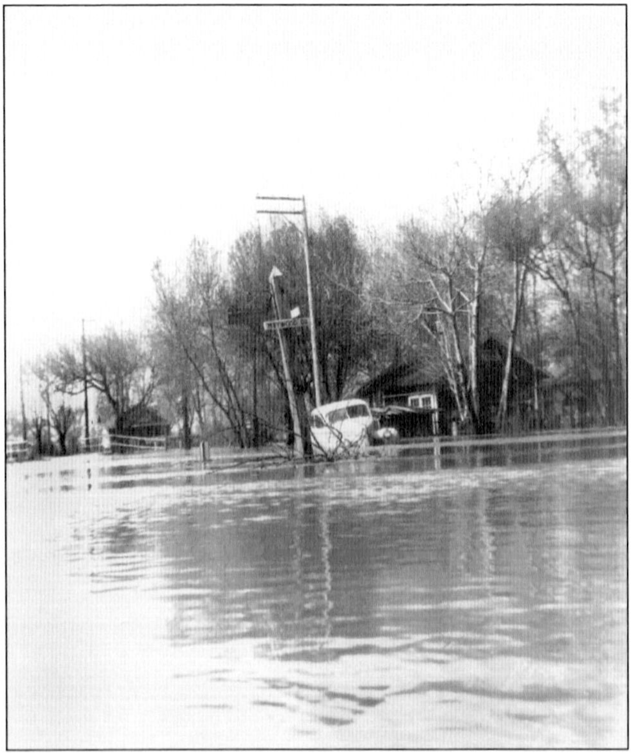

Today's television reports warn of the dangers that lurk in flooded homes. High water is more than an inconvenience. Bacteria and black mold can cause very real health problems. In the 1930s, residents like William Beaderstadt didn't worry about Stachybotrys. They worried about finding the narrow road and getting home or to higher ground without ending up in a ditch or in the river.

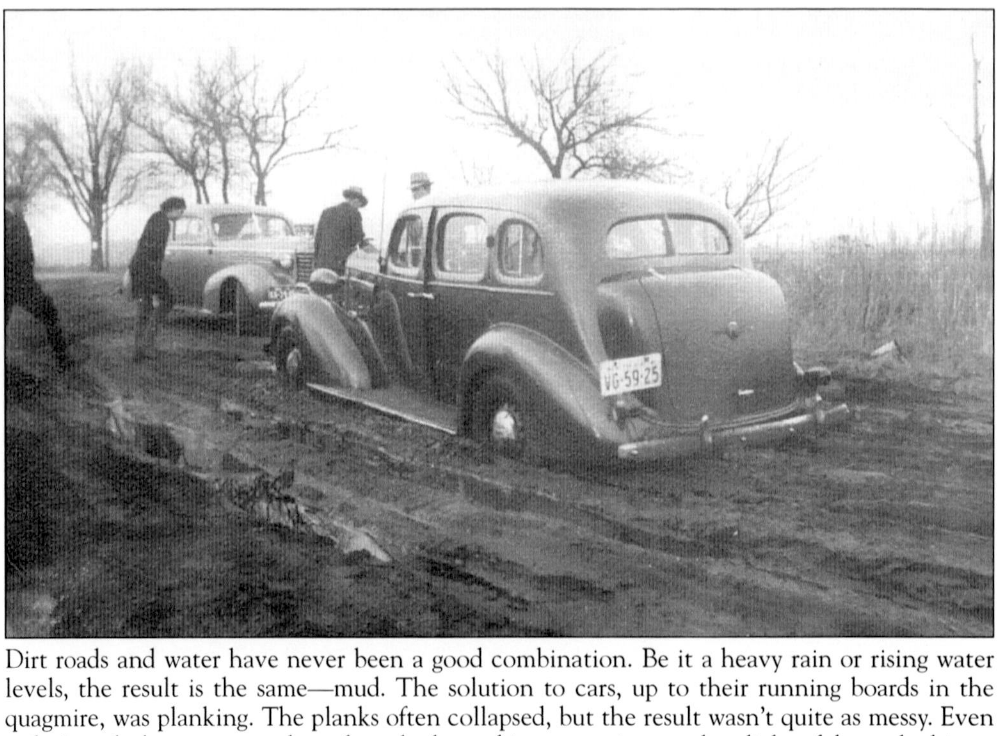

Dirt roads and water have never been a good combination. Be it a heavy rain or rising water levels, the result is the same—mud. The solution to cars, up to their running boards in the quagmire, was planking. The planks often collapsed, but the result wasn't quite as messy. Even today's potholes, no matter how deep, look good in comparison to the plight of the early drivers who couldn't even call a tow truck.

Five

Education and Religion

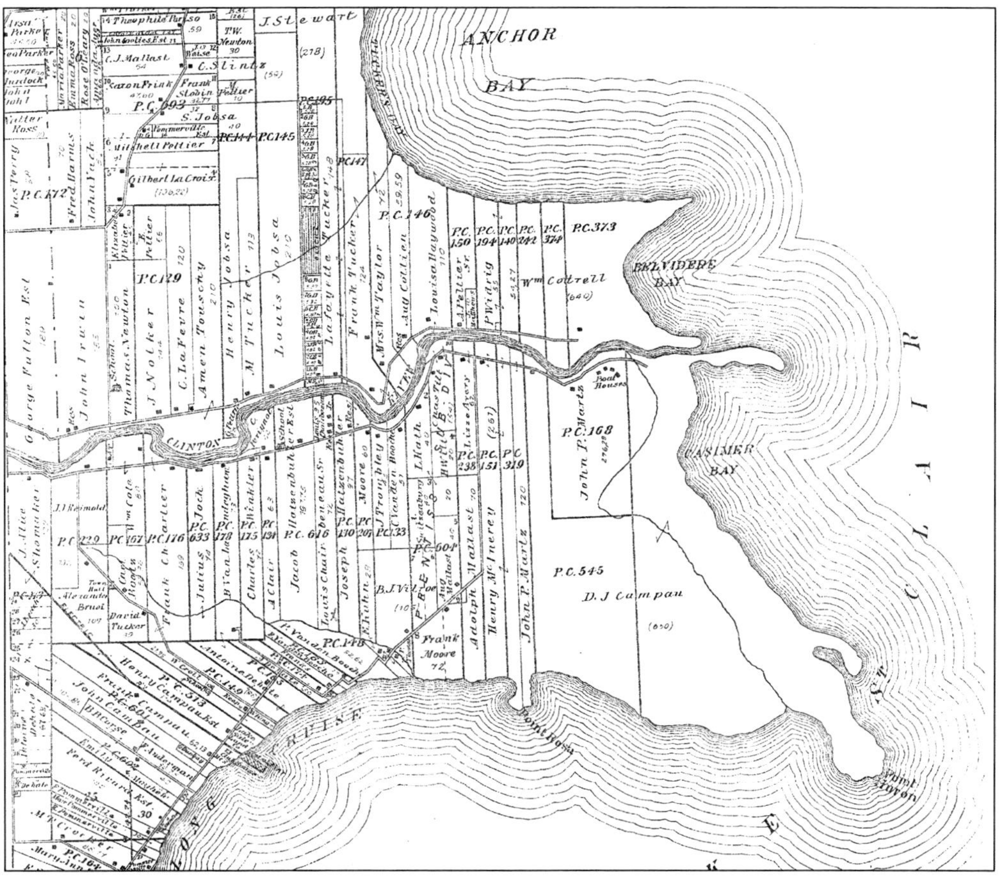

This 1895 map shows the location of the early one and two room schoolhouses. In the middle of the map near the river is the South River Road School on Jacob Hatzenbuhler's property. Also on the river, but closer to Mount Clemens, is the Irwin Road or North River Road School, on Thomas Newton's property. Harder to find is the Jefferson School, near the lake, next to Henry Campau's property.

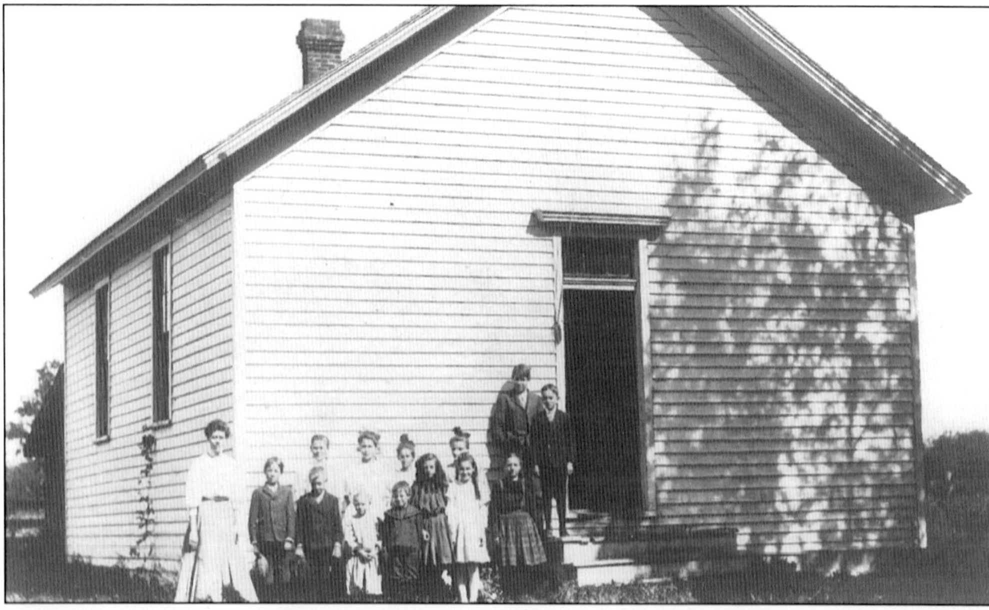

In October of 1874, Jacob Hatzenbuhler sold a corner of his farm for $25 as a site for the South River Road School. The one-room schoolhouse was on a lot 8-chains deep and 5 1/2-rods wide. Classes were, undoubtedly, a challenge when the teacher received $7 a week and had to compete with the excitement of the Native-American Indians who regularly camped near the school.

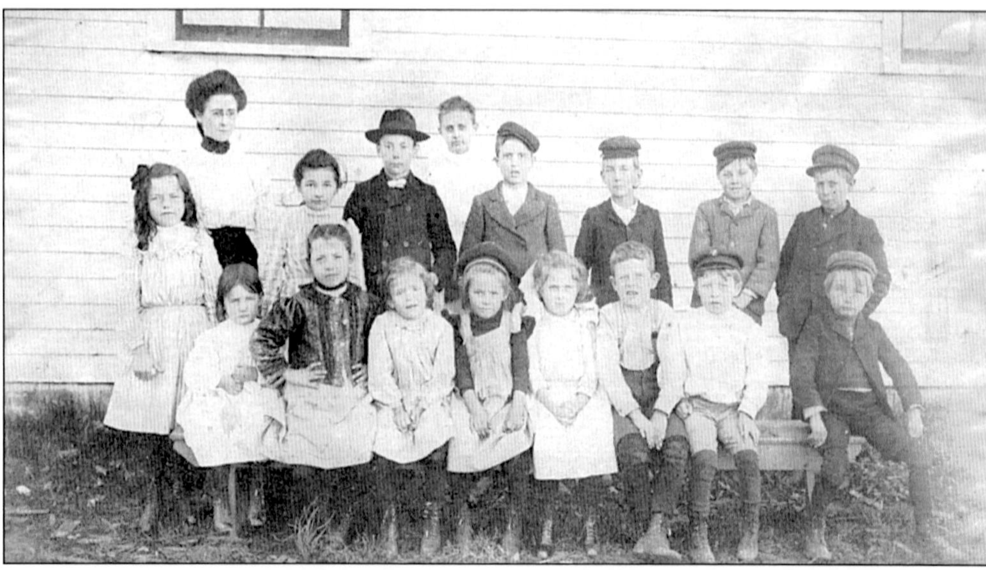

The list of students at South River Road School in 1903 may explain why the Hatzenbuhler farm was chosen as the site of the new school. The K–8 class included, from left to right: (front row) Dulsie Hatzenbuhler, Mabel Charbeneau, Ruth Chartier, Emmie Verstyn, Beatrice Koroff, Billie Koroff, Arthur VandenBossche, and Jacob Hatzenbuhler; (back row) Stella Hatzenbuhler, teacher Jennie Pomaville, Catherine Hatzenbuhler, Henry Charbeneau, Charlotte Teats, Norman Koroff, William Hatzenbuhler, Joseph VandenBossche, and Arthur Verstyn.

Originally known as the Lakeside School, the schoolhouse on Jefferson, seen here, was a popular place. Although some of these students in Miss Williams' 1924 class don't look too excited about being there. Virginia, in the center of the middle row, had to prove herself in order to stay. Since she was only four years old, she had to keep up with the reading level of the older students. Alga Ballard also spoke of sneaking away from her mother in the early 1900s to join her older siblings at the school. Apparently the early teachers or Alga's parents weren't quite as understanding. Alga was always hauled home.

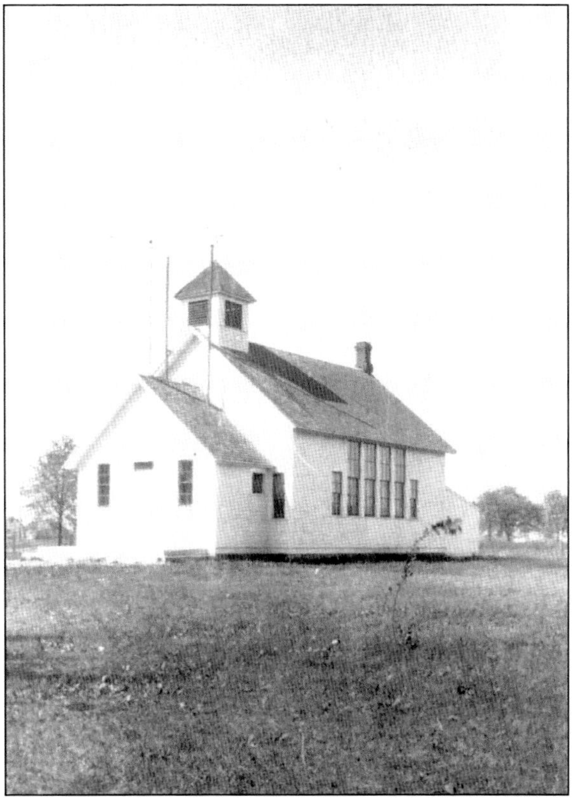

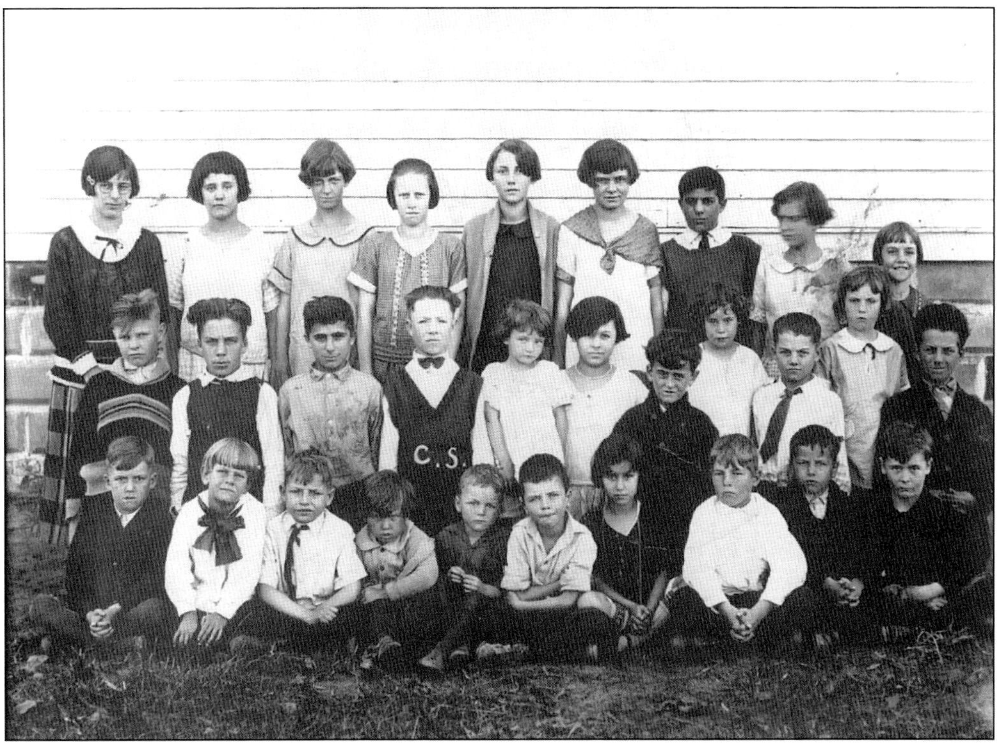

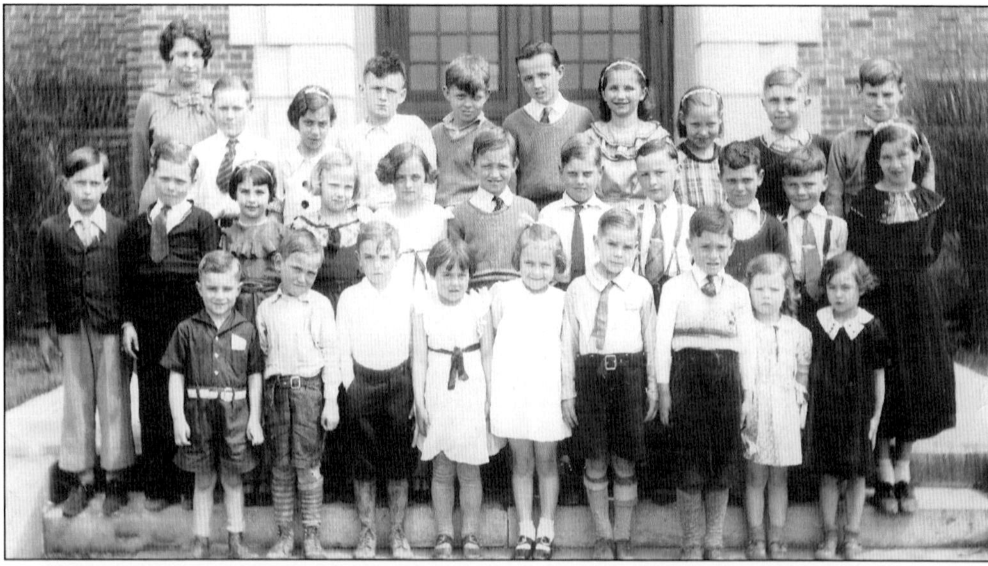

By 1927, the one-room South River schoolhouse was too small to handle the growing needs of the community. The new school, however, presented a problem. With 60 students in 1930, the school needed to employ two teachers. The School Board felt a man was needed to handle the older, "rough" boys. Fearing the scandal a man and woman teacher working together would cause, they found the perfect solution, Lester Schutt and his sister, Thelma. The class of 1935 is shown above.

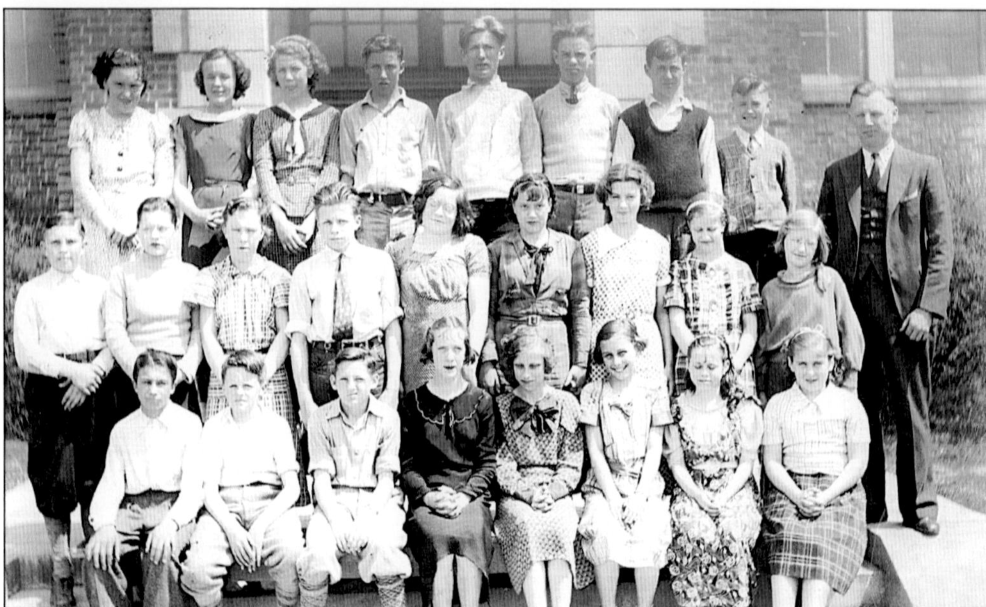

When Selfridge Field expanded, absorbing the Irwin Road School, students moved to the "big school" on South River Road. Lester Schutt, seen above with one of his classes, was promoted to principal. Several additions have been built on to the original four-room school, including the Lester J. Schutt Wing completed in 1972. In 1954, Mr. Schutt did have to share his school with Principal Fred Pankow until the high school was completed.

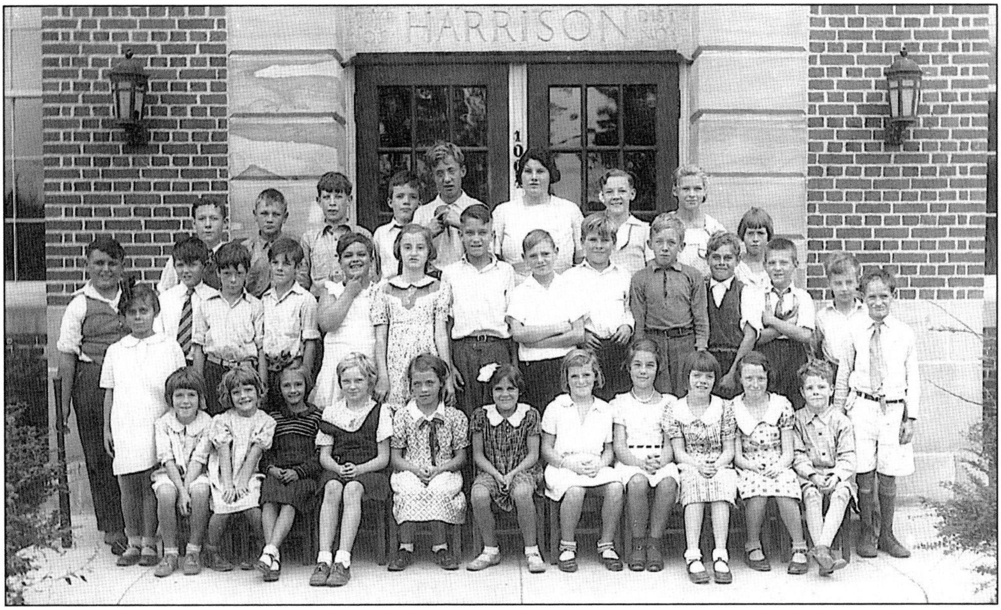

Before there was a L'Anse Creuse School District, students in the south end of the township attended school in the Jefferson Primary School District. Jefferson Primary School, seen here in Henry Callewaert's school pictures, was constructed in approximately 1930. Small additions were made, but by 1950, a major classroom addition was needed. This addition included restrooms, a receiving and storage room, and a boiler room. The 1971 bond issue was expected to provide renovation and modernization for what was then known as Jefferson Elementary. Instead, the Board of Education decided to build a new elementary and transform the old school into the L'Anse Creuse Administration Building. Today, the Administration is still located in the old schoolhouse.

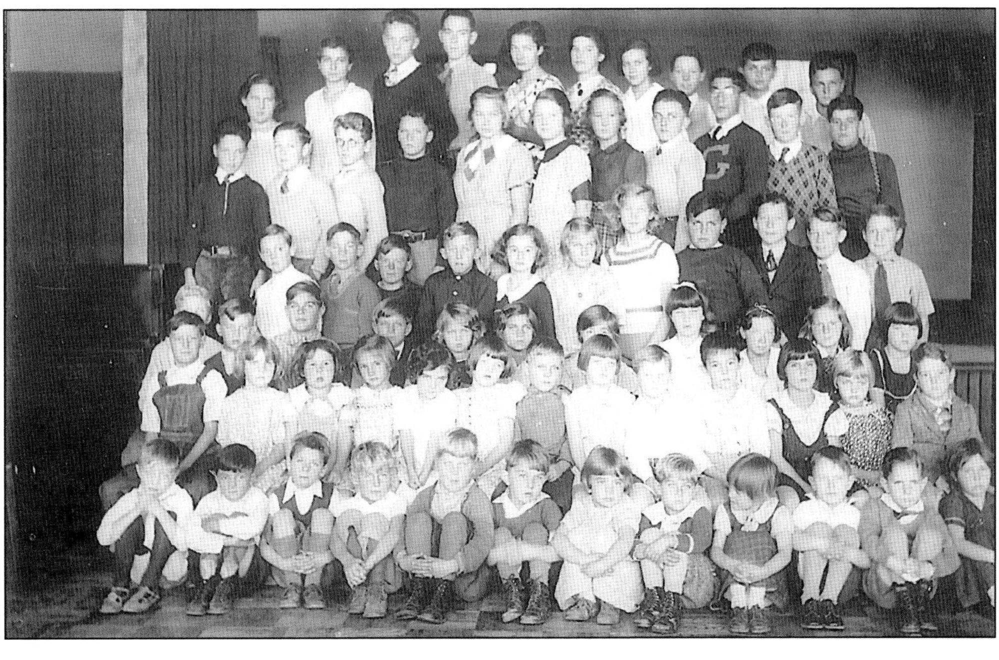

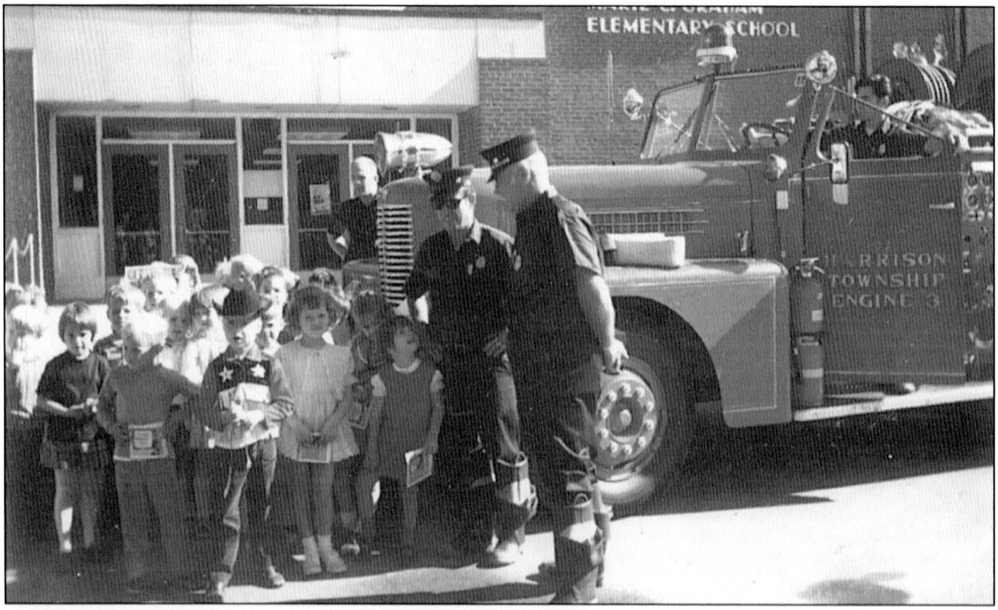

The L'Anse Creuse School District has maintained a close relationship with township government. Here, firefighters give students at Marie C. Graham Elementary a lesson in fire safety. They also held babysitting classes. The school, completed in 1965, was named after Marie Graham, who was the only female member of the district's first Board of Education.

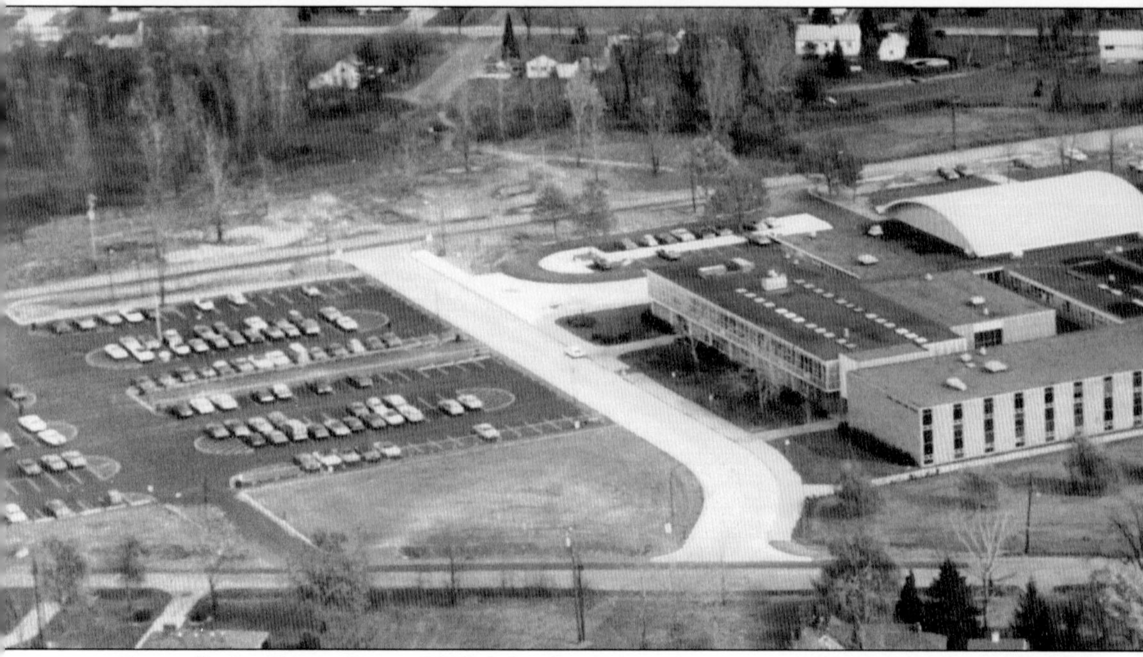

Originally the L'Anse Creuse High School's academic wing, it was the two-story section across from the parking lot, and consisted of 16 rooms and a library. A glassed hallway ran from front to back with offices, cafeteria, and gym on the left side. Opposite the gym was the non-academic wing, with rooms for drafting, wood shop, metal shop, art, and homemaking. Across the back of the building were the locker rooms, boiler room, and music room. The photo above shows

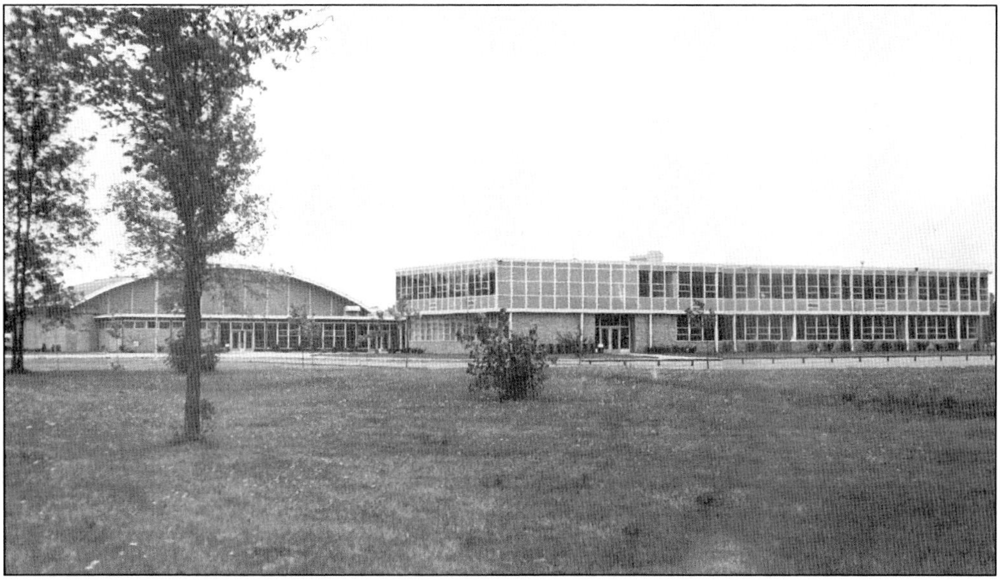

In 1953 the Mount Clemens School District notified its tuition students that they would no longer be accepted into city schools. The K–8 districts in the townships of Harrison, Macomb, Chesterfield, and Clinton organized to create a fourth class school district designated Harrison Township No. 4 Fractional. The official legal name then became L'Anse Creuse Public Schools. The dedication ceremony for L'Anse Creuse High School was held on May 13, 1956.

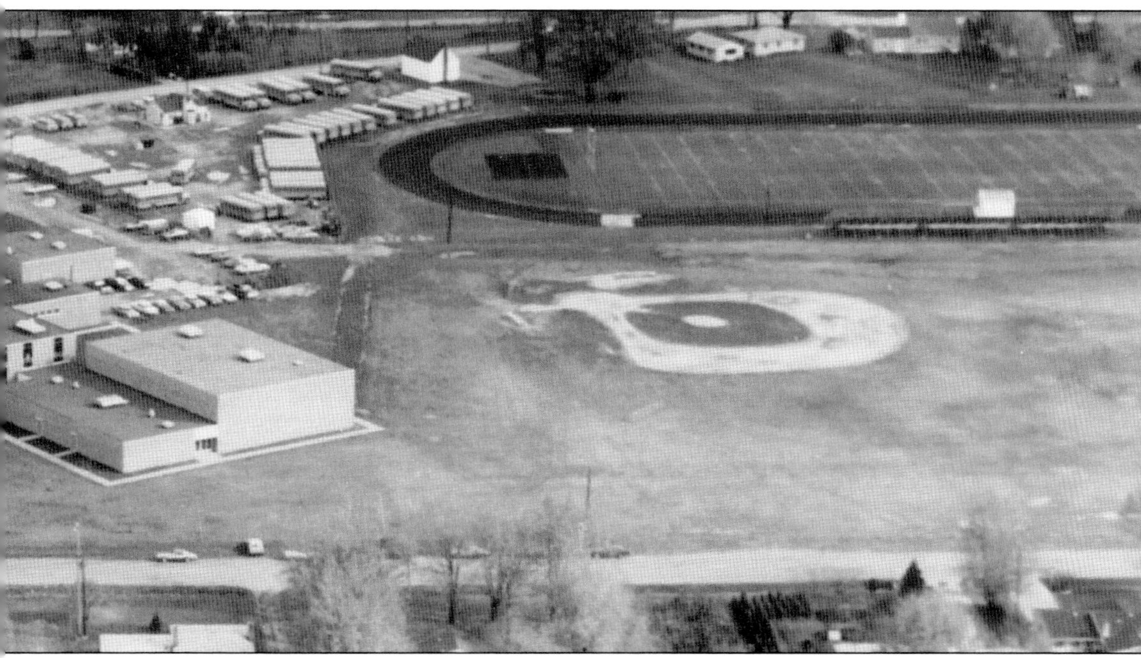

the addition of a two-story academic wing, a smaller gym and locker rooms, and a library in the center in what was an interior courtyard. Today more classrooms, a pool, and a new library have taken up most of the available land including what was the bus lot. Property for the high school was donated by residents and then swapped for this land that used to be a pig farm.

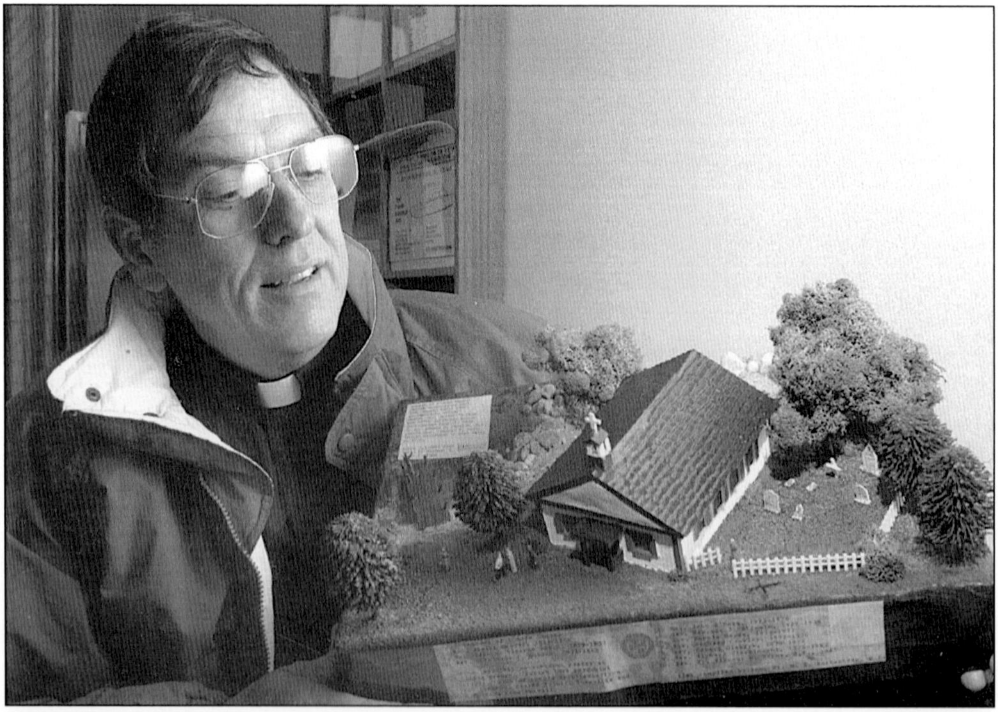

Father Pierre DeJean was a missionary priest who came to the township from France in 1824. He was in charge of La Petite Chapelle, which was built by Father Gabriel Richard in 1800, but he wanted a bigger and better church. Actually, he wanted two churches. He built St. Frances de Sales Church on the Clinton River and St. Felicitas on Lake St. Clair. In the photo above, taken by Larry Peplin, Father Michael B. Ruthenberg displays a replica of St. Felicitas.

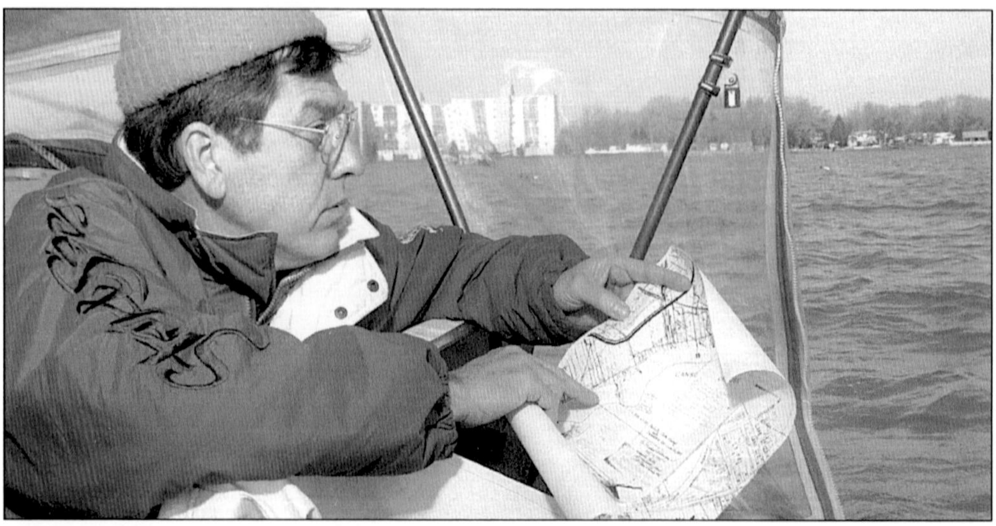

Many stories are told about the fate of the church better known as St. Felicity. Some involve a curse and others advice about rising waters, but everyone agrees that the water rose and covered the small church and its cemetery in 1855. It was lost but not forgotten. Father Ruthenberg, a priest at St. Gertrude Catholic Church in St. Clair Shores in the 1990s, was obsessed with finding the remains of the early parish.

Working with the research of Father Stanley Ulman who preceded him, Father Ruthenberg was determined to do what Father Ulman hadn't, find the church. After eight years of research, he contacted the Dossin Great Lakes Museum dive team. On November 5, 1995, Dossin curator, John Polaczk, and the divers followed Father Ruthenberg's directions to a site in Harrison Township near the St. Clair Shores border. In about 10 feet of water, some 2,000 feet from shore, the divers located several large stones covered in zebra mussels. Convinced they had found the cemetery, they recorded their location and announced the discovery of the lost church. Despite further exploration by amateur divers the following year, the church foundation was not found. The original discovery, however, was lauded by Cardinal Adam Maida as a "great, wonderful find."

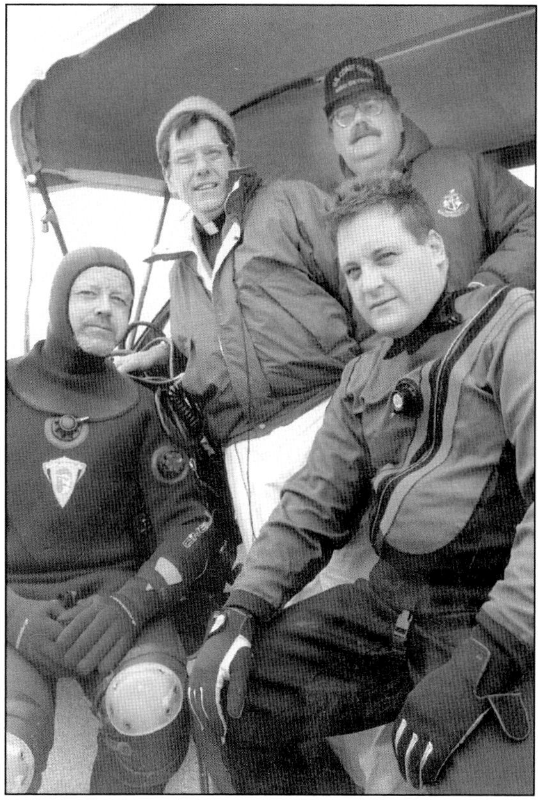

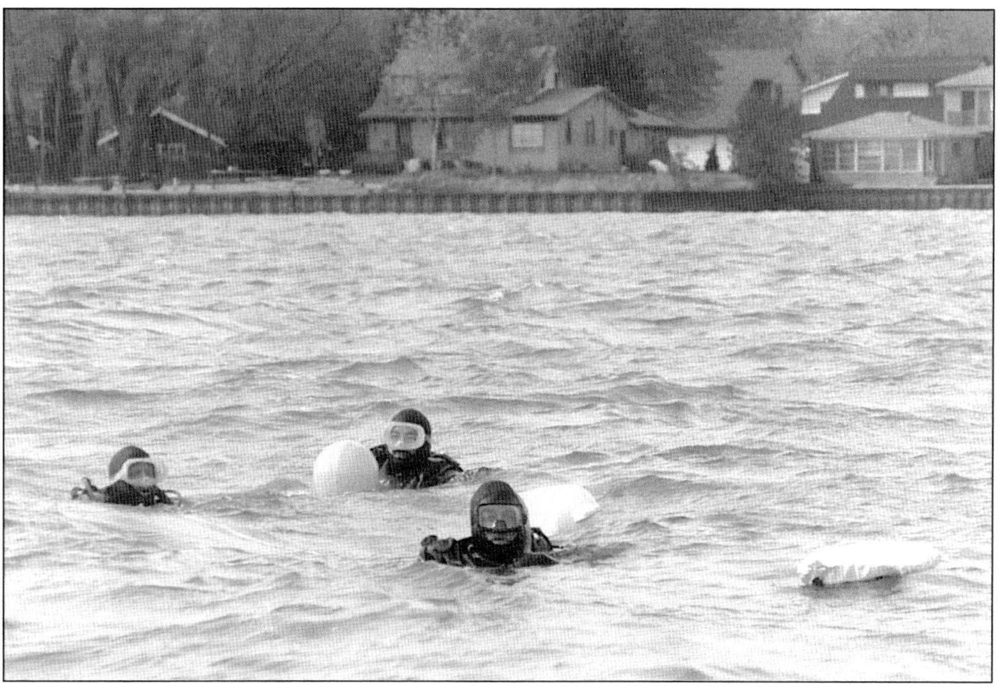

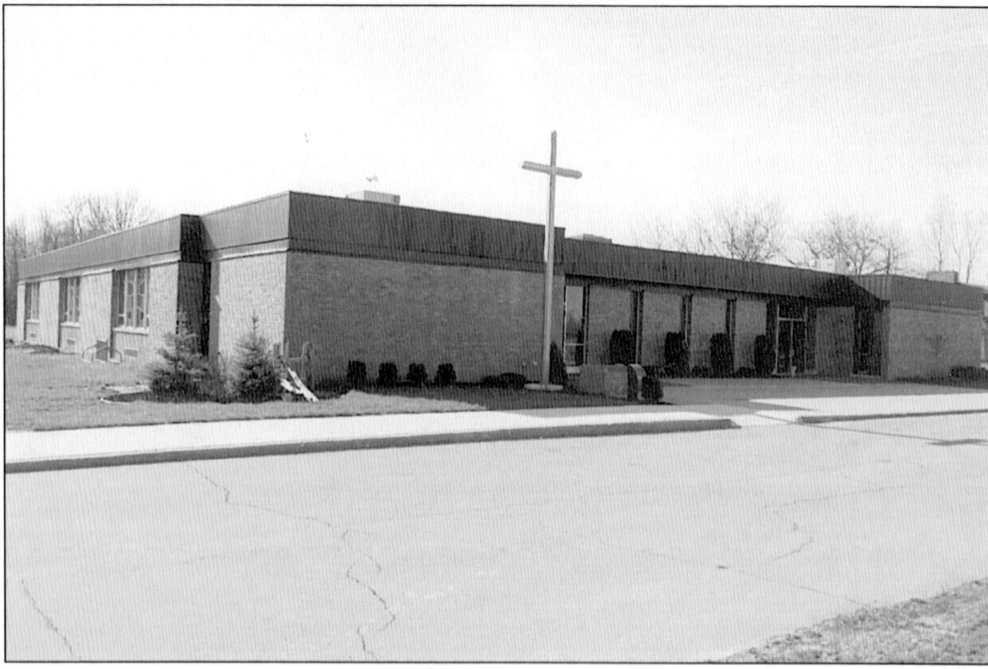

St. Hubert Parish was officially established on June 14, 1966. The first St. Hubert Church building was dedicated on October 21, 1967. Father Bill Borowski was pastor until 1983 when he was transferred to Gibraltar. He was replaced by Father Bauer who served the congregation from 1983 until 1985 being replaced by Father James J. O'Leary. In 1996, the parish celebrated its 30th anniversary and dedicated the new church pictured below. The original church, above, was converted into an activity center and named for the congregation's first priest. The latest addition is a magnificent oratory for private worship, the first in the state. Last September the church held its 16th-annual festival to raise money for church activities. Another special project was the building of a second Habitat for Humanity home for a family in the parish.

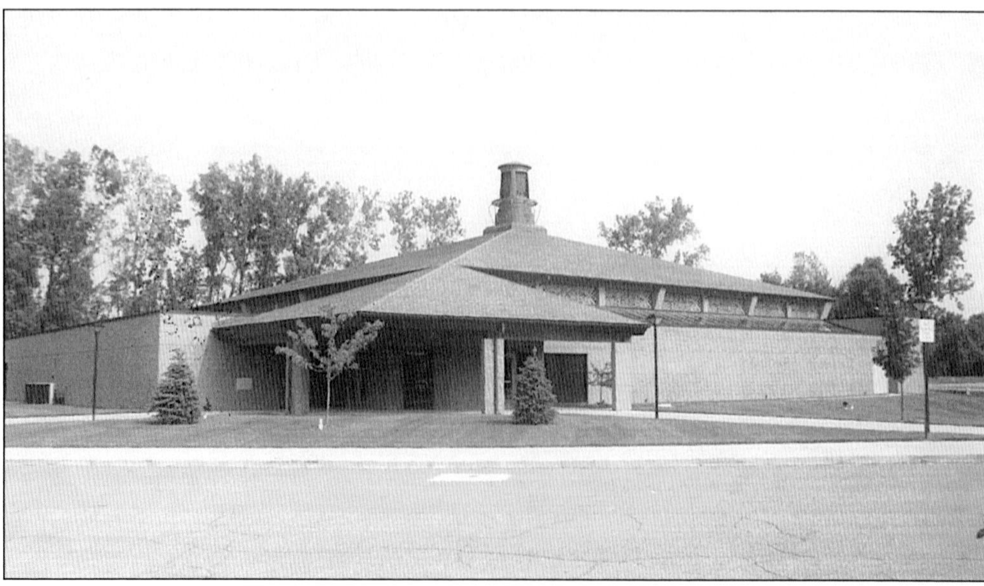

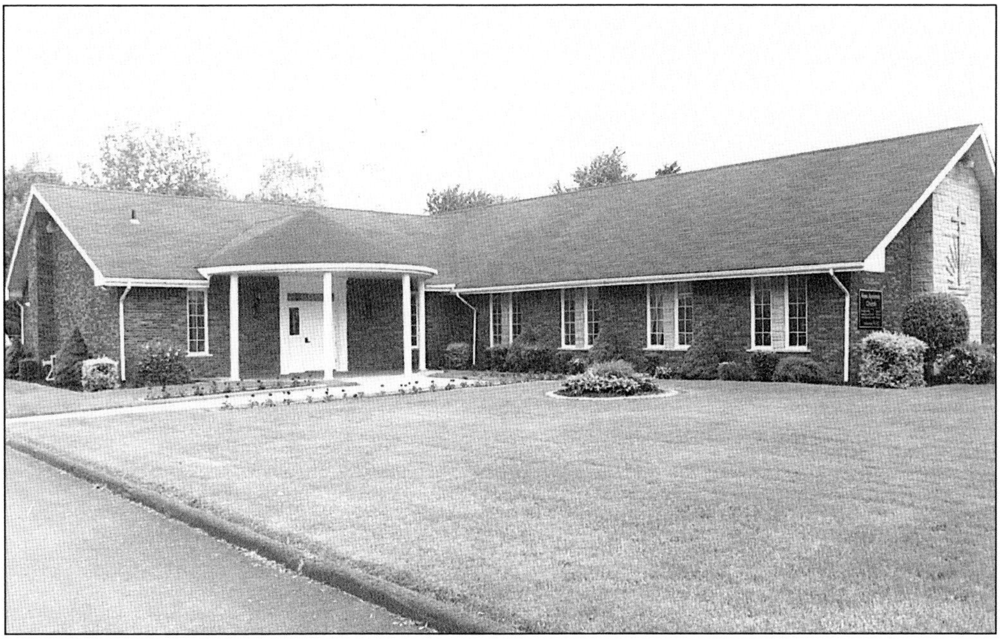

The New Apostolic Church traces its origins to England in the 1830s. By the turn of the last century, the denomination had spread to North America. In 1932 the first service in this area was held in a private home on Grand Avenue in Mount Clemens. The congregation of approximately 18 members was served by a priest from a church in Detroit. Membership soon grew, however, and in 1939 a church was built on South Walnut. In 1973, the congregation moved to its present location on Townhall near South River Road in Harrison Township. Today, membership has grown to approximately 200, and the church plays an active role in the community. The church building was recently renovated.

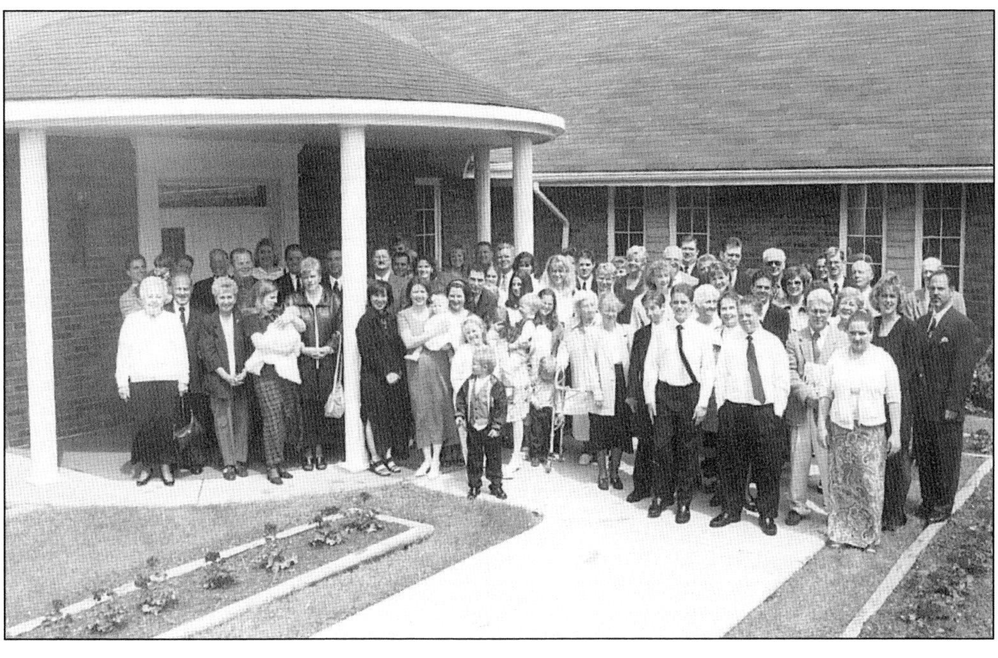

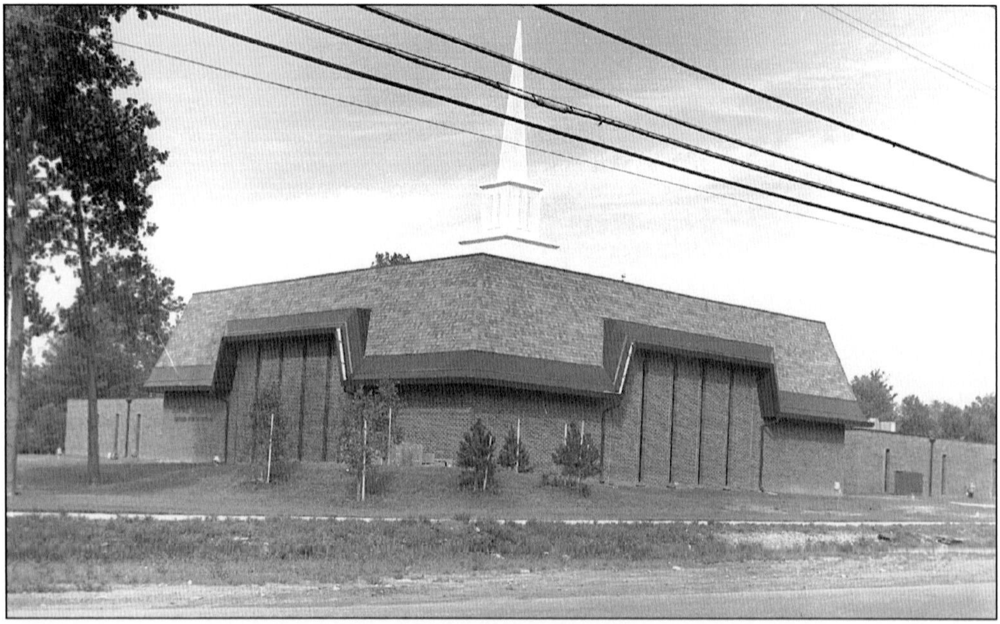

The Knox Presbyterian Church at the corner of Crocker and Metropolitan Parkway was dedicated on February 1, 1976. George W. Woodcock preached the last sermon in the former Detroit location and the first sermon in the Harrison Township church. In July of 1980, the congregation withdrew from the United Presbyterian Church in the USA and became a charter member of the Evangelical Presbyterian Church. The Reverend John Tenjack came later that year as assistant pastor, and by 1984 more land was needed for expansion. The addition included two classrooms, the Patterson Room, and the Jonathan Cary Memorial Athletic Field. Reverend Mark Hudson joined the staff in 1987, and in 1990, seven more classrooms were added. Reverend Chris Gibson joined in 1988, and Pastor Wayne Uppendahl in 1996. The church continues to grow and expand its church and family-oriented activities.

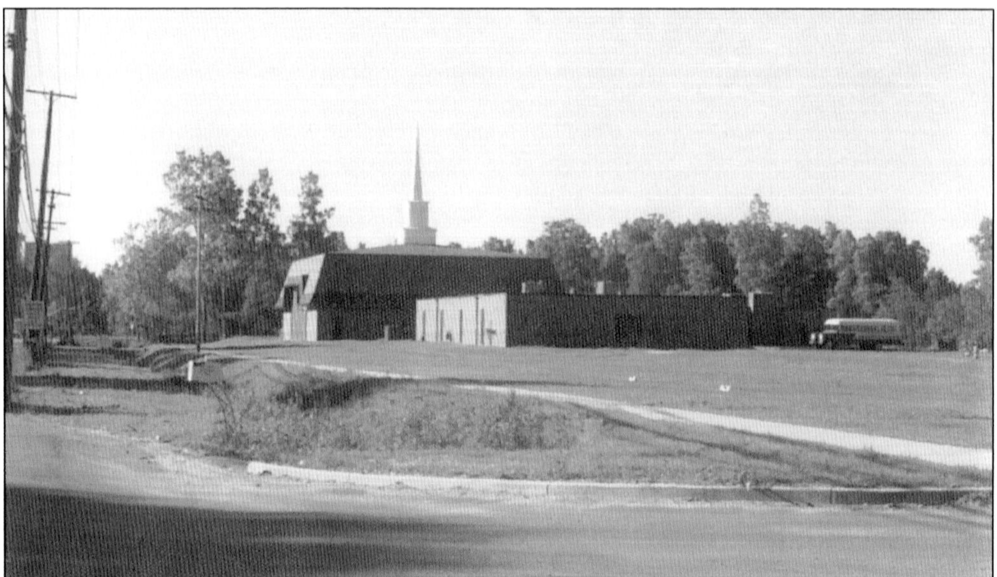

Six

House and Home

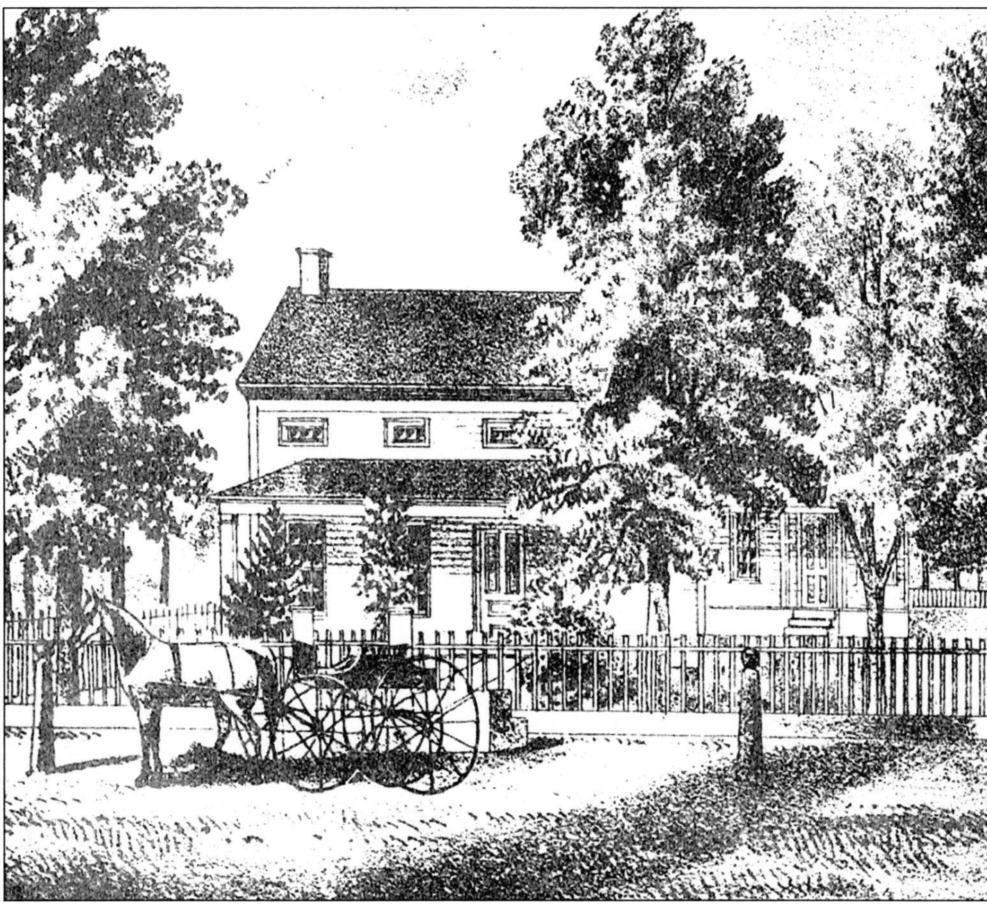

Henry Fries was listed in the *1875 Atlas* as one of the old citizens and prominent farmers in Harrison Township. He was born in New York and settled here in 1850. Unlike the other settlers listed, Fries was only a part-time farmer. His chief responsibility was as superintendent of the county poor house. His home, shown here, was west of Irwin Road.

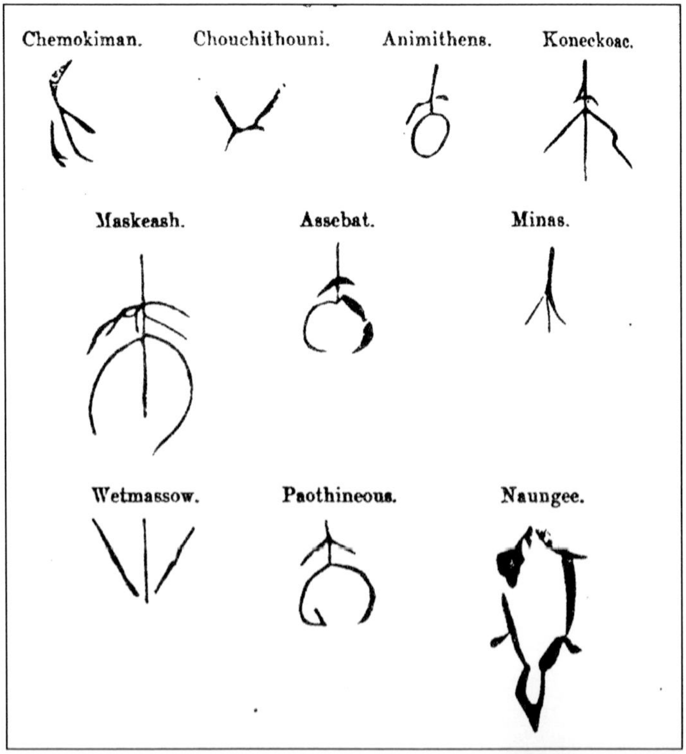

William Tucker was the first English-speaking white man to make his home in Harrison Township. Unfortunately, despite the deed, which contained the signatures on the left, he did not get to keep all of the property given to him by the Native Americans. The English and later the American government did not recognize the Native-American deed. Fortunately, the Tuckers were allowed to keep the land they and their many children had settled and improved, including the orchards.

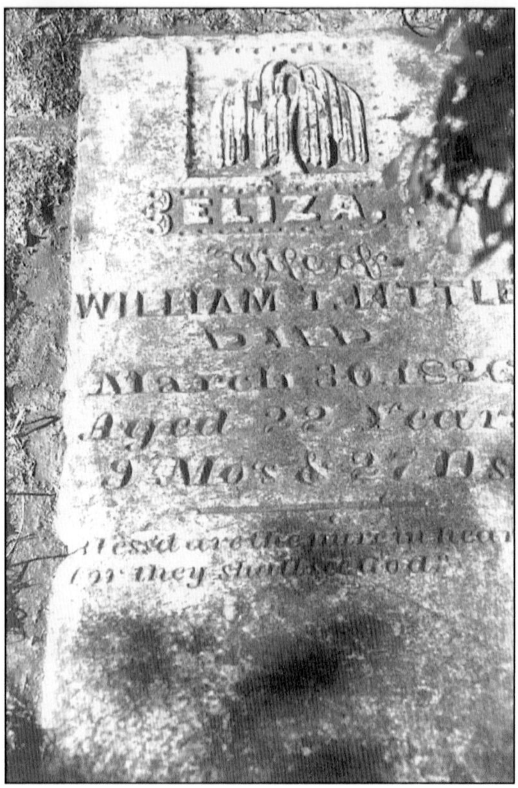

One of the remnants of the Tucker family is a white marble gravestone that reads, "Eliza, wife of William T. Little, died March 30, 1826, aged 22 years, 9 Mos, and 27Ds. Blessed are the pure of heart for they shall see God." Since William Tucker's only daughter married Mr. Robert Little, it has been assumed that Eliza must have been the wife of one of Tucker's grandsons.

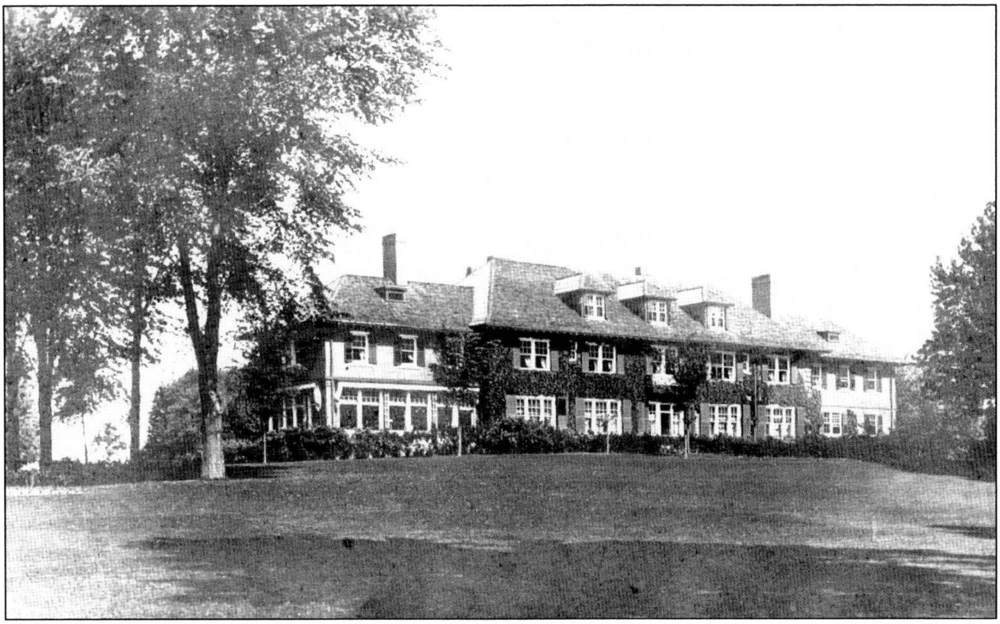

In the early 1900s most Harrison Township residents lived in farmhouses or cottages. Henry Bourne Joy, however, built his "estate" on the northern edge of his 800-acre marshland. When he leased 642 acres to the government in 1917, he kept enough land to insure that the base wouldn't infringe on his waterfront home.

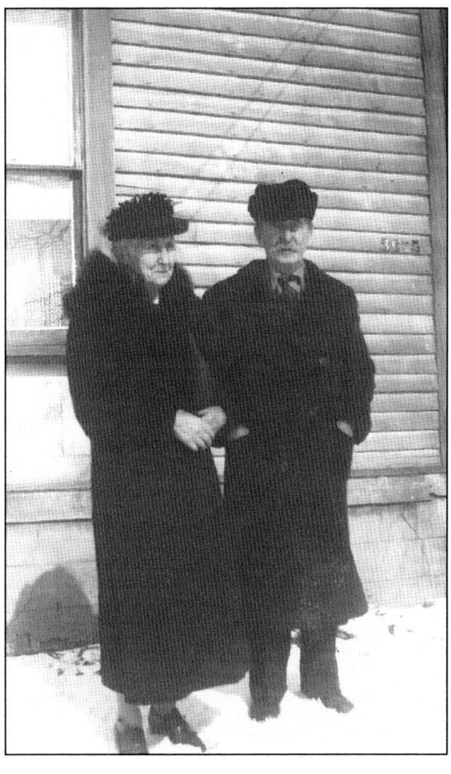

The township's last dairy farm was the Lowenstein Farm, which ran from the river to Metropolitan Parkway. The 165-acre farm is remembered because of the silos that remain long after the cows were gone. Here, Lawrence and Ann Duggan stand in front of their son's home. Martin Duggan and his family were sharecroppers on the farm, but Martin also drove the school bus while his wife, Mae, taught third grade at South River School.

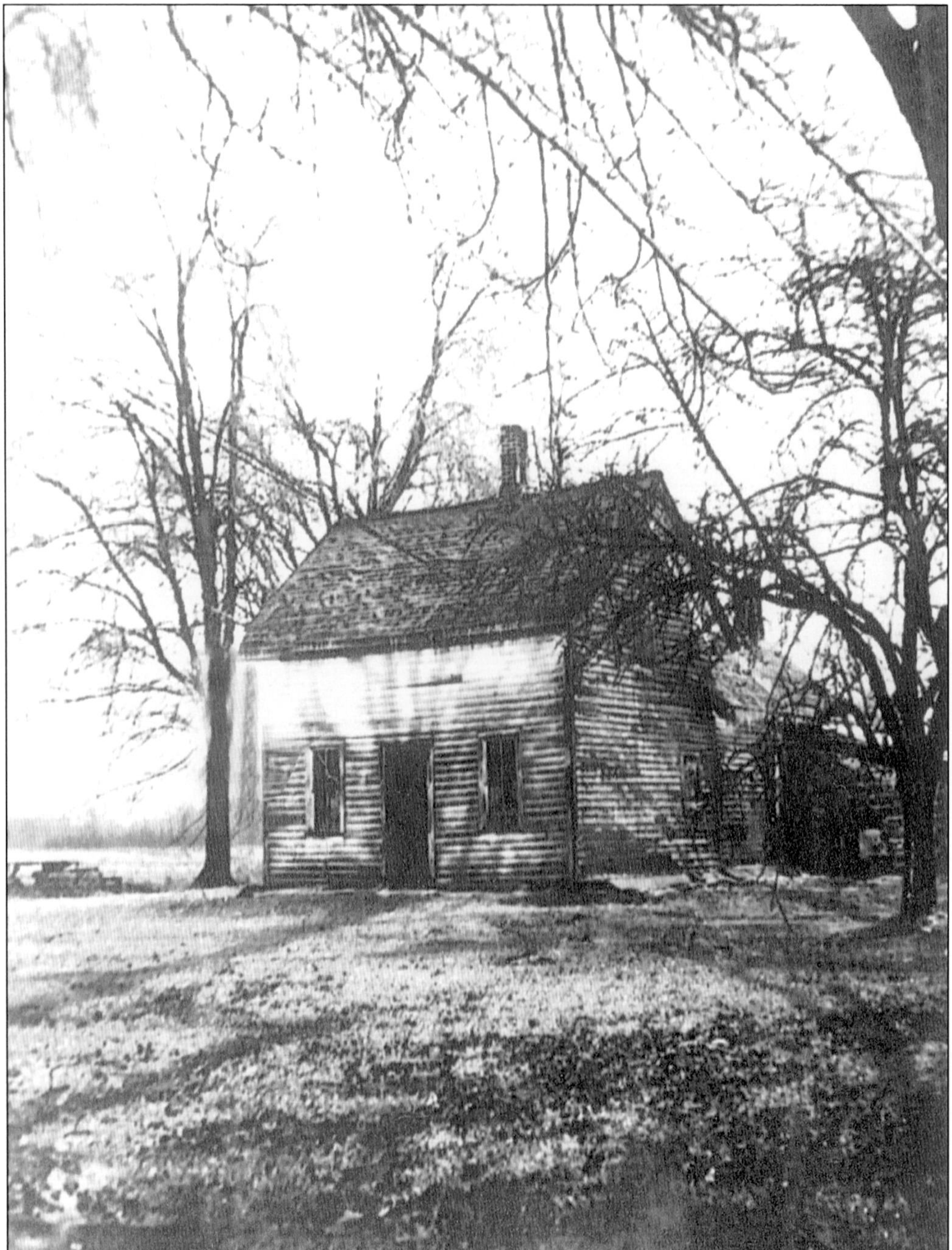

In 1925, Fred Mallast decided to sell his home, seen here, to Chuck Callewaert. According to Rita Callewaert, Chuck's daughter-in-law, it was an interesting house. The family lived there for 15 years despite the fact that when the wind blew, the linoleum flapped up and down. Rita's husband, Hank, used to tell stories about how the neighborhood kids would sneak over because the house was filled with good times. "It was a rough life," Rita said, "but it was good for the kids." In 1940, Chuck built a new house which stands today near the soccer field that replaced the cabbage and pumpkin fields.

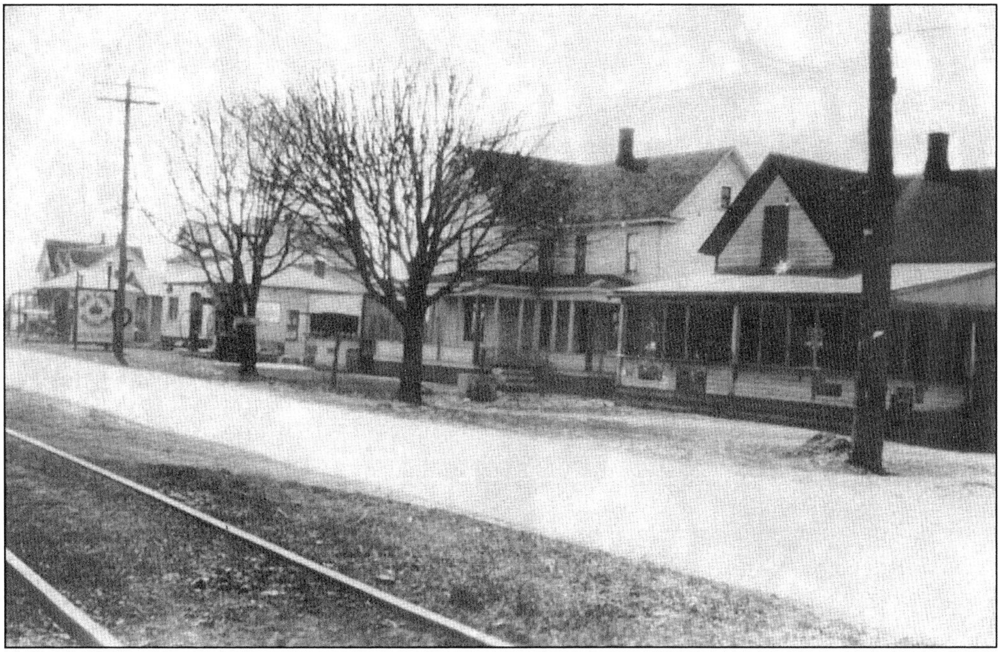

In 1922 Jefferson Avenue was a gravel road with the track for the Rapid Railway running along side it. The homes between Campau Lane and Ballard belonged to Joe Campau, William and Berdina Lowe, Tom Flynn, and William Johnson. The Lowe Bake Stand can be seen in the center of the picture. It was later expanded into the neighborhood grocery of Wilfred and Gertude Lowe.

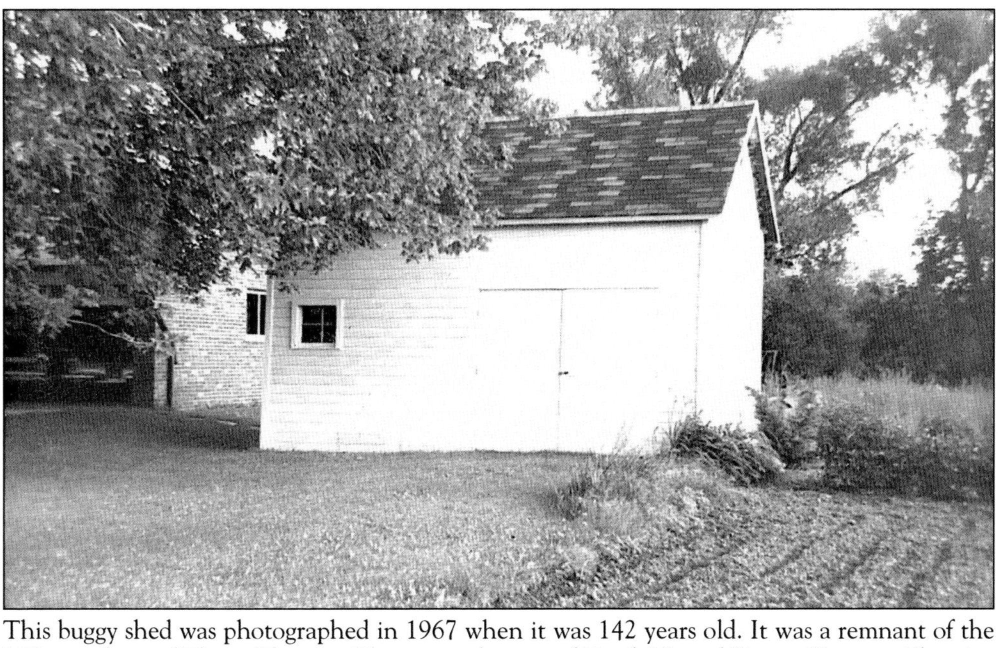

This buggy shed was photographed in 1967 when it was 142 years old. It was a remnant of the 160-acre farm of Elmer Chartier. Elmer was the son of Frank N. and Emma Campau Chartier. He was a farmer and building contractor. A life-long resident of the township, he was born in 1885 and died in 1970.

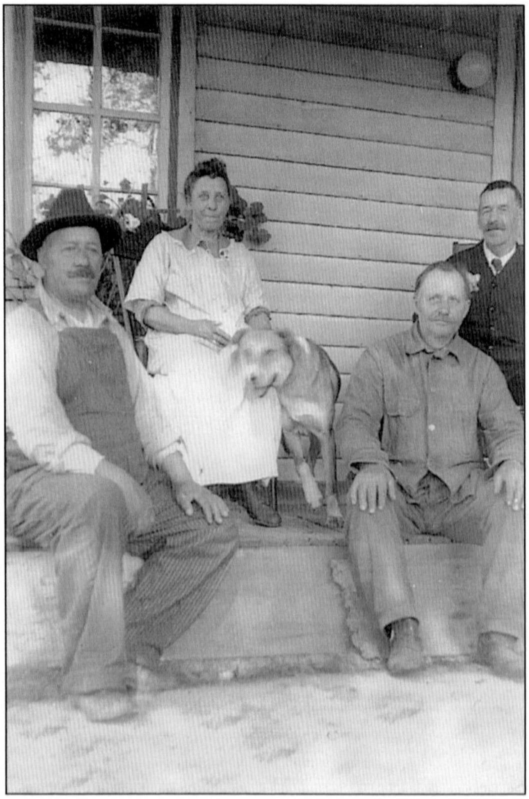

This picture was taken on May 19, 1925, apparently just before Fred Mallast sold the old homestead. The Mallast family—Fred, Amelia (Mallast) Bobcean, Emil, and Amelia's husband, John—appear to be enjoying a chance to relax after a hard day on the farm. The Mallast name is one of many that can be found on the old strip farm maps and today's street maps as well.

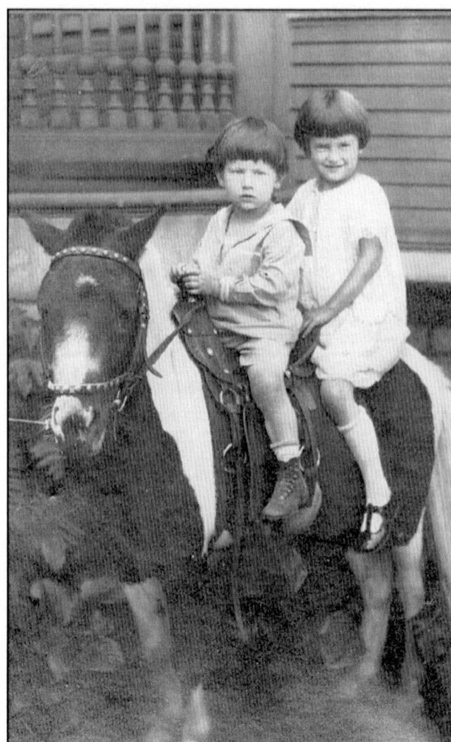

The farmers in Harrison Township saw horses as a part of life, but for weekend resorters, a pony and a cute kid or two made the perfect photo opportunity. Many families in the area can find a pony picture in the old album. The picture to the right came from township trustee Barbara Urban's family photo collection. The children are Barb's Uncle Donald McKillop and her mother, Patricia McKillop.

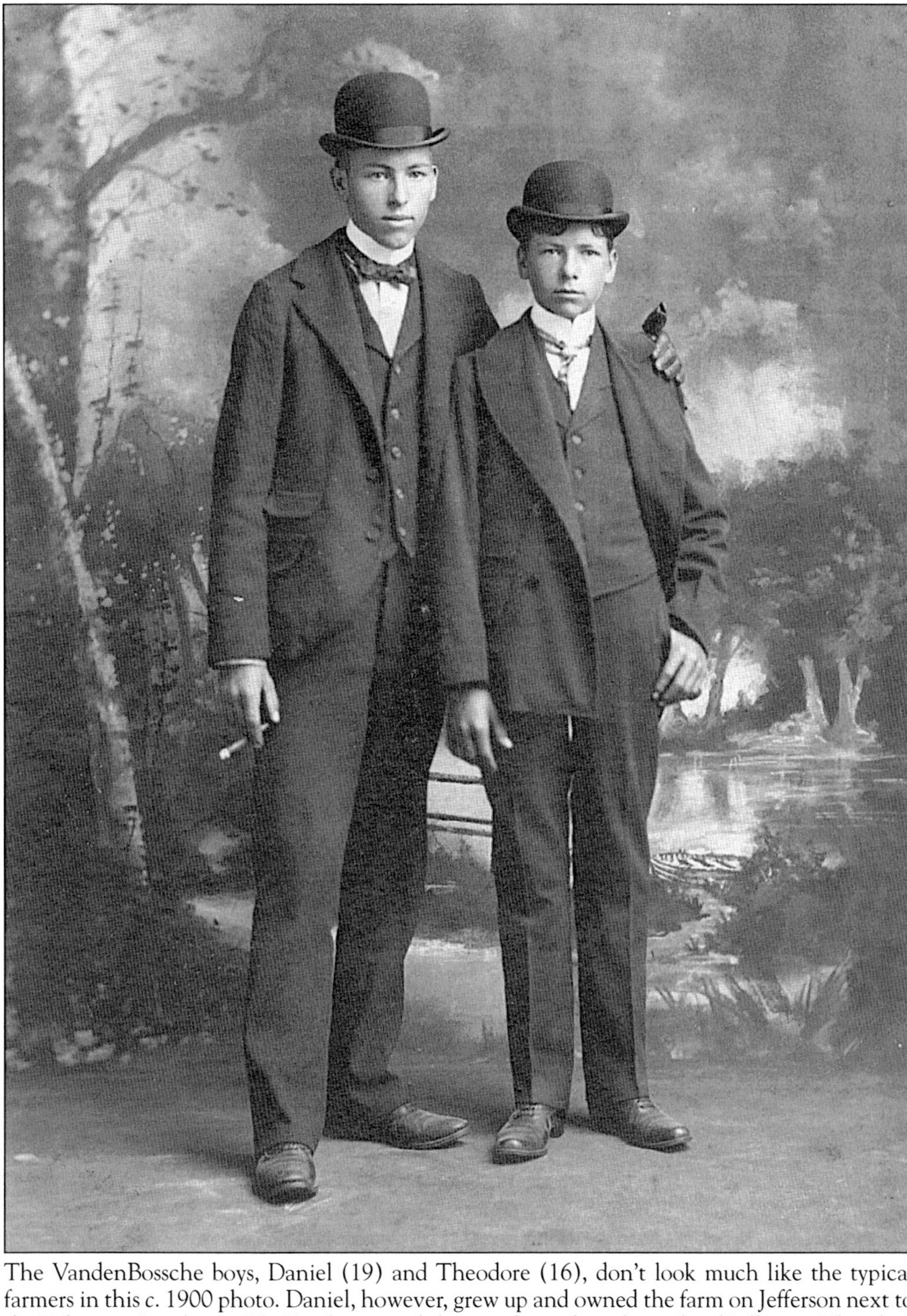

The VandenBossche boys, Daniel (19) and Theodore (16), don't look much like the typical farmers in this c. 1900 photo. Daniel, however, grew up and owned the farm on Jefferson next to the Lakeview Inn (page 37). He also owned the woods on the other side of Jefferson. Theodore ran Jefferson Motor Service, and brother Pete (not pictured) was the proprietor of the Lakeside Boat House (page 16). The VandenBossche name has been prevalent in the community for more than a century.

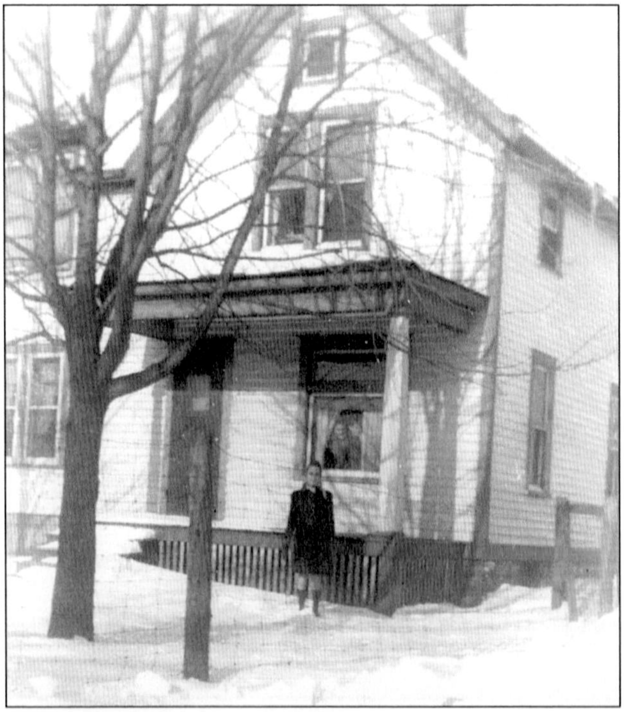

Charles Campau was proud of this home he built for his family. In the early 1960s, however, he was forced to relocate to a home built for him by the State of Michigan. Actually, the state insisted that he move into the new house. They needed to demolish the farmhouse to make room for the entrance ramp at 16 Mile and I-94. Charles moved, but not willingly. He had to be escorted.

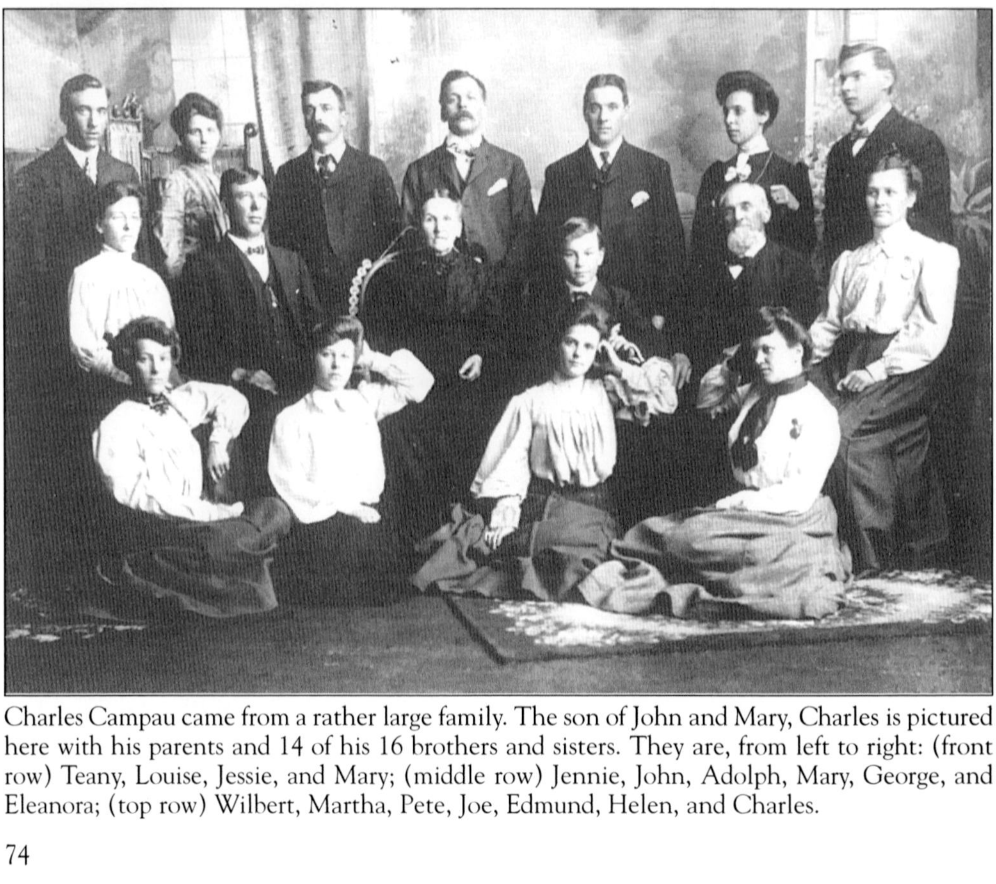

Charles Campau came from a rather large family. The son of John and Mary, Charles is pictured here with his parents and 14 of his 16 brothers and sisters. They are, from left to right: (front row) Teany, Louise, Jessie, and Mary; (middle row) Jennie, John, Adolph, Mary, George, and Eleanora; (top row) Wilbert, Martha, Pete, Joe, Edmund, Helen, and Charles.

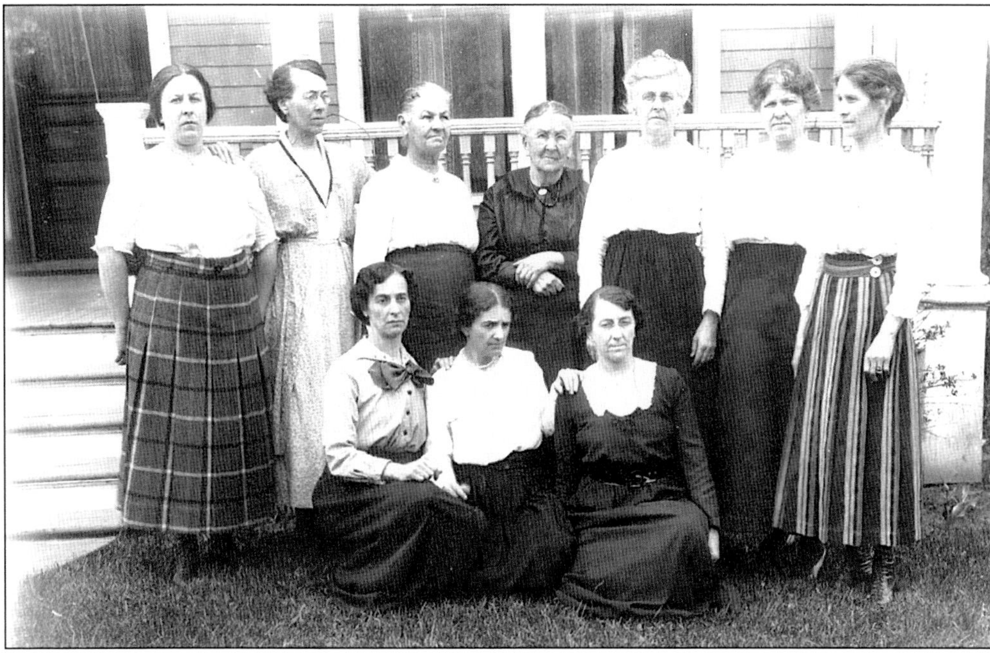

The farm of John and Mary Campau was also known as the John Campau Subdivision. When the property was sub-divided into lots, the streets were named for Campau family members. Three streets that ran off of Ballard were called Mary, Edmund, and Adolph. Today they are known as Homeview, Marilac, and Malone. In the picture above, Mary Campau (top row, middle) is shown with her nine daughters. Charles Campau, shown to the right, in his earlier years, was married in 1916 to Margaret Forton. In 1966, Charles died at the age of 83, having been a lifelong resident of the township. His wife died in 1980 at the age of 82.

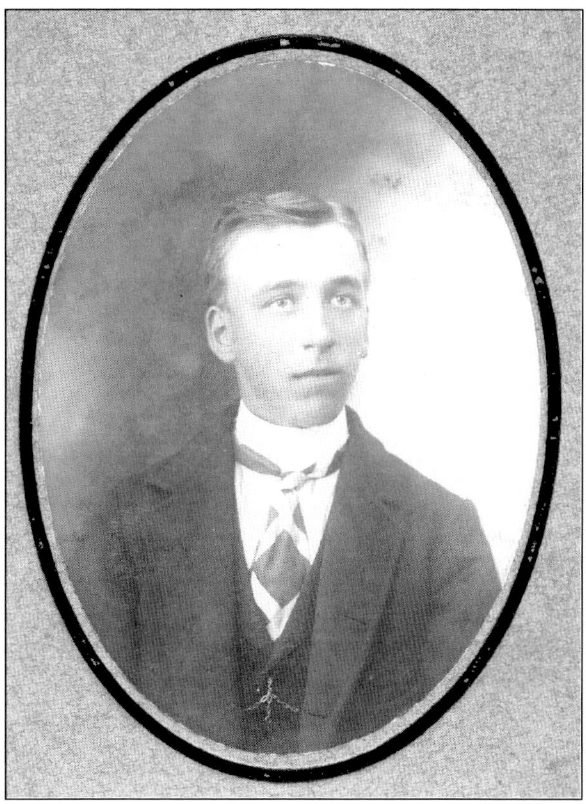

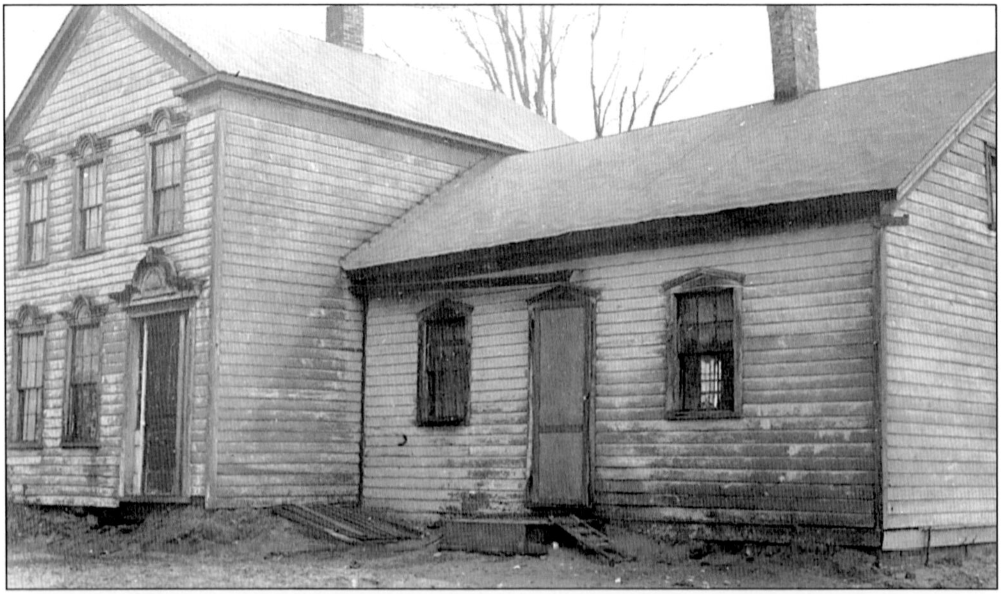

The home of John and Mary Campau is another structure that has stood the test of generations. It was the home of Alga (Campau) Ballard, seen on the following page. It was also home to her son, Historical Commissioner Bob Ballard, when he was very young. In recent years it was known as the Utash home. The hand-hewn logs that support the structure can still be seen in the basement.

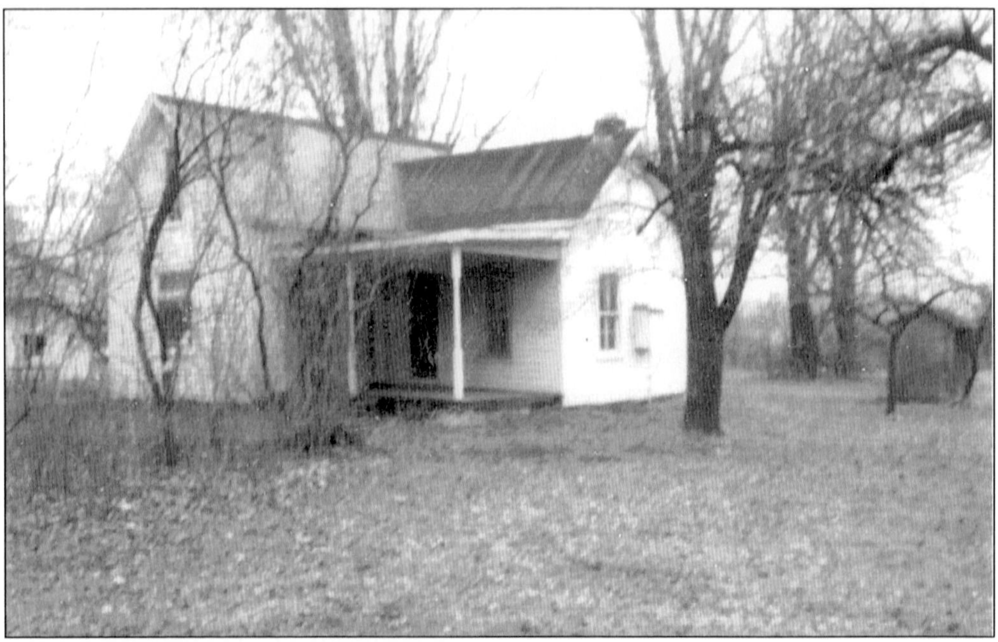

The home of Peter and Emma (Rettell) Ballard, pictured above, was originally at the wrong end of Ballard Road. When Sigma Gamma decided they needed a hospital in the area, they also wanted the property this house was on. It wasn't easy to move a house in those days, but with the Hatzenbuhler Stonebot and a team of horses, the house—which was built in the early 1870s—was taken to the far end of Ballard.

When Alga (Campau) Ballard died on March 4, 2000, she was 101 years old. Most of those years she lived in Harrison Township. In many ways she epitomized the farming women of her generation. The common factor, according to Dr. Patricia Meyers, was grit. Her memorial words seem to have captured that zest for life. "These were tough people. They did not have time to gripe and complain about their lot in life. They had to feed the animals, bake the bread, plant and harvest the crops, bear and bury children, mend clothes until each piece was little more than patches upon patches, and get up the next morning to repeat the drill. Alga saw the first automobile and the first man on the moon....a life lived in three centuries.... Her life was not the easiest, but she lived it to the fullest."

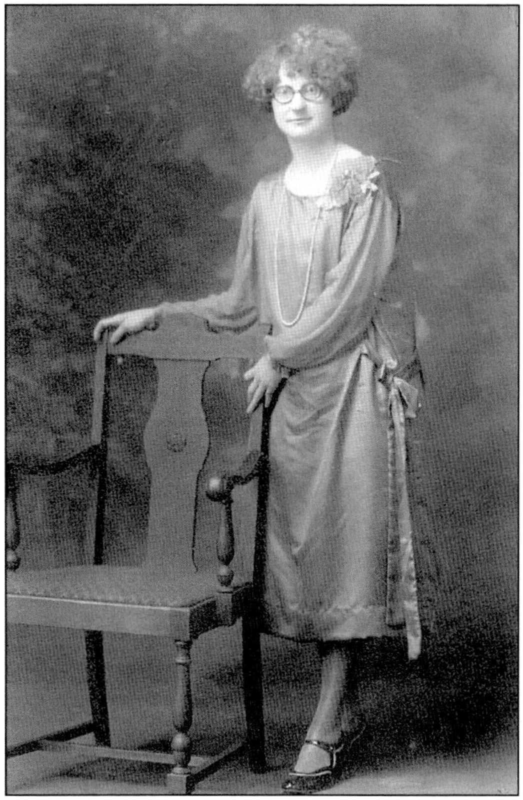

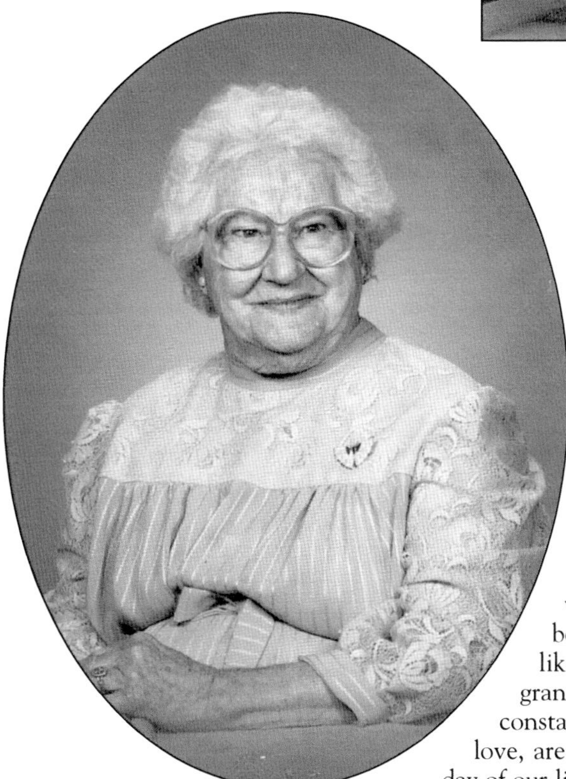

Above, Alga is seen in her younger years. To the left is the Alga who will be remembered by her grandchildren like Candace White. Her memorial to her grandmother read, "Her lessons of fidelity, constancy, loyalty, faith, and last, but not least, love, are models for each of us to strive for each day of our lives."

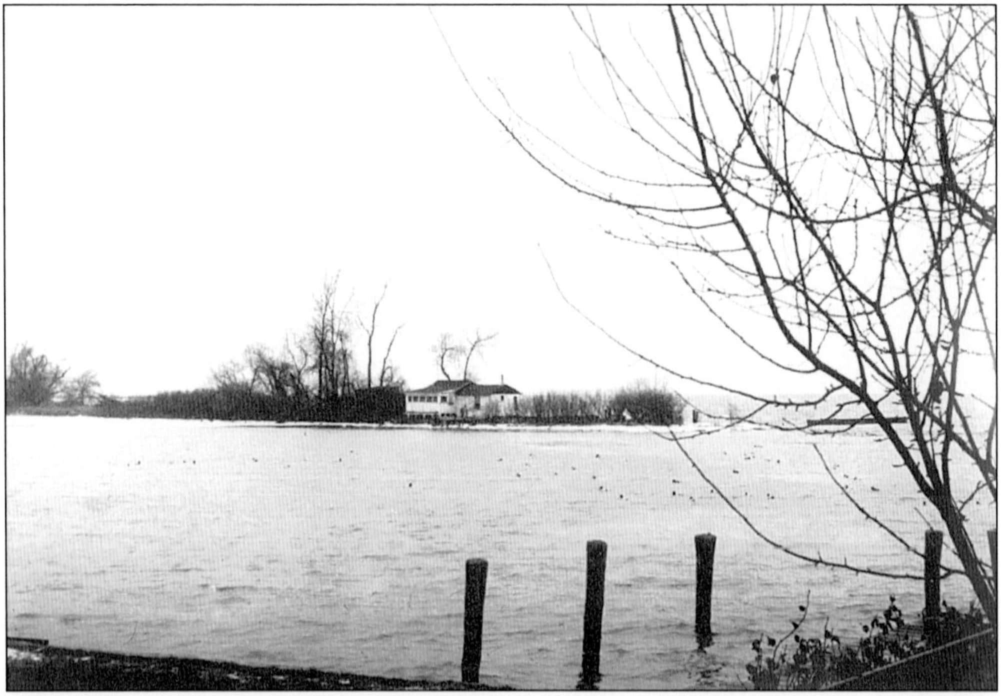

Grass Island is a dot on the map today, but the personal watercraft owners in the area know it well. With the recent low water, its old pilings and dock have become hazardous for those who have been skimming past the island for years. It looks more like an island now, but few would believe that it once held three buildings. It was called Wallich Island, after the Detroit family that spent weekends there.

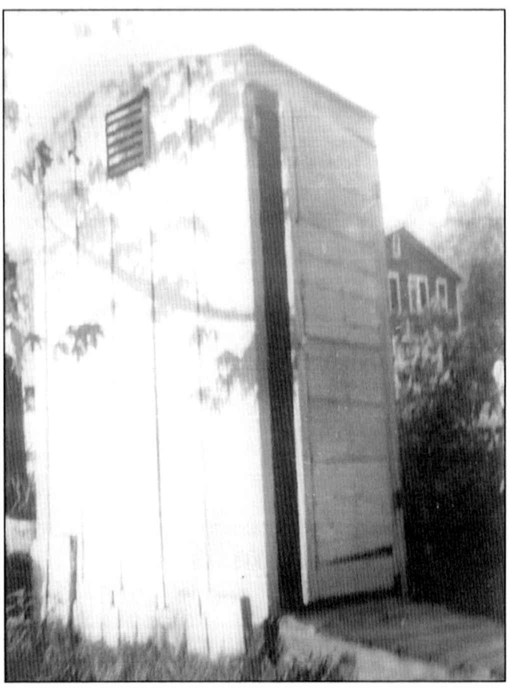

Today, major problems in the township involve septic fields and water pollution. In the old days, the problem was getting to the outhouse in the dark. In their home on Mast Court, the Hosler family had an outhouse, shown here, right on the edge of the canal, but Shirley was proud of it. "It was special," she said. "It was pink with red carpet. It had the most beautiful painting inside." Those were the good, old days.

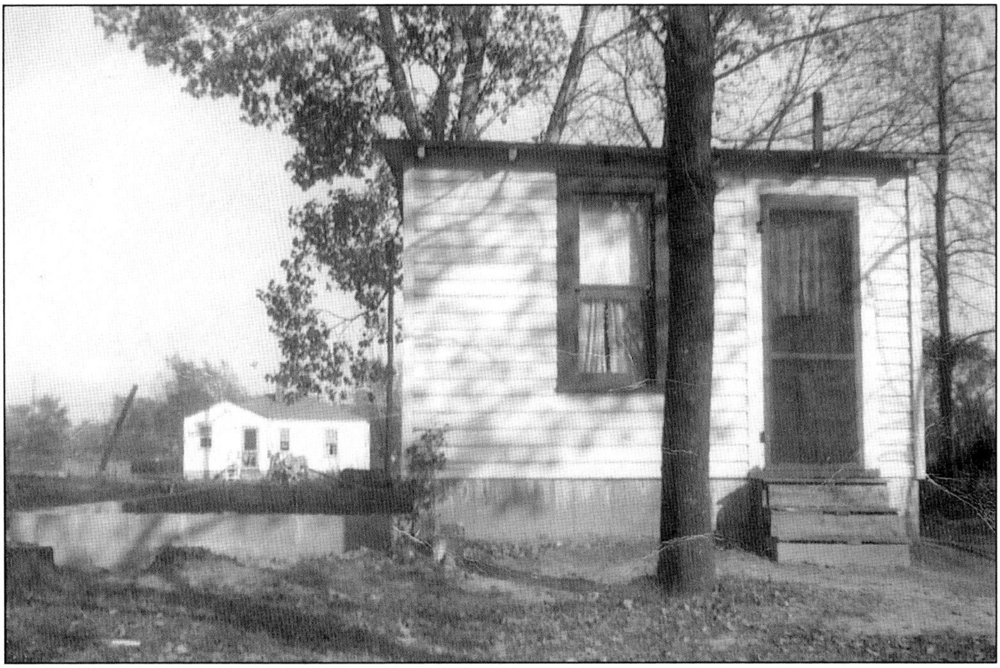

Many township homes were originally built as summer or weekend cottages. The house on Townhall that the Hoslers moved into was small but convenient. Located next to the Fire Station, it was not only close for firefighter Virgil Hosler, but also for his wife Shirley. She was one of the women who took the emergency calls. She then ran to the station to call the volunteers. Every minute counted.

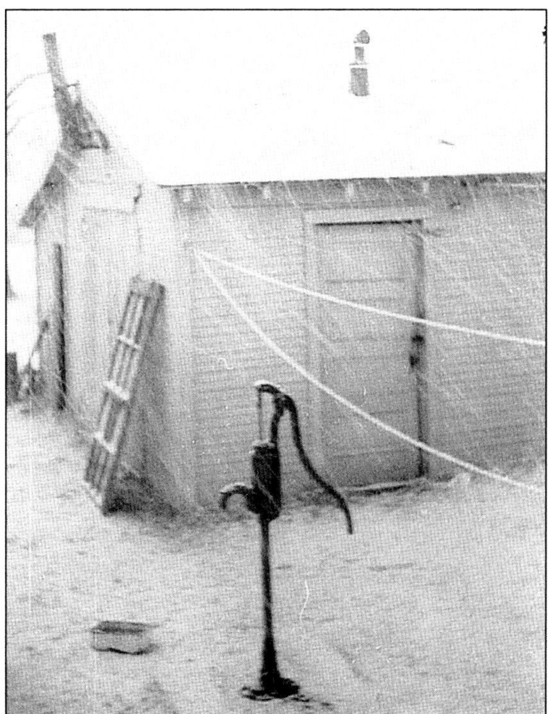

Kids today think it's fun to get water from a pump like the one pictured here. Township seniors, however, remember fighting over who had to fetch the water because, for them, pumping the water was just another daily chore. The pump house near the old township hall was one of the most popular places to get water, but the actual pumping and carting the water home was not so popular.

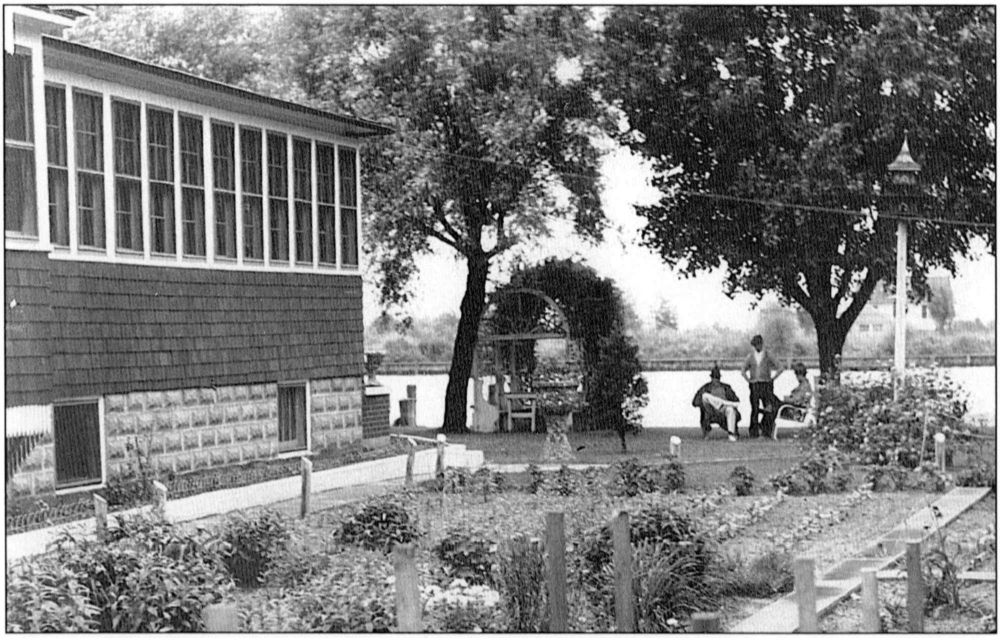

Residents today take those little bumps in South River Road for granted. Many don't even realize they are going over a bridge. The Barney family, however, came to the mouth of the Clinton River when no bridges connected the islands to the mainland. It was at times lonely, but the pioneers had to see each chore as an adventure. From getting wood for cooking and heating to fetching water, most tasks had to be done by boat.

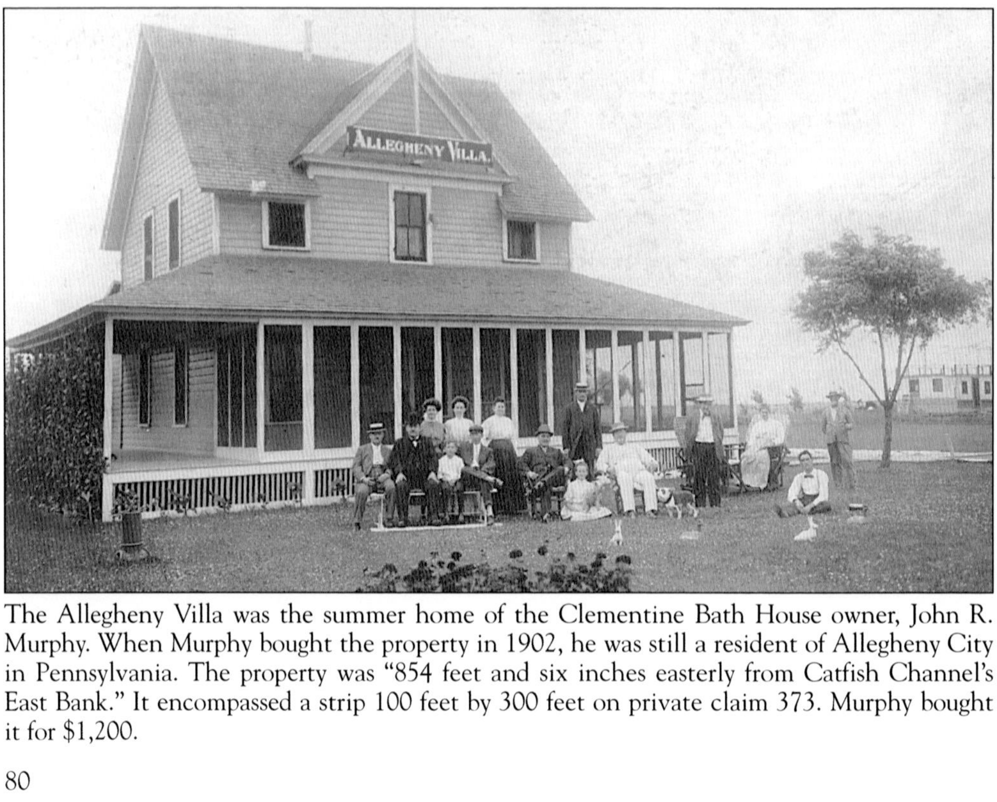

The Allegheny Villa was the summer home of the Clementine Bath House owner, John R. Murphy. When Murphy bought the property in 1902, he was still a resident of Allegheny City in Pennsylvania. The property was "854 feet and six inches easterly from Catfish Channel's East Bank." It encompassed a strip 100 feet by 300 feet on private claim 373. Murphy bought it for $1,200.

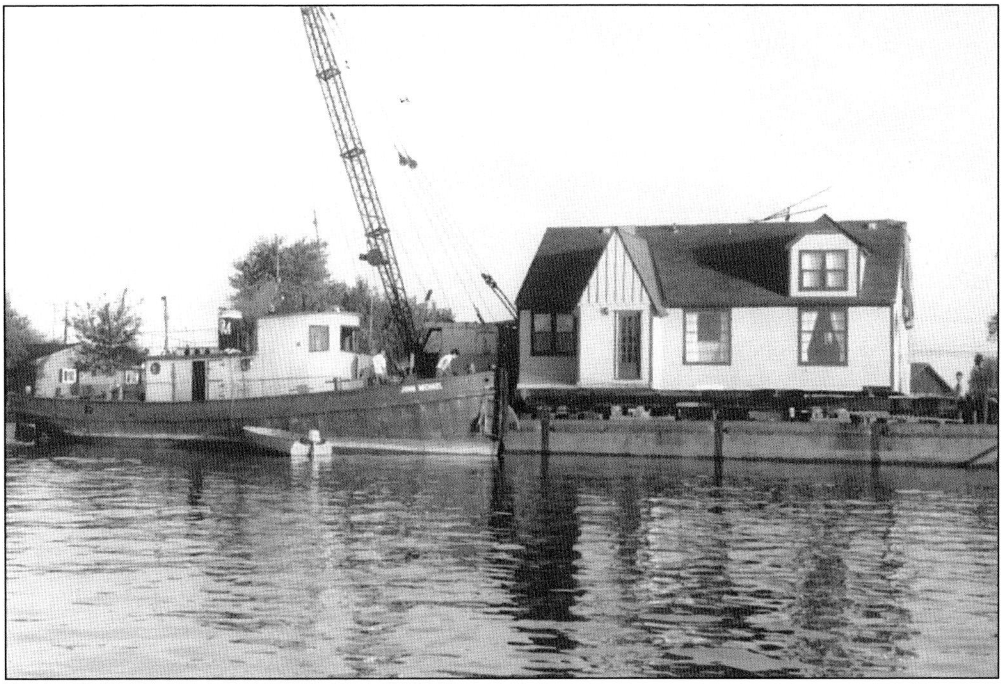

Living in a waterfront community has many advantages, but not many residents make use of the water for transportation of their house. According to Ron Kahn, who moved the house seen above from Harrison Township to Algonac in 1983, creativity can pay off. He pointed out that no power lines had to be moved and it was cheaper and safer than using the roadways. Carol Krause, who sold the house to Kahn, was planning to tear it down in order to make better use of the three lots it was sitting on. Moving it seemed like a better option. Luckily the township doesn't lose a lot of houses. As a matter of fact, the houseboat shown below was moved from Detroit to Sunshine Point at the end of North River Road. It is still standing.

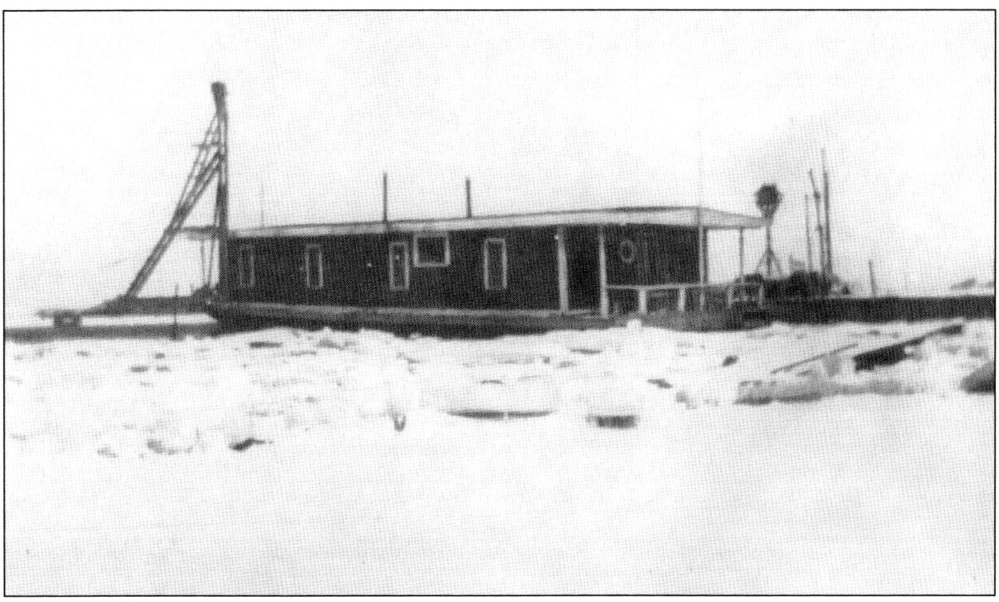

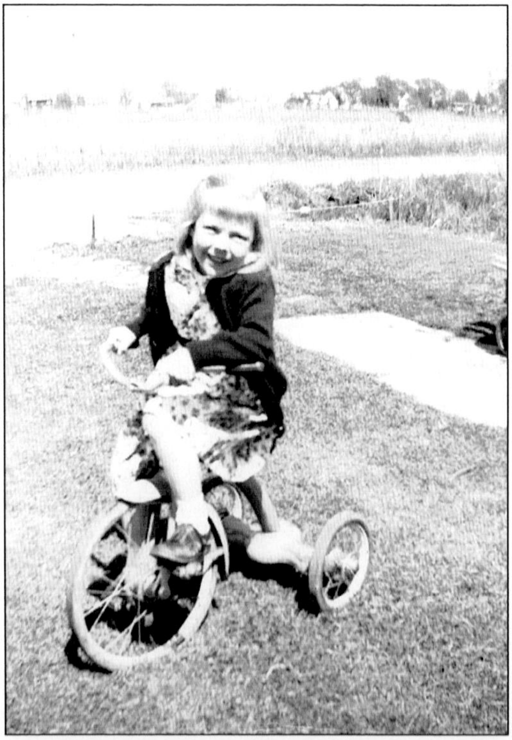

Subdivisions are replacing farms, but over the years another change has been slowly but just as relentlessly appearing. In this early 1950s photo, if Louise Rood had turned her tricycle in the opposite direction, she would have seen the houses on Lakeshore. Today there are several rows of houses between Lakeshore and Huron Pointe Drive. As a matter of fact, vacant lots in most of the older subdivisions are becoming scarce.

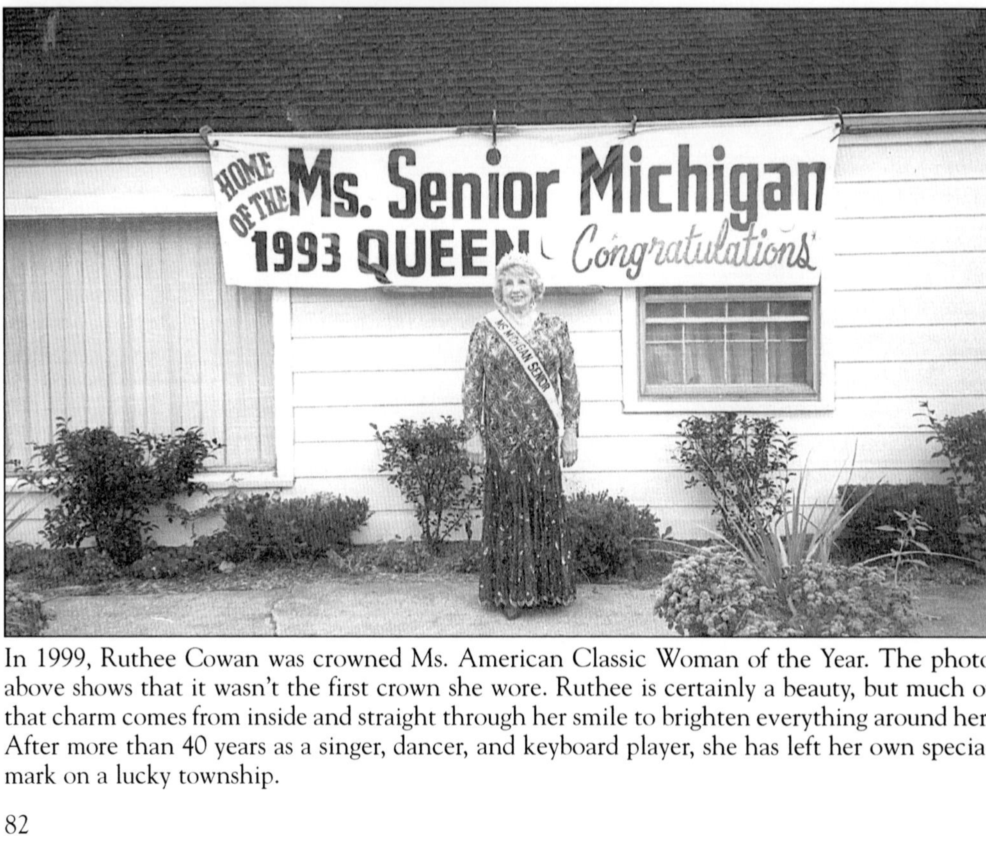

In 1999, Ruthee Cowan was crowned Ms. American Classic Woman of the Year. The photo above shows that it wasn't the first crown she wore. Ruthee is certainly a beauty, but much of that charm comes from inside and straight through her smile to brighten everything around her. After more than 40 years as a singer, dancer, and keyboard player, she has left her own special mark on a lucky township.

Seven

The Base and the Beach

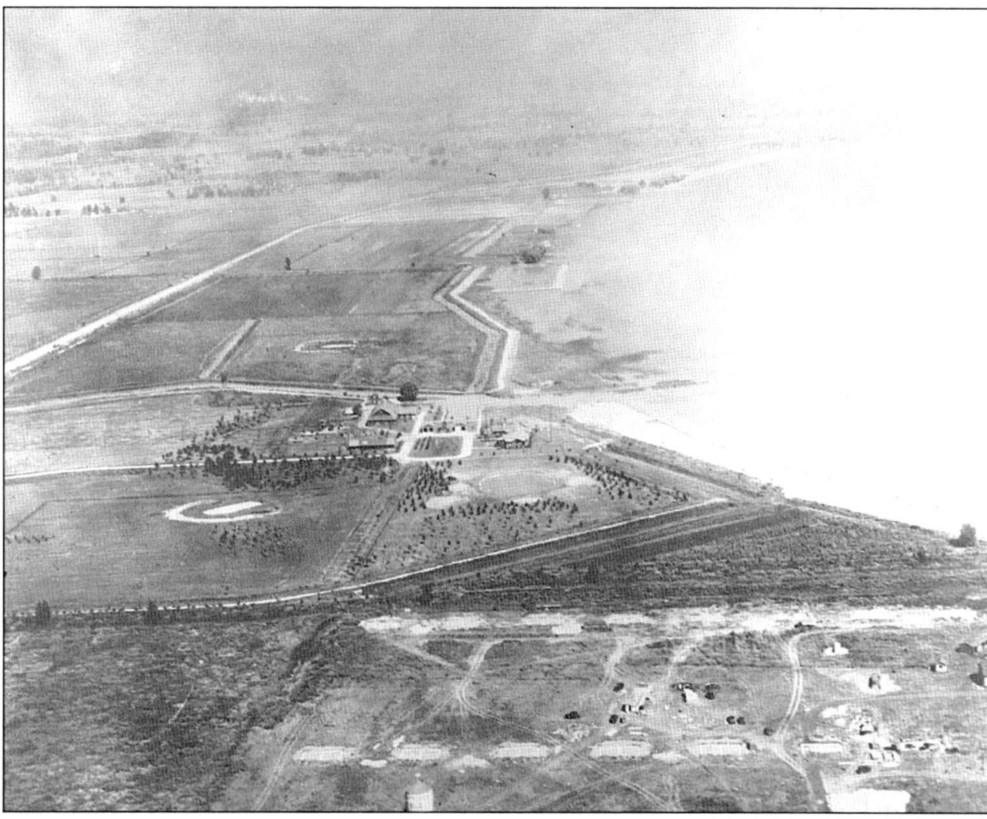

When Packard Motor Car executive Henry B. Joy came to the township, he had high hopes for the more than 800 acres of land he planned to turn into a testing ground for cars and those new-fangled flying machines. When Packard turned down the idea, Joy made the property into Joy Aviation Field. In 1911, the Army's first radiotelegraphic transmission was made from a plane 100 feet over the field.

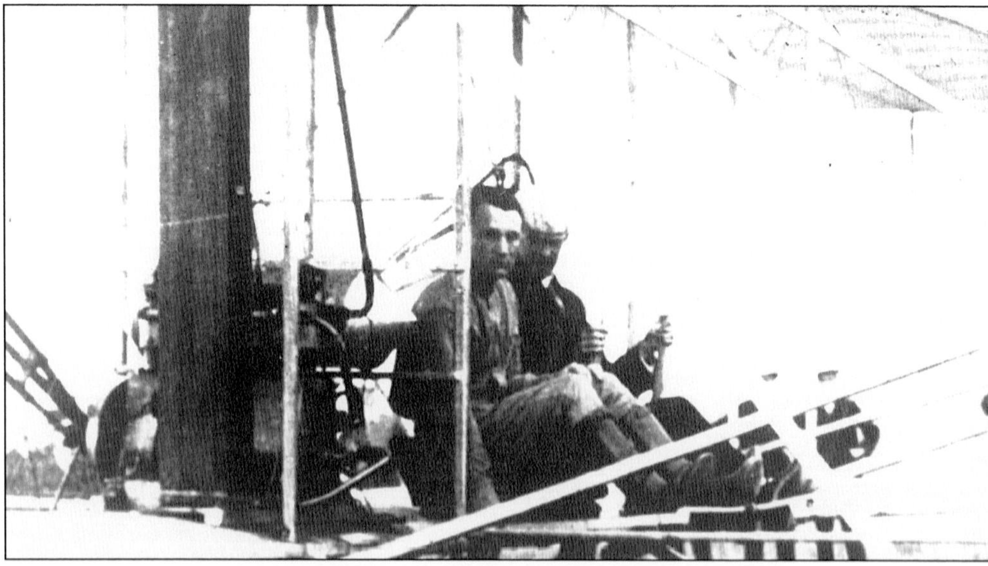

Lieutenant Thomas Etholan Selfridge was fascinated by the new flying machine. When he found no place in the Wright brothers' organization, he turned to Alexander Graham Bell. His first seven-minute flight was in a Bell kite. They went on to develop "aeroplanes," and in 1908 Selfridge became the first Army officer to fly an airplane. The plane rose 3 feet from the ground and in 10 seconds covered 100 feet. Unfortunately, Selfridge did get a chance to fly in a Wright Brothers plane. In 1908, Orville Wright arrived in Fort Myers, Virginia, to introduce the Army to his Wright Flyer. Selfridge was so excited that when new orders came in, he switched flights with a friend. That mistake put him on the plane that circled the field 4 1/2 times at 150 feet and plummeted to Earth, making him the first military casualty of powered flight.

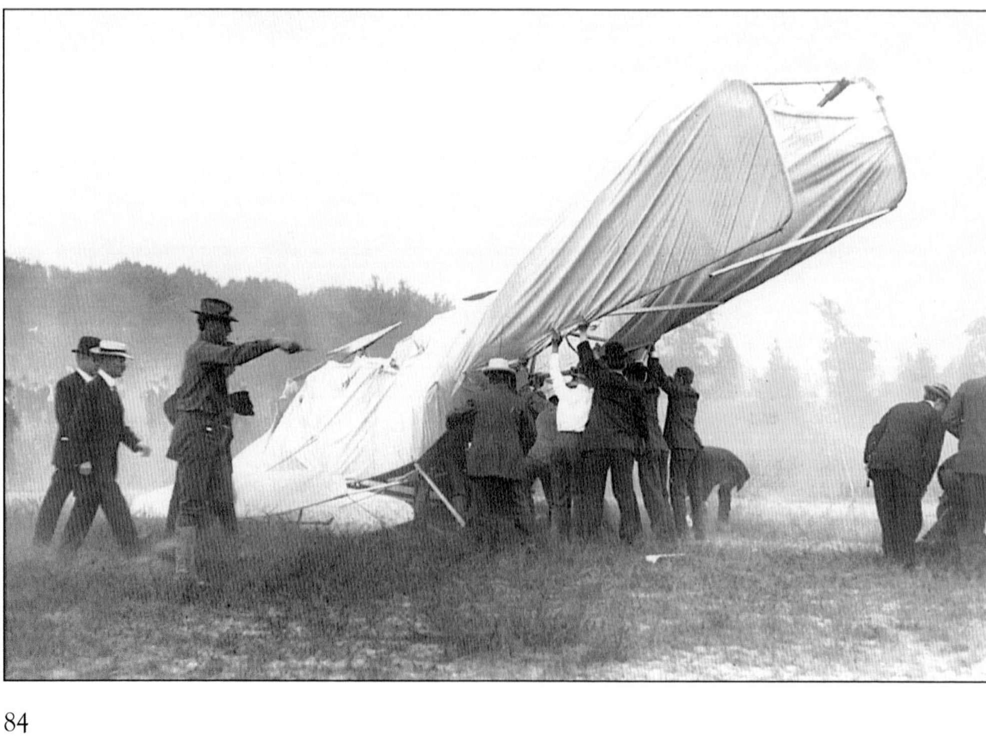

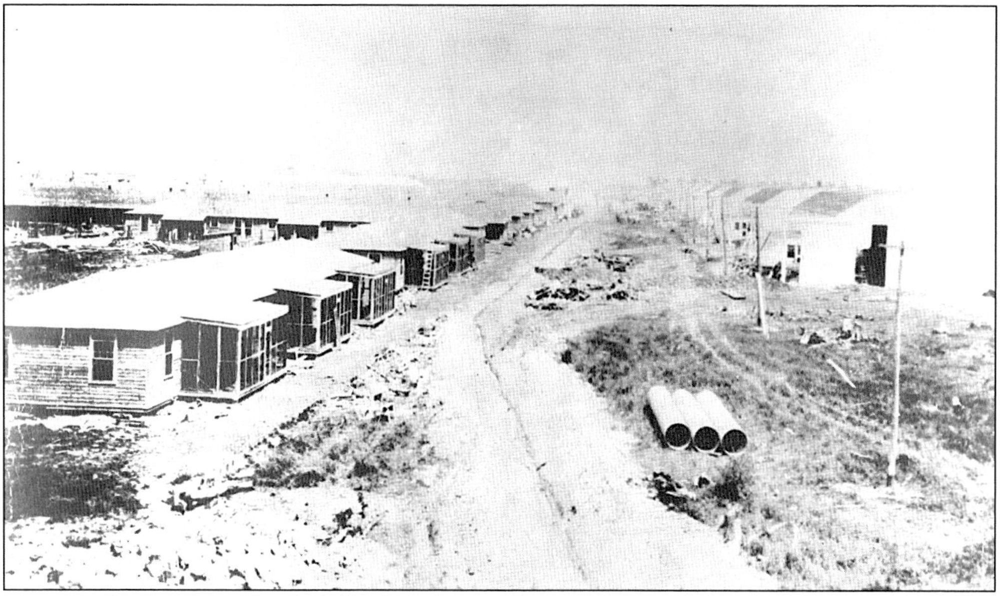

In 1917, the government needed a new air base, and it needed the facility fast. Luckily Henry Joy had an aviation field he was willing to lease to them. Unfortunately, it was a sea of mud. The only way in was the river road, and tractors had to be brought in to pull the trucks through the mud. The planking of the road helped for a while, but then it collapsed from the stress.

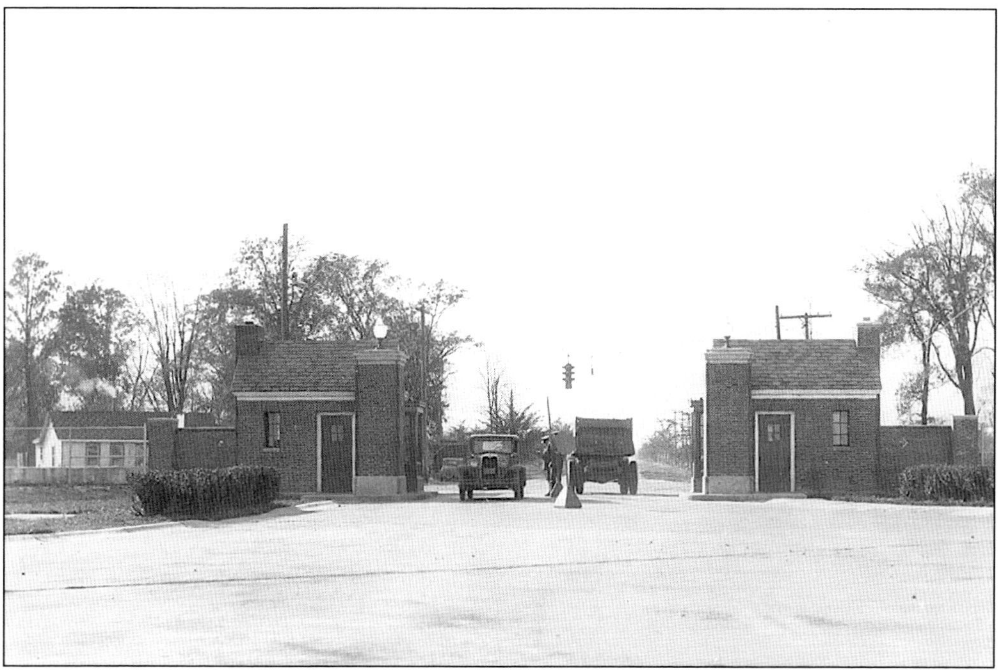

In the 1930s, the main gate to Selfridge was located at Joy Boulevard and Jefferson. Originally known as Aviation Road, Joy was built to solve the problem of how to get building equipment and supplies in without the use of North River Road. The road crew came through the farmers' fields, taking down anything in their way. Later, the farmers were compensated. Jefferson originally crossed the river.

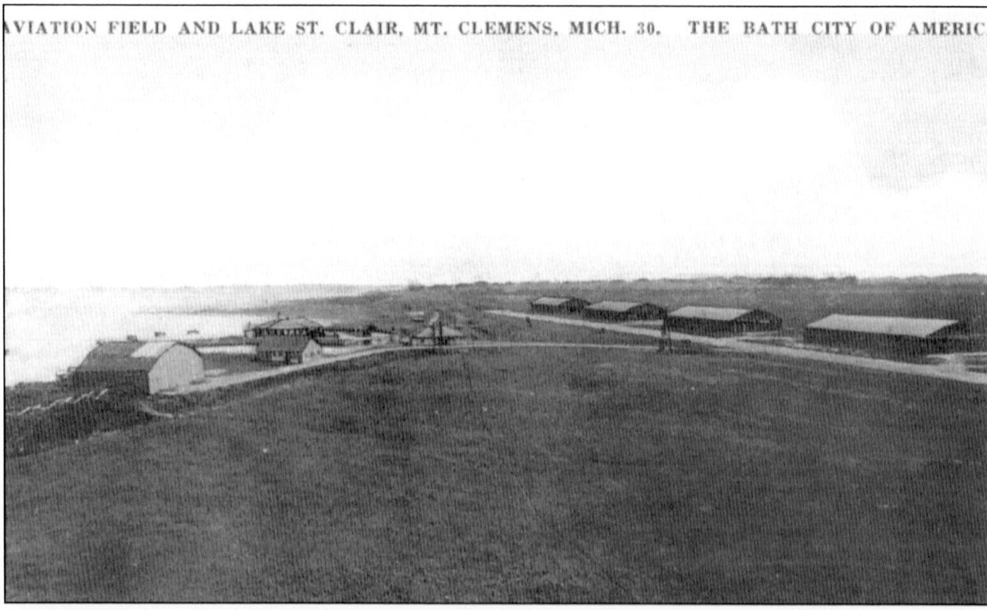

The airfield has had many name changes since it was known as Joy Aviation Field. It was referred to as Selfridge Aviation Field, the Selfridge Reservation, and simply Selfridge Field in its earliest days. In 1947, when the Air Force was recognized as a separate department of the military, Selfridge Air Force Base was born. In the 1960s and 1970s, the base went through many transformations. In 1971, the Air Force Base became Selfridge Air National Guard Base. Eventually its diversity gave it the distinction of being the only base in the country that is home to all branches of the military. The Army, Navy, Air Force, and Marines are represented, as well as the Coast Guard and, of course, the Air National Guard.

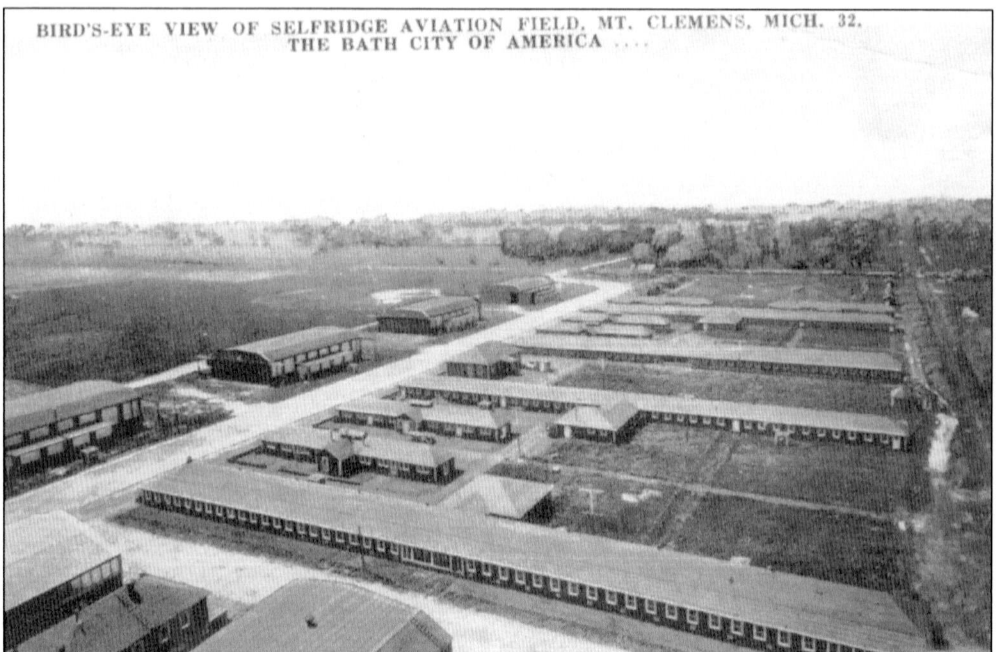

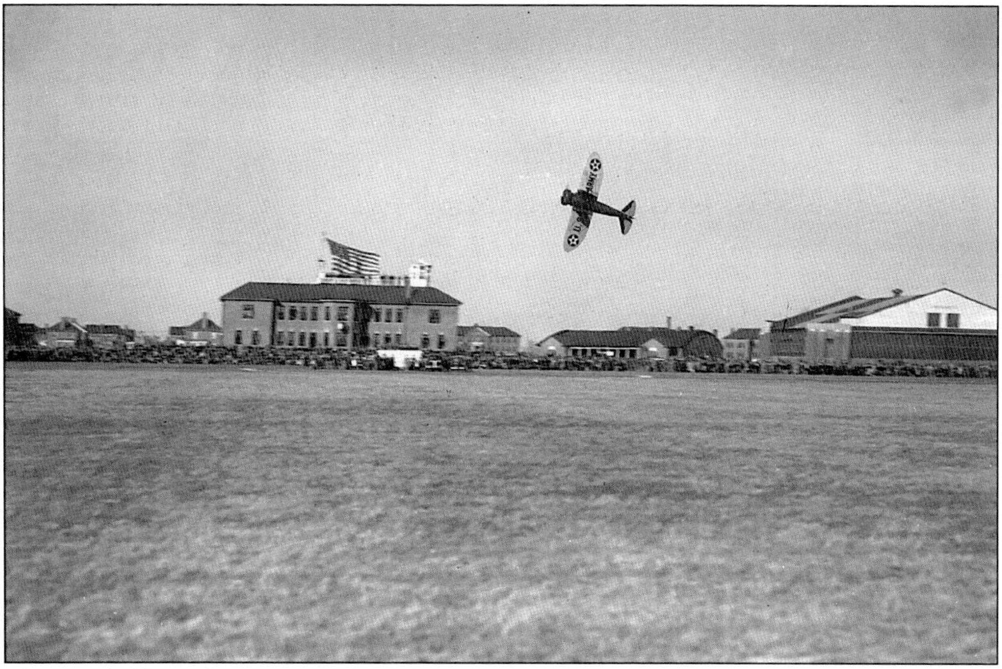

The Mitchell Trophy Air Races brought international attention to the township air base. To be eligible for the Mitchell Trophy Race itself, a pilot had to be a member of the First Pursuit Group, have over 1,000 flying hours, have been on duty at Selfridge for one year or longer, be an officer in the Regular Army, and never have flown in a Mitchell Trophy Race before. The plane above flew in the 12th race in 1936.

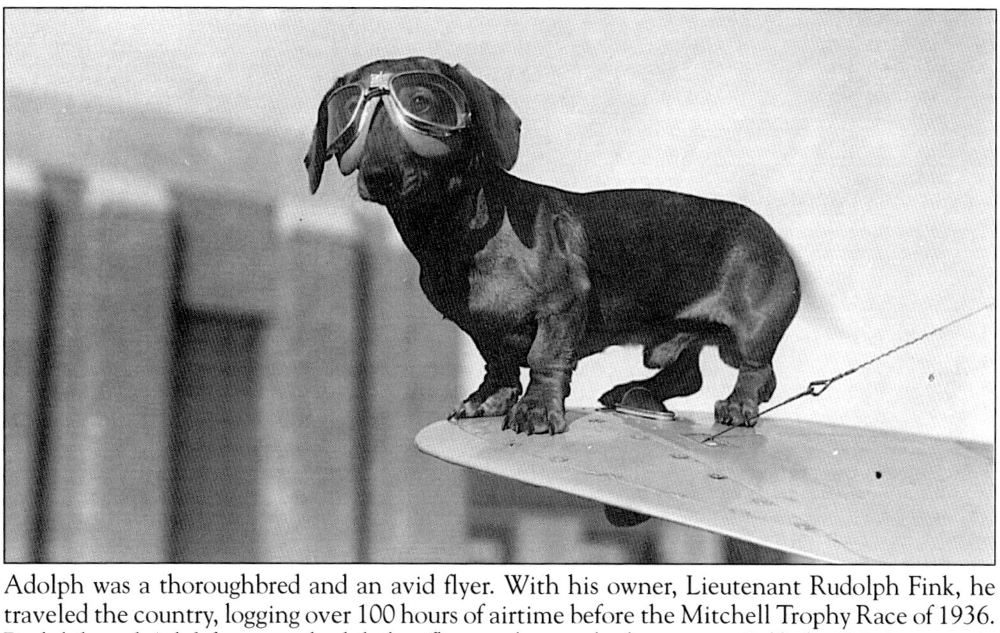

Adolph was a thoroughbred and an avid flyer. With his owner, Lieutenant Rudolph Fink, he traveled the country, logging over 100 hours of airtime before the Mitchell Trophy Race of 1936. Rudolph and Adolph were scheduled to fly together in the big race at Selfridge. Unfortunately for Adolph, a few weeks before the race, he tangled with another mode of transportation, the automobile. Adolph was still recuperating at the time of the race.

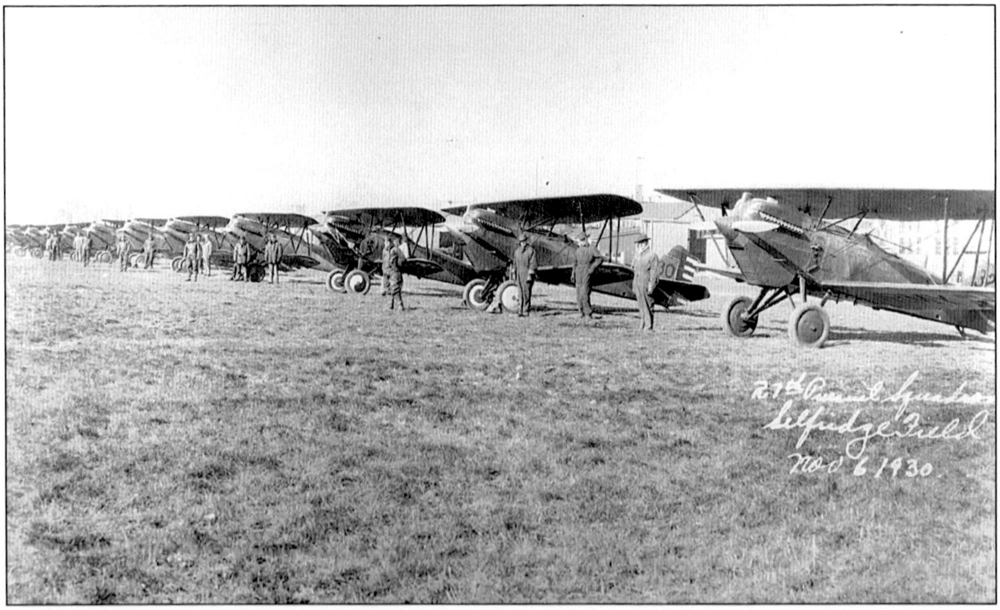

The planes pictured above are part of the 27th Pursuit Squadron, but it was the 1st Pursuit Group that brought national attention to Selfridge. These flyers were number one in more than just name. They were the heroes of World War I and considered the best. After the attack on Pearl Harbor, however, the planes were transferred to San Diego, leaving Selfridge without its major claim to fame.

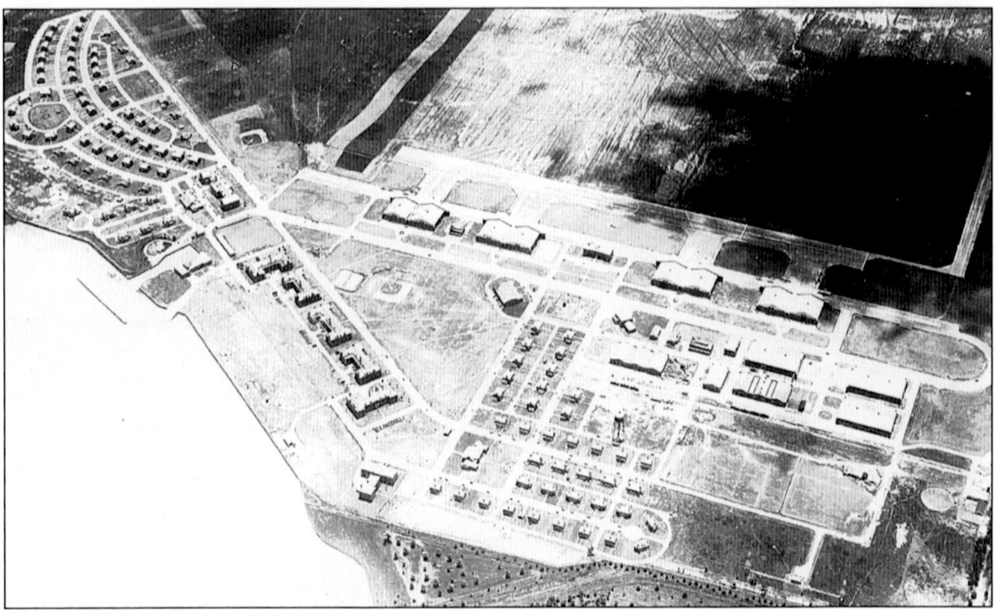

Selfridge is a military base, and local residents have been determined to keep it that way. Efforts to convert it to a joint military and civilian facility have failed for decades, thanks to a group called CAJUN (Citizens Against Joint Use and Noise). The group that has fought so tenaciously has recently announced they are disbanding and donating their funds to the Selfridge Air Museum.

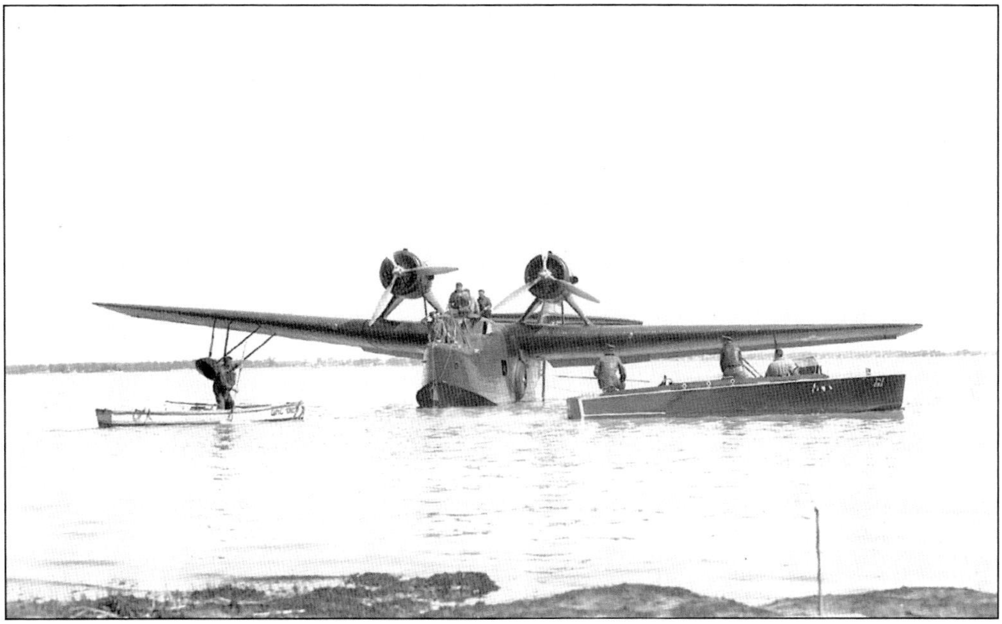

Rescue missions are a very important aspect of training at Selfridge. The combination on this page of the rescue plane and the rescue boat were the early version of the helicopters that are often heard overhead in the township. The seaplane had its own concrete ramp, but it needed the towboat to help maneuver it onto the ramp since it had no brakes. The 1927 Chris Craft can be identified as an Army boat because of the V number on its hull. Although this duo was an obvious asset at the time, the advantages of accessibility and maneuverability make the helicopter a major improvement.

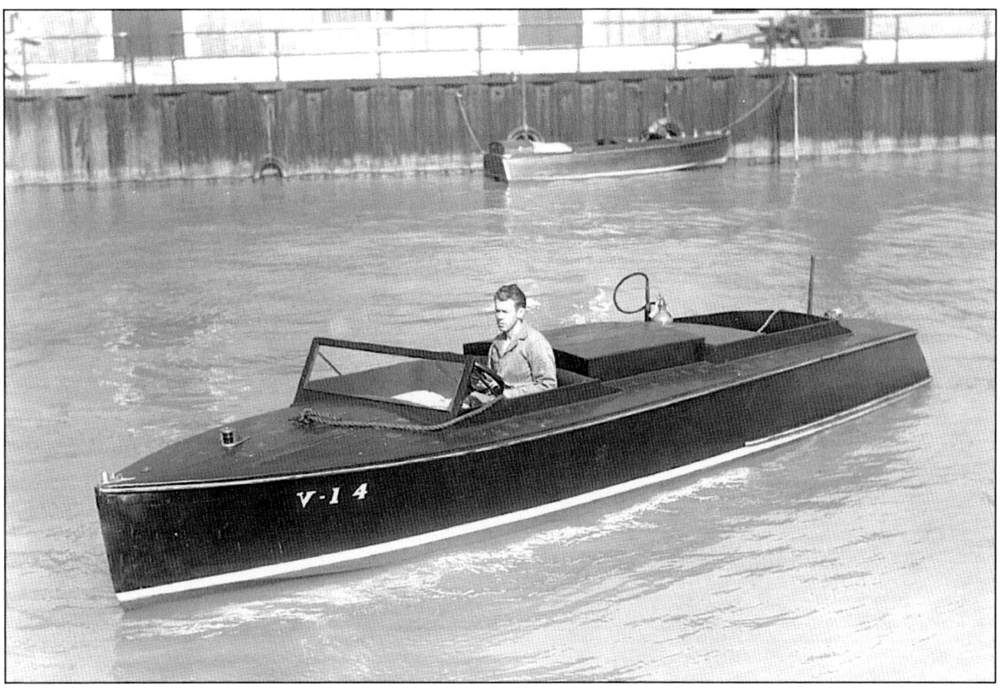

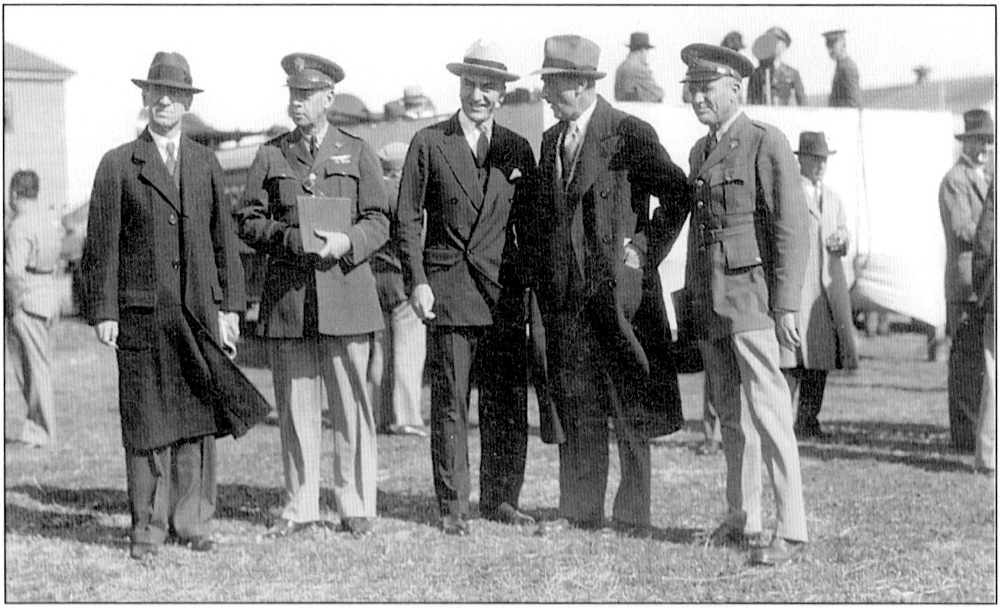

In the 1960s, the base was dubbed "The Home of Generals." It was home to America's ace pilots like Eddie Rickenbacker, seen here at the base in the 1930s. Throughout the years, more than 150 soldiers that trained at Selfridge became generals. Even Charles Lindburgh stopped at the base two months after his historic flight. His plane had to be guarded as local residents flocked to the base with food and gifts.

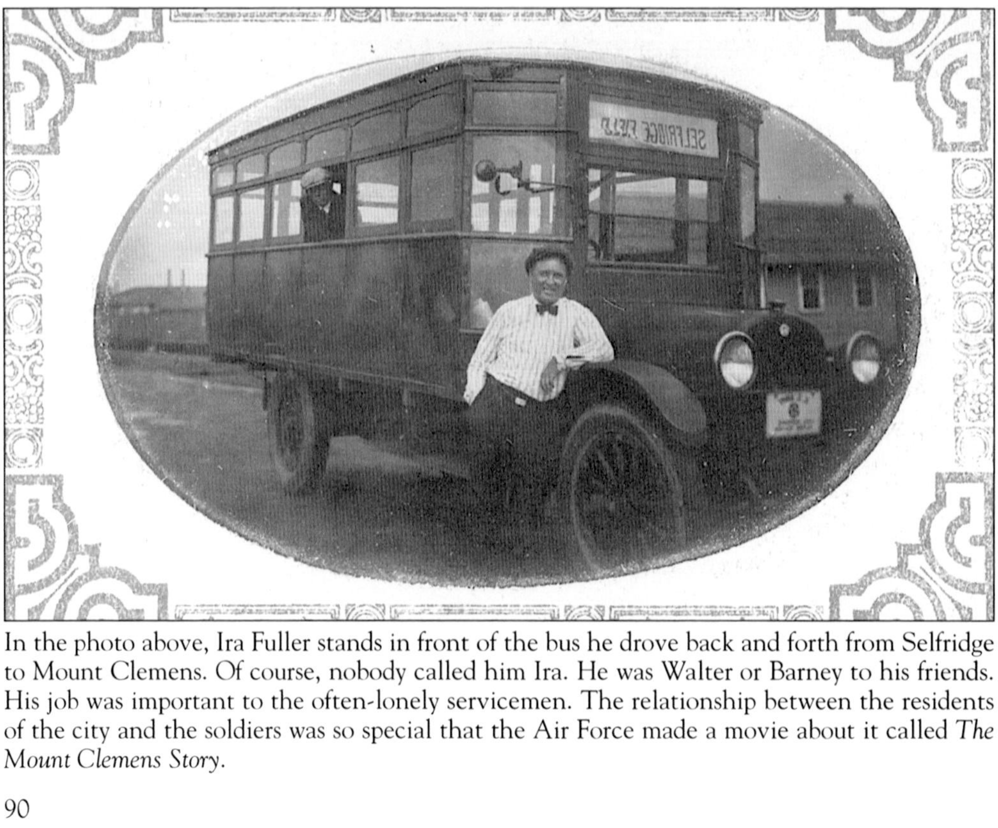

In the photo above, Ira Fuller stands in front of the bus he drove back and forth from Selfridge to Mount Clemens. Of course, nobody called him Ira. He was Walter or Barney to his friends. His job was important to the often-lonely servicemen. The relationship between the residents of the city and the soldiers was so special that the Air Force made a movie about it called *The Mount Clemens Story*.

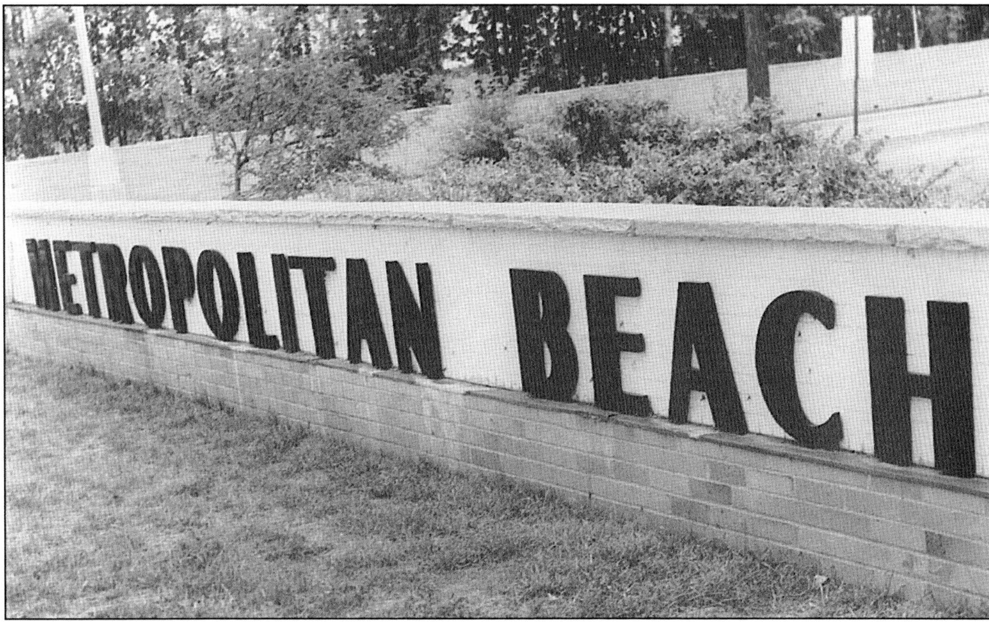

In the late 1940s, the board of the Huron-Clinton Metropolitan Authority released a plan to "provide beach and swimming facilities commensurate with the needs and desires of the three million people living within the (Detroit) metropolitan region." Their first project was to acquire 550 acres of the Huron Point property at the terminus of the Huron-Clinton Parkway plan for a park to be known as St. Clair Metropolitan Beach. The photo above shows the original brick sign at the entrance to the beach property. Since motorists had a tendency to hit the sign, it was later replaced with a wooden version. The aerial below shows the early progress.

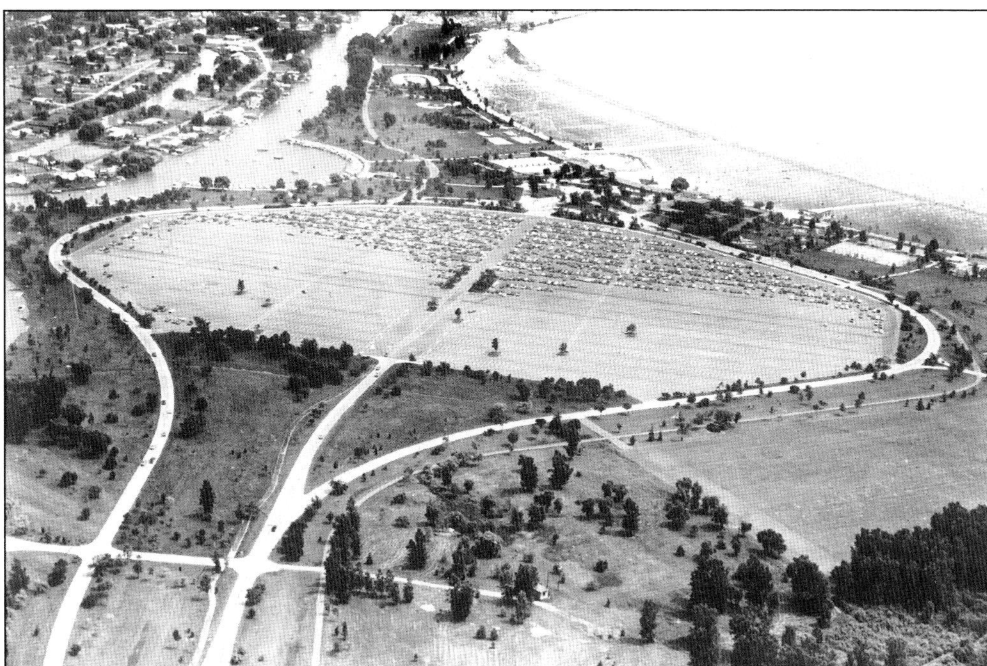

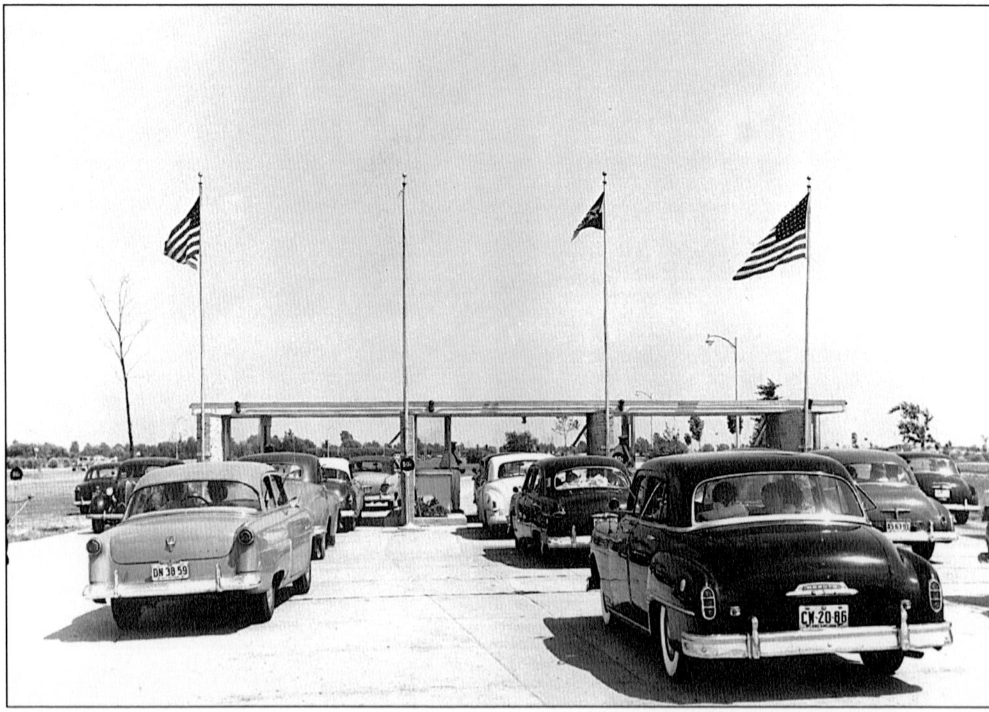

The sign on the tollbooth says 50¢ was the parking fee for each car, no matter how many occupants. In the 1950s, however, the cost was only 25¢ on weekdays. The only better deal there is would be free Wednesdays. Today's rates of $2 on weekdays and $3 on weekends and holidays look better in perspective. In the 1950s, there was no "Squirt Zone."

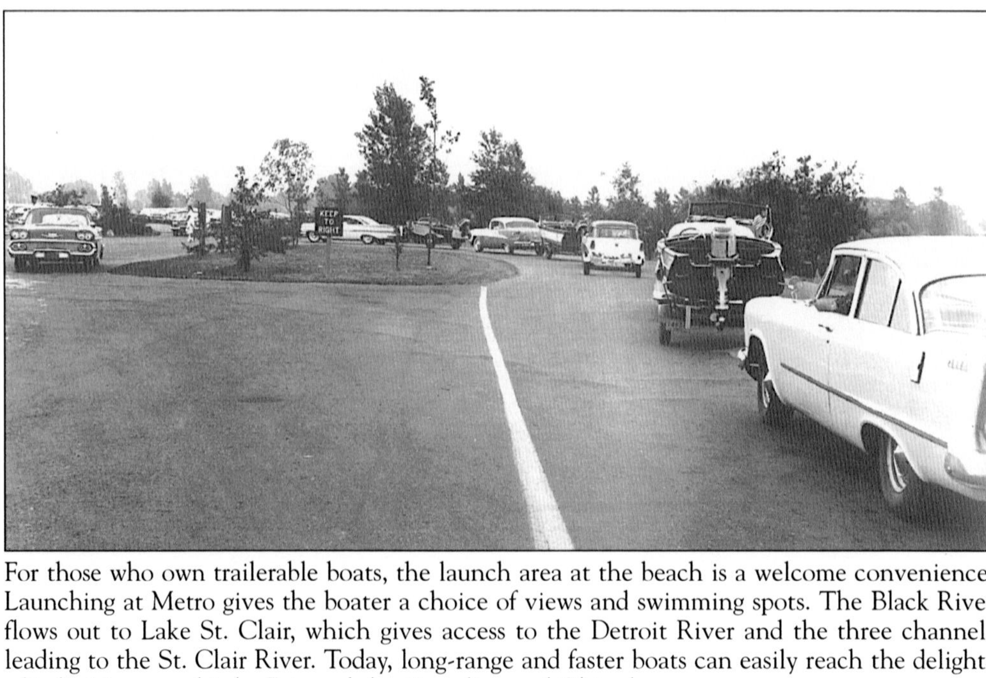

For those who own trailerable boats, the launch area at the beach is a welcome convenience. Launching at Metro gives the boater a choice of views and swimming spots. The Black River flows out to Lake St. Clair, which gives access to the Detroit River and the three channels leading to the St. Clair River. Today, long-range and faster boats can easily reach the delights of Lake Huron and Lake Erie and the Canadian and Ohio shores.

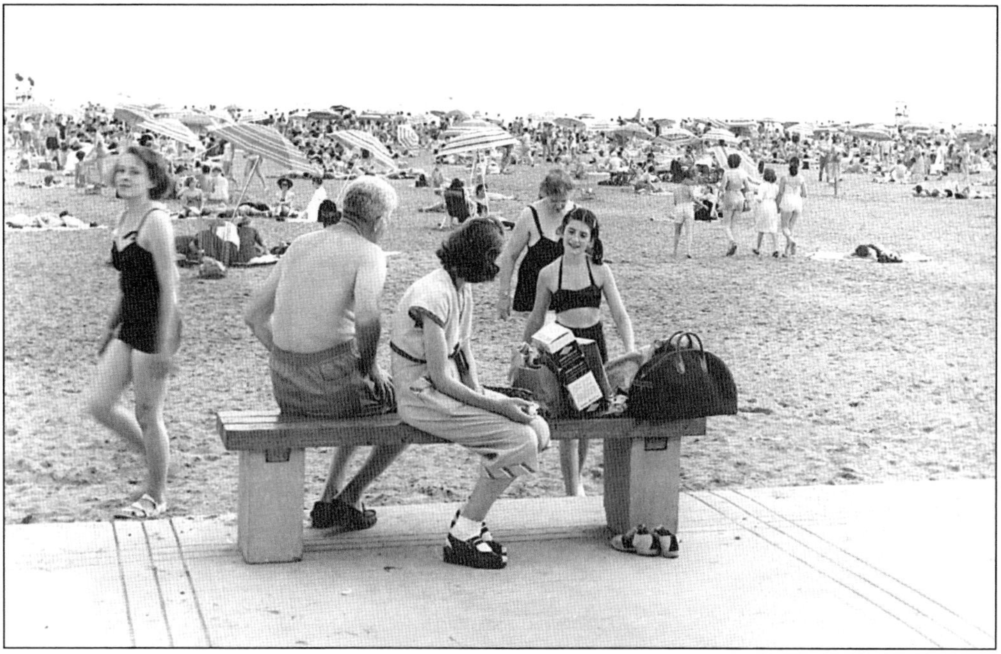

The master plan called for "a 50-acre beach, more than a mile long and average 300 feet in width." A 3,500 foot-long "beach walk" provided a connection between all public and service areas. In the early days, the sand ran from the boardwalk to the beach. Today, much of it has been grassed.

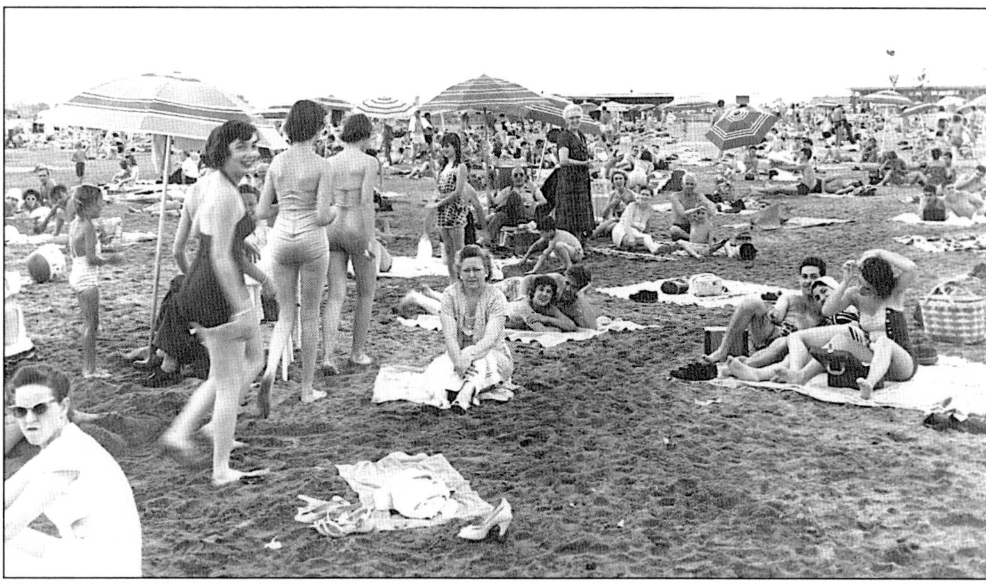

According to an early Huron-Clinton Metropolitan Authority report, the crescent-shaped beach was created when " thousands of yards of clean, white sand was pumped from the lake bottom to form the 6,000 foot-long beach." The Authority planned for the beach to be "one of the largest and most adequate swimming areas in the Central United States." The umbrellas rented for 50¢, then $1.00, and then $2.00 until 1989. Today, a small canopy for picnicking rents for $50.

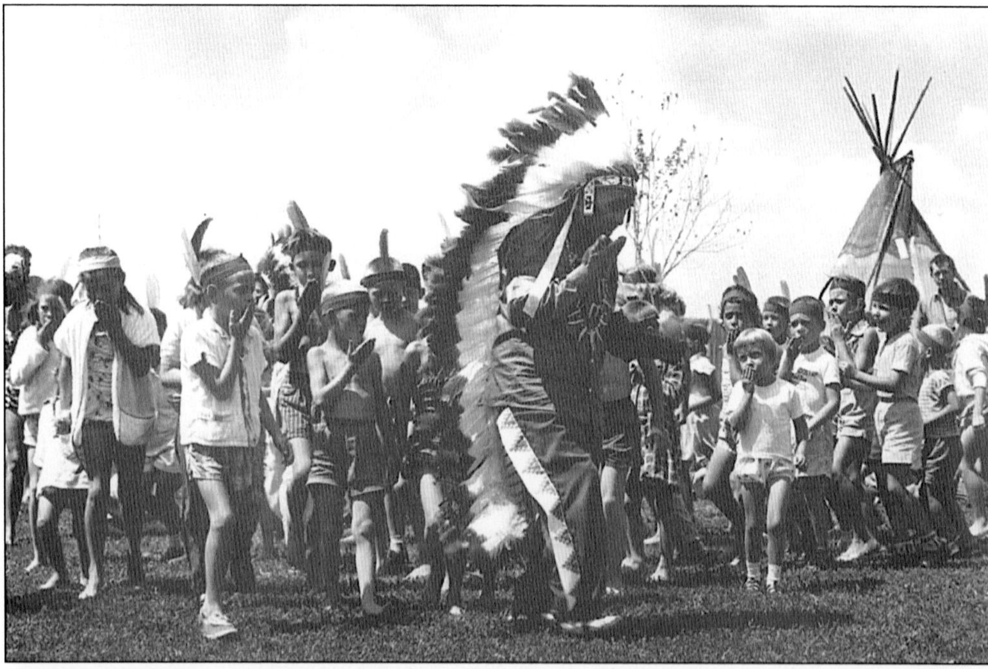

In 1956, Chief White Sands was billed as the "sole remaining chief of the Wyandotte Tribe." Above, Chief Blue Cloud led a war dance during the first children's Pow Wow on August 8, 1959. Below, Chief Yellow Sky Eagle poses with Children's Day winners in 1965. In the 1950s and '60s, children enjoyed pretending to be Native-American warriors. Today, they would more likely paddle the Voyageur Canoe and learn about the traditions and ways of the Native Americans at a Voyageur Encampment.

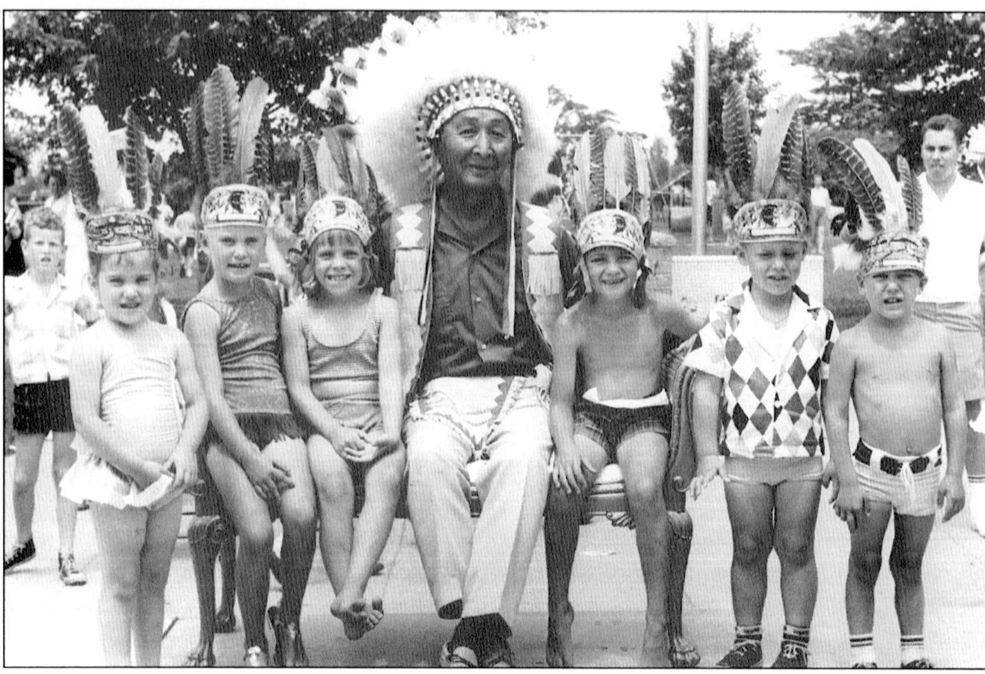

Special events at the beach included celebrations like the Summer Festival, the Children's Day or Festival, and the Fall Festival. Held at different times in given years, the crowning of a Miss Metropolitan Beach and a Tot Lot King and Queen or Prince and Princess was an annual highlight.

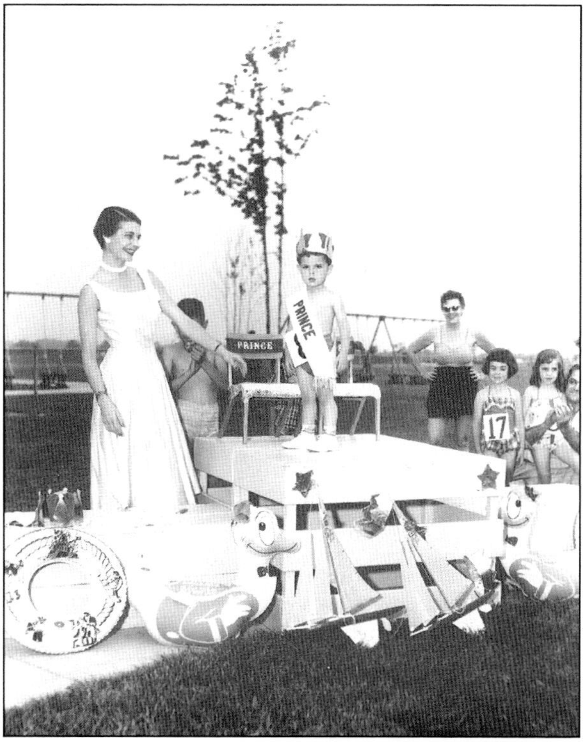

Originally known as the Children's or Kindergarten area, the Tot Lot was an exciting place for the younger visitors. The beach offered a daily children's program from 11 a.m. to 5 p.m. for two to six-year olds and another for youngsters six and over. Play was supervised and featured a mini-car racetrack, games, nature study, crafts and a favorite of kids and parents alike, the Native-American Tee Pee.

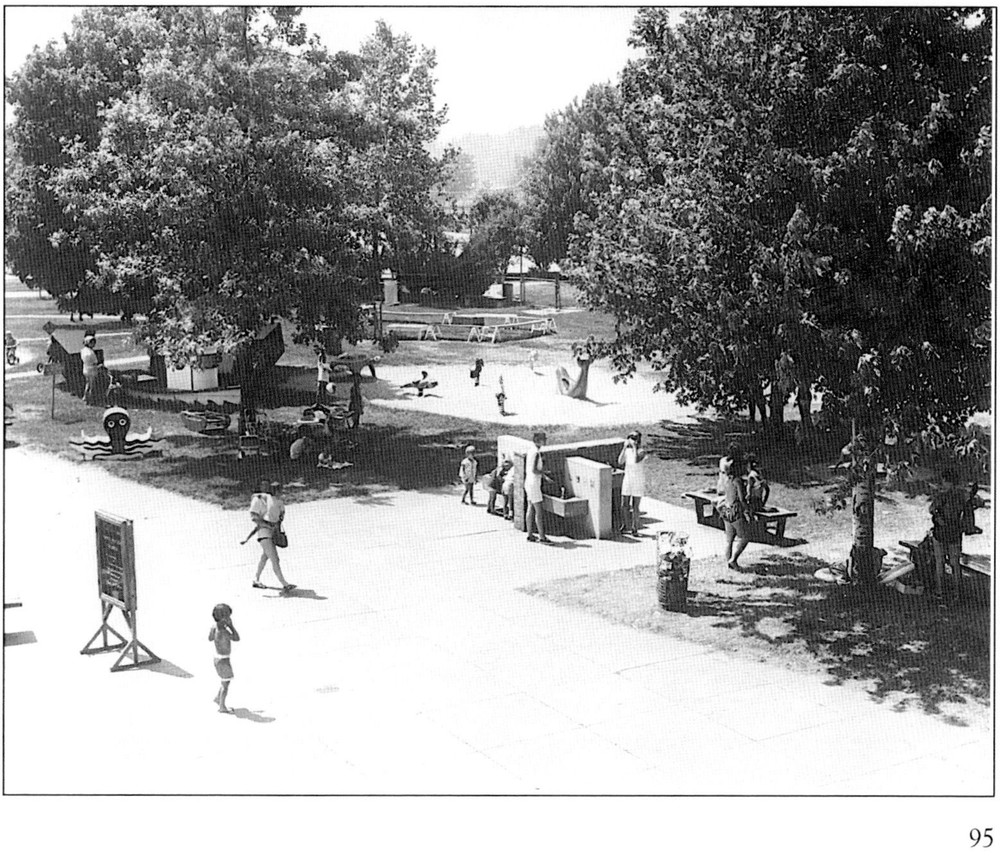

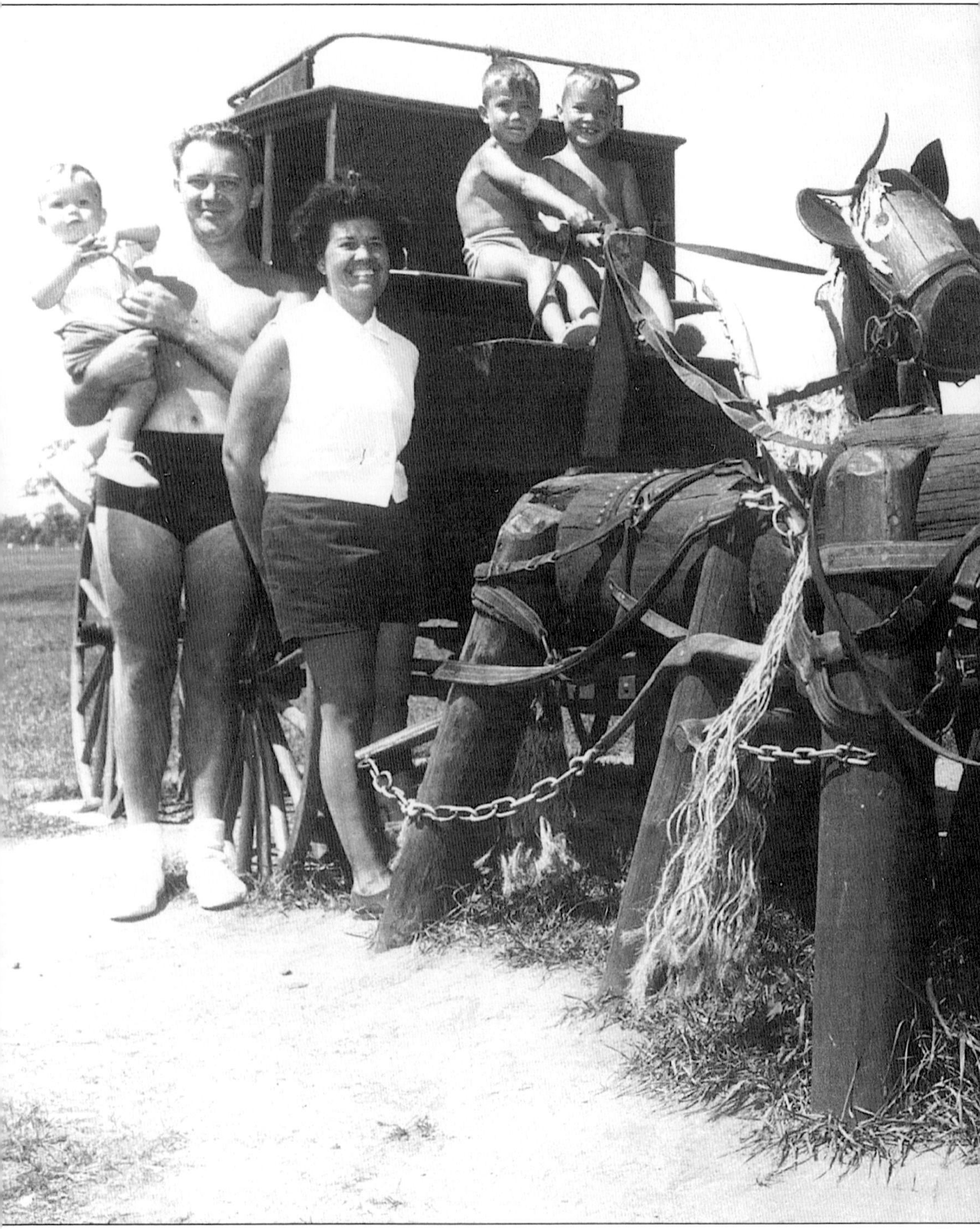

Nobody could mistake these horses for the real thing, but the Tot Lot's stagecoach was still a big success. In the days when "Cowboys and Indians" were giving way to video games, youngsters with vivid imaginations could ride the stage into Dodge all day if they chose. Township native, Pete Williams, remembered the stagecoach being his favorite place when he

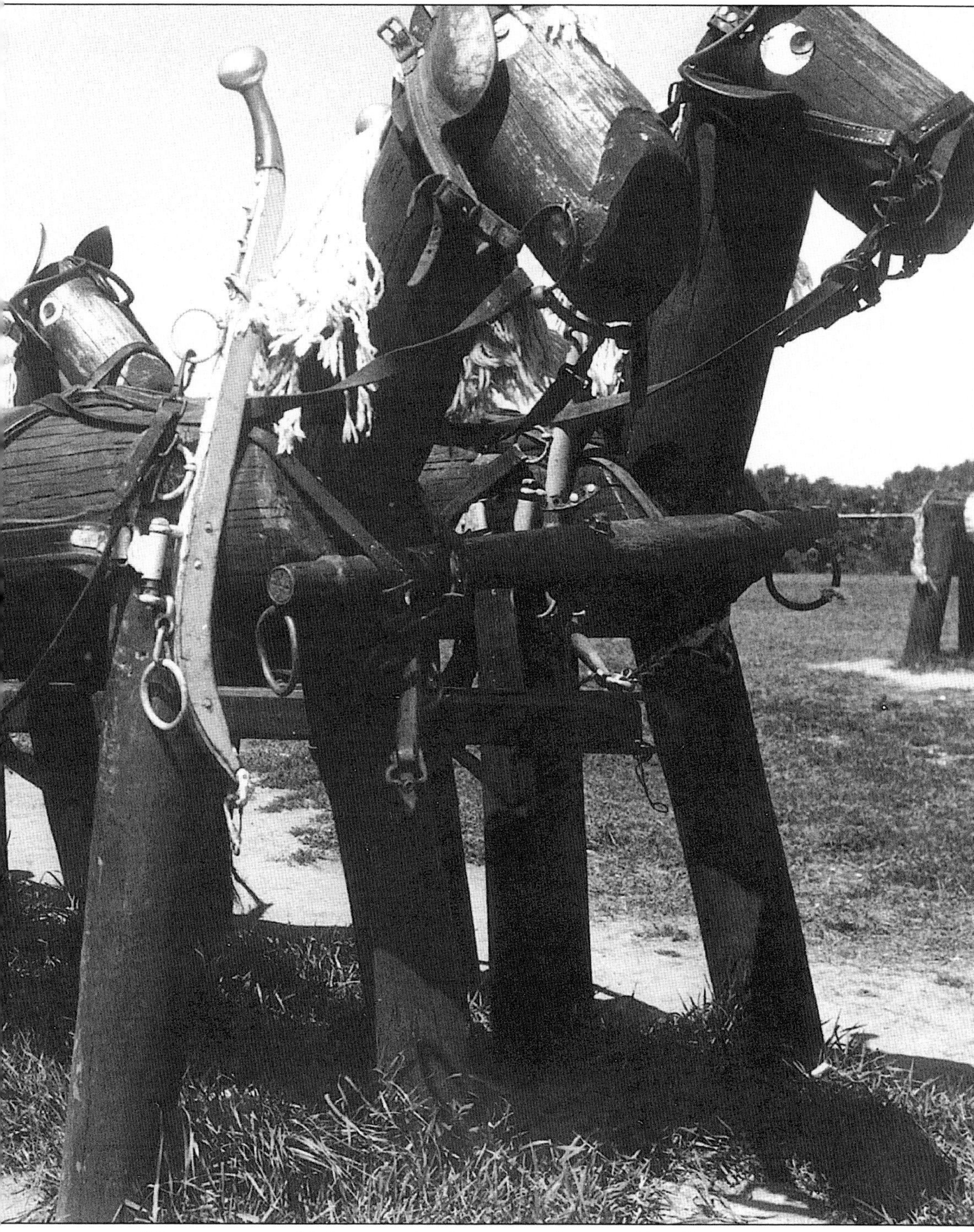

was young. "Our parents would drop us off at the gate, and we would walk into the park to save the admission fee. Then we would meet them back at the gate." Today, the bike path leads right to the gate. Local youth don't even have to worry about traffic.

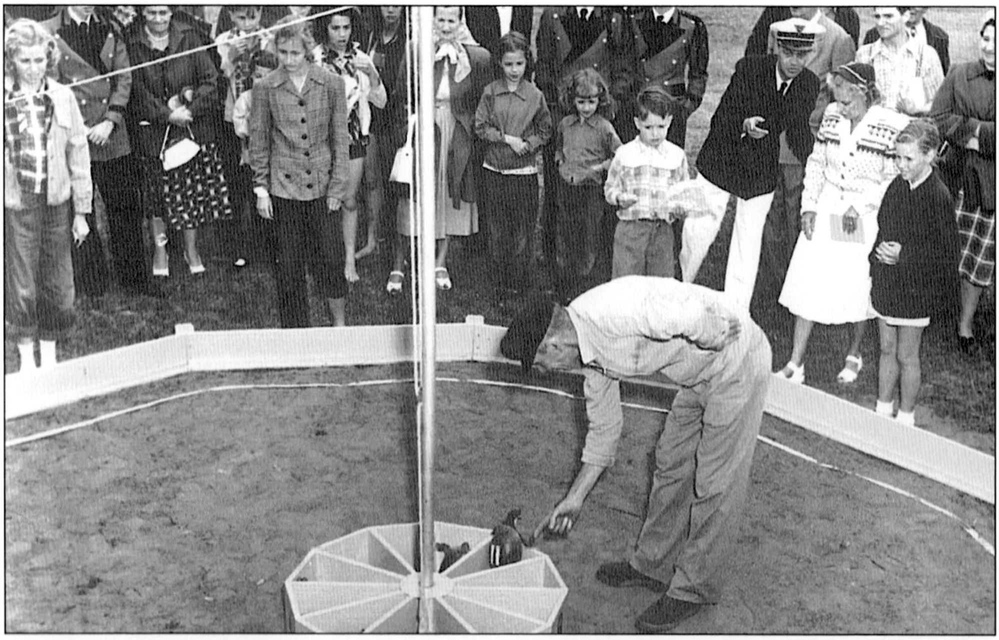

One of the early special attractions for all ages was the Turtle Race. The races must have been popular since they were held three times a week in 1953 and became a daily event in 1954. Local resident, Arlene Rood, remembers that the beach supplied the turtles for the free races. "Each turtle had a number. You picked the one you wanted. If your turtle won, you got a prize."

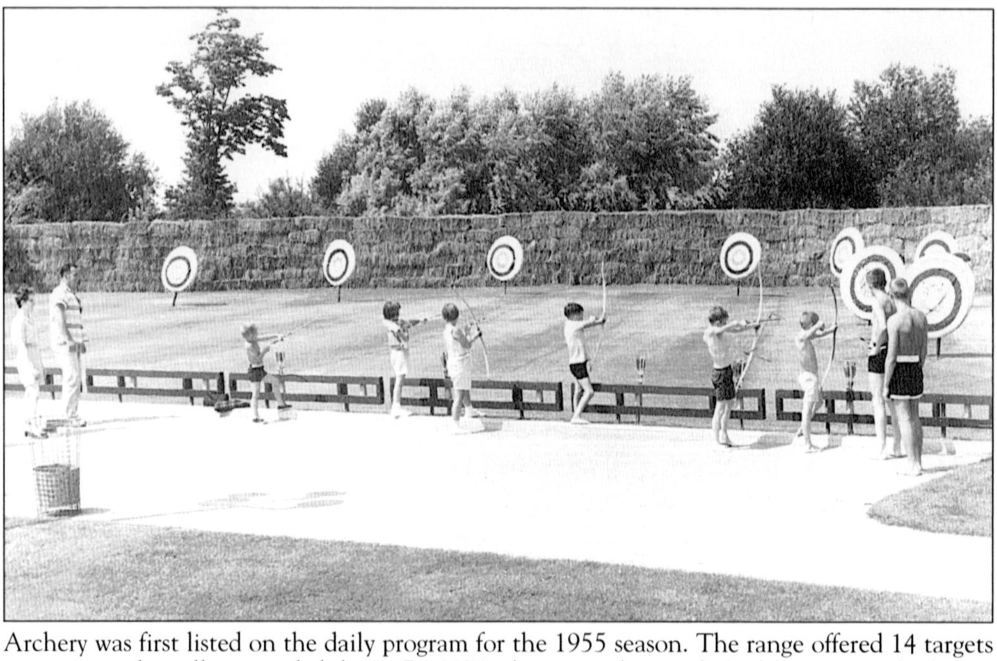

Archery was first listed on the daily program for the 1955 season. The range offered 14 targets to accommodate all ages and abilities. By 1970, the original cost of 10¢ for 10 arrows had risen to 15 arrows for 25¢. Unfortunately, the archery range was destroyed by fire of an unknown origin. Perhaps someone didn't read the beach rules that clearly state, "Fires permitted only in grills at picnic areas."

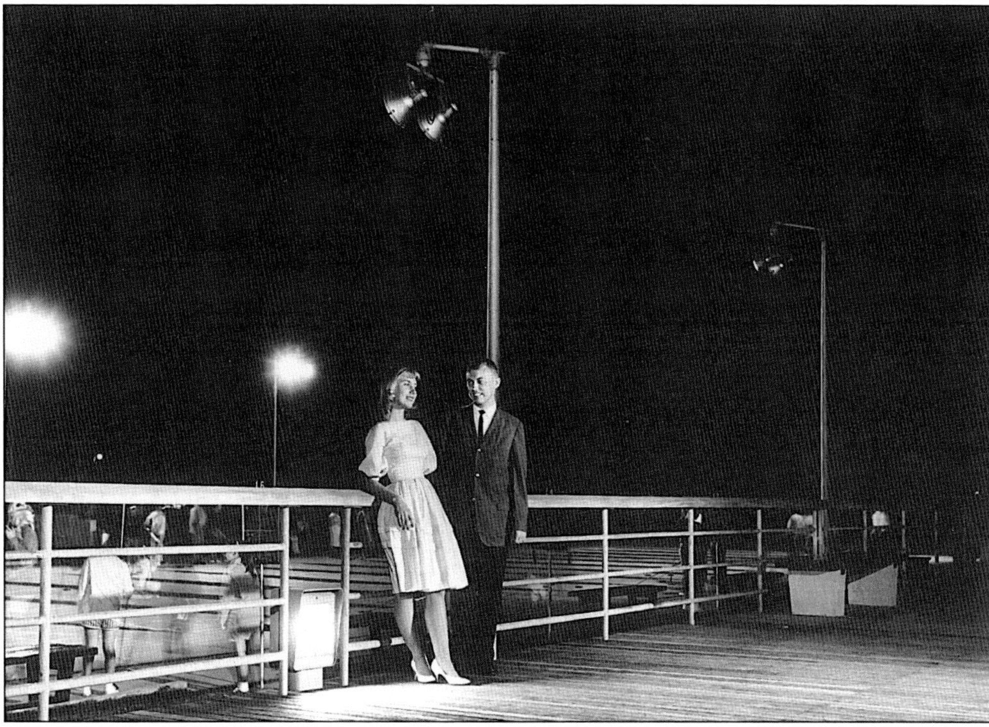

On a sunny day the boardwalk was packed with visitors, moving from one attraction to the next. In the evening, it was strictly for romance. Even the lights of the shuffleboard courts couldn't detract from the atmosphere or the view of the lake on a balmy summer evening. For the less romantically inclined, the 20 shuffleboard courts provided free entertainment. Also free were basketball, badminton, tetherball, volleyball, horseshoes, Ping-Pong, and softball.

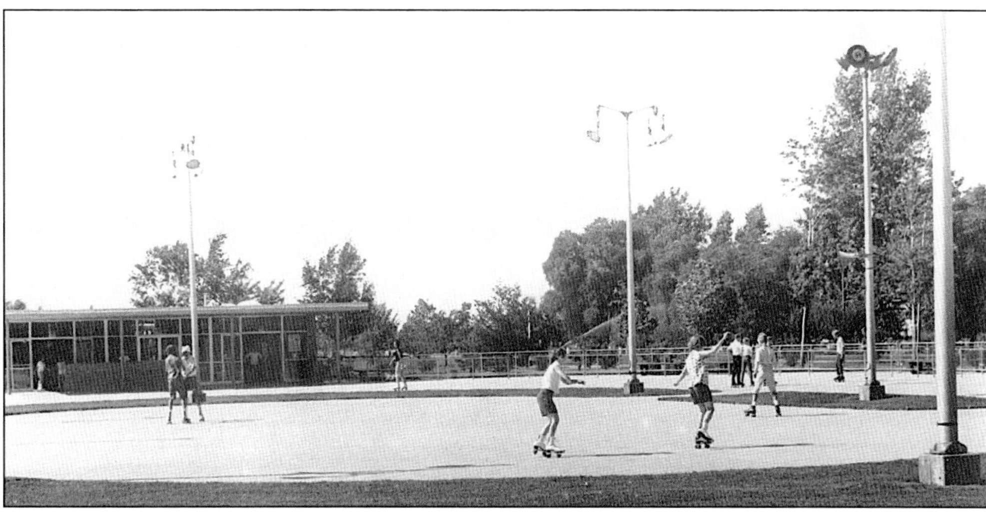

The roller rink was a popular attraction in the earlier days at the beach, but today's roller bladers find a sidewalk or bike path more to their liking. Music now plays for private parties instead of skaters, and umbrella tables dot the circular rink. Whether it's graduation parties, class reunions, or just good friends getting together, the old roller rink is still a site that provides good times.

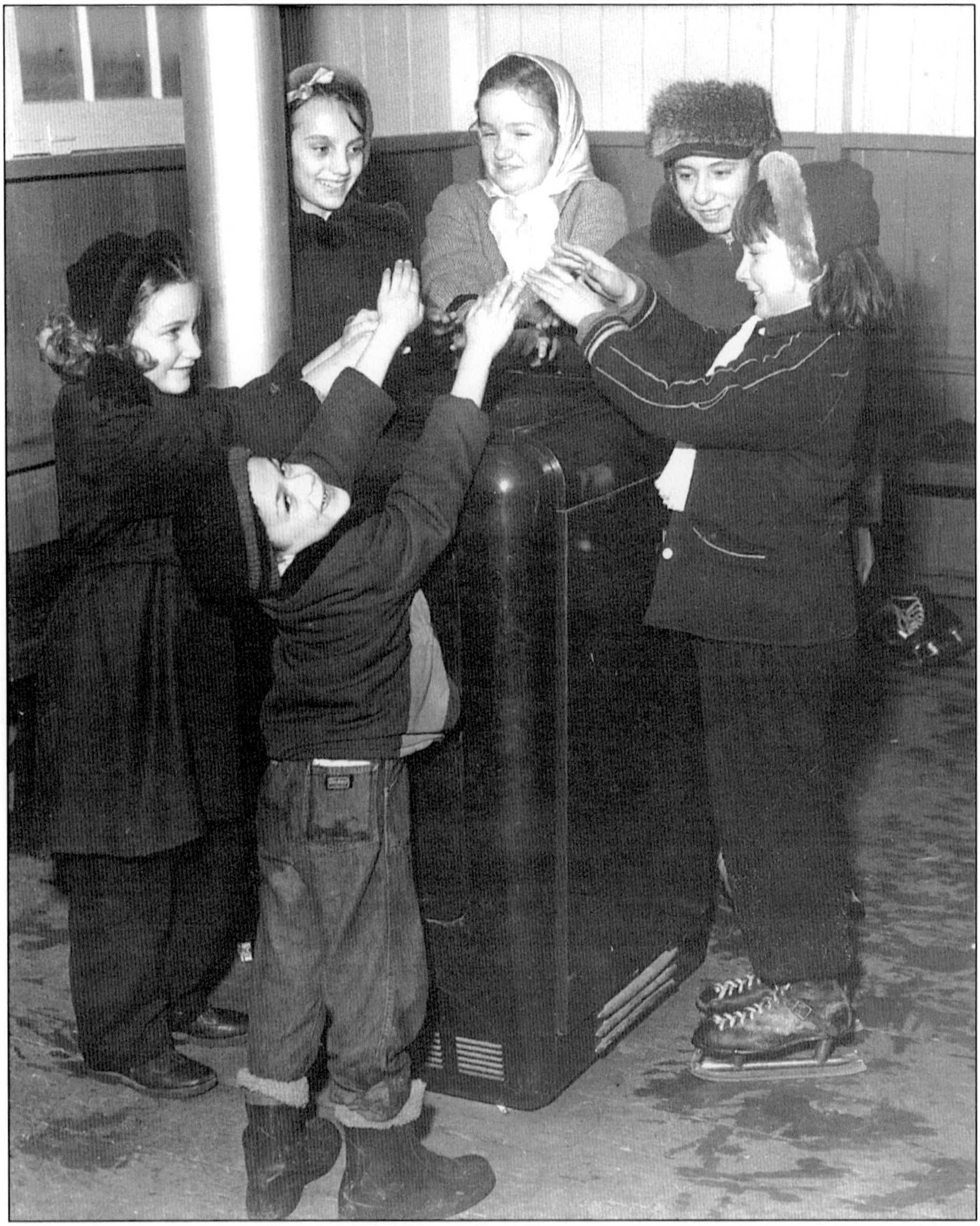

Where there is water in Michigan, there will likely be ice. Ice skating, ice fishing, and ice boating have all been enjoyable winter activities at Metropolitan Beach. Although the beach is not officially open in the winter months, the hearty souls still come. The young folks pictured here know there is no better place to gather on a chilly afternoon than the toasty old warming shed. The program for the Seventh Annual Ice Fishing Derby in 1959 points out one of the advantages of the beach in winter. "All facilities free except food and fishing equipment." The tollbooths are even unmanned in the off-season. Classifications for the derby were men, women, and juniors. The categories included longest perch and total perch entry poundage (not exceeding legal limit of 50). Even the unluckiest fishermen had a chance of going away with a prize—a door prize drawn from registration stubs.

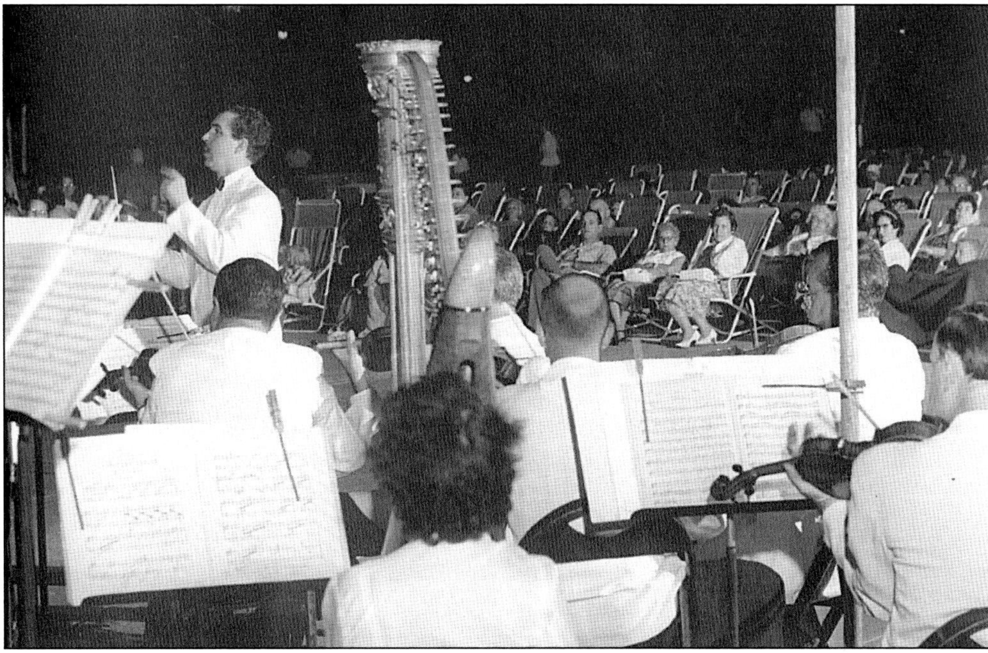

A 1957 program announced the addition of the Detroit Little Symphony to the beach's summer program. The Little Symphony was made up of "outstanding artists from the Detroit Symphony Orchestra, resulting in a perfect balance of strings, woodwinds, and brass." This free innovation made the beach one of the few in the world to present symphonic music. Francesco DiBlassi was the conductor.

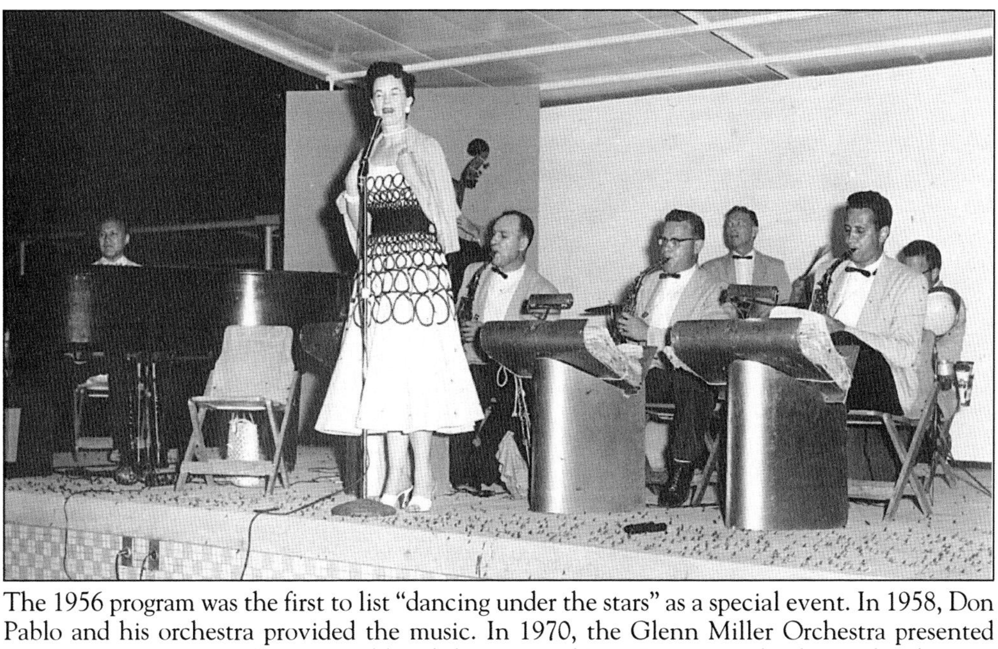

The 1956 program was the first to list "dancing under the stars" as a special event. In 1958, Don Pablo and his orchestra provided the music. In 1970, the Glenn Miller Orchestra presented "Jumping Swing Time," but Don Pablo, Phil Gram, and Jerry Ross were also featured orchestras. Dancing has always been a crowd-pleaser, but Harrison's notorious fish fly season was not making life easy for this band and singer.

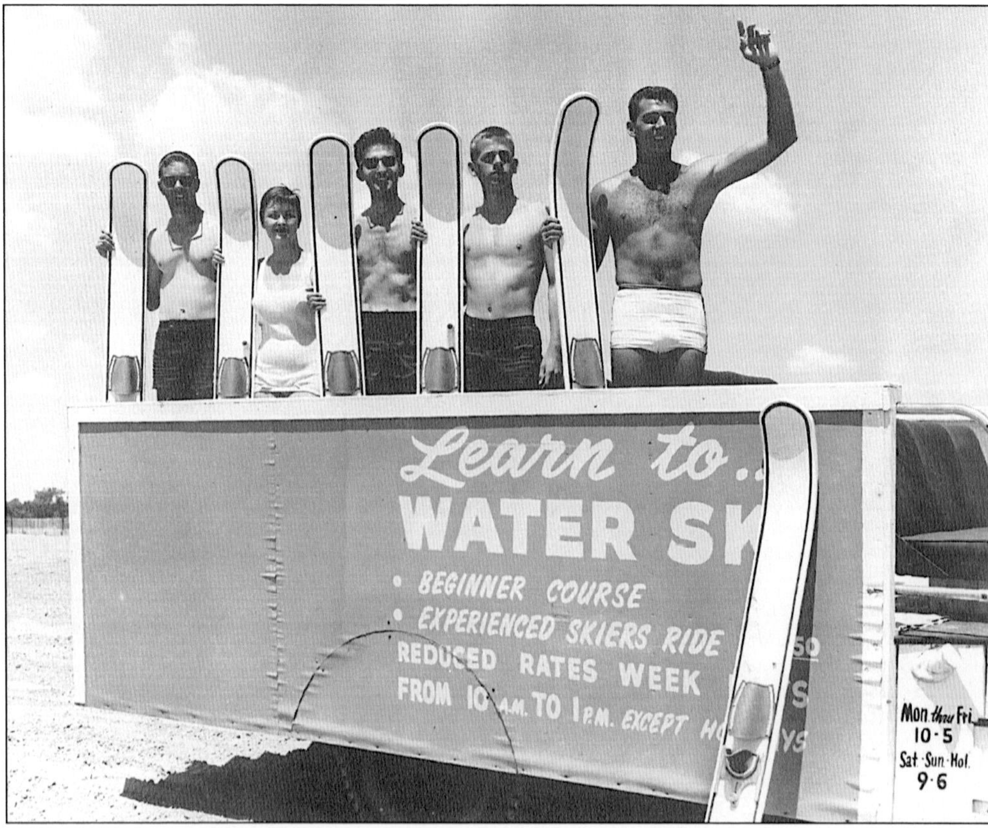

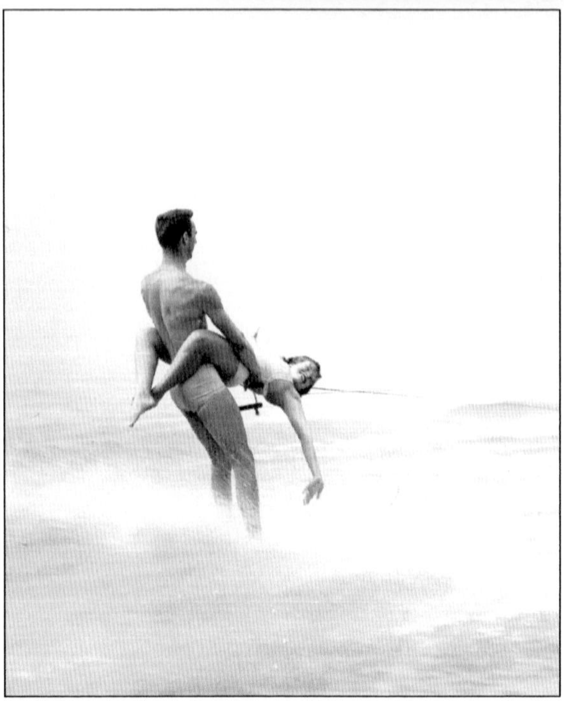

Dick Sligh, one of America's top seven ski champs, and Willie Williams, America's number one woman skier, were in charge of the Water Ski School at Metro in 1953. On Wednesday through Sunday, from the end of June to the first of September, they offered lessons at the large boat basin. Unfortunately, the program listed "rates on inquiry," and a well-placed ski in the picture above leaves the question of cost unanswered. Apparently the school was closed from 3:30 to 4:00 p.m. for a 20-minute water-ski exhibition performed on the same days. Once a year the International Championship Troupe from Lake Macatawa, Michigan, presented a special show with the president of the National Water Ski Association, Charles Sligh, providing the comments.

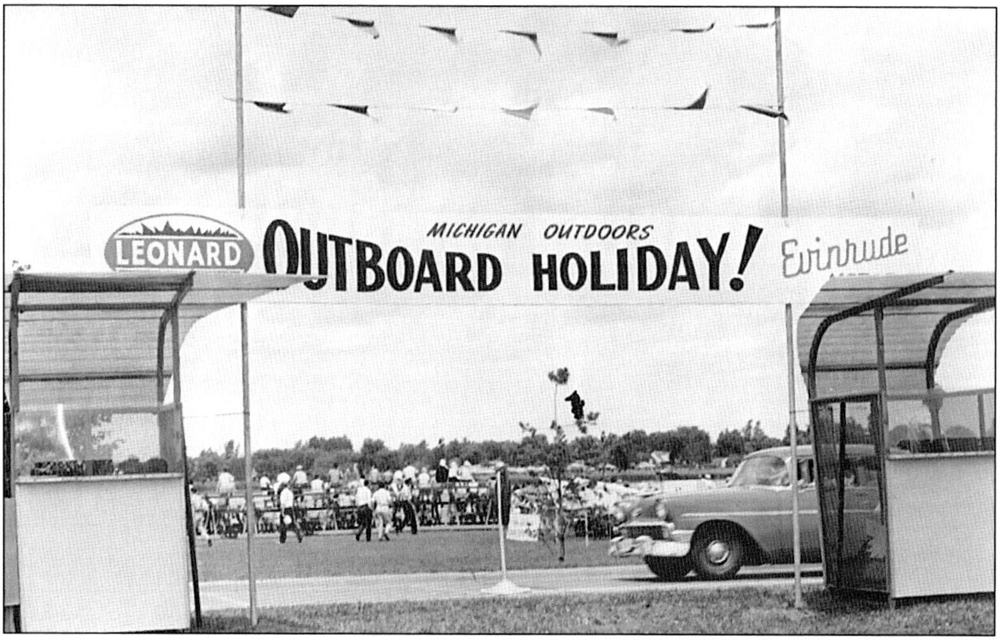

Special events have always drawn a large crowd. On Saturday, July 19, 1958, Mort Neff's Michigan Outdoors show, Outboard Holiday, made a one-time stop at Metro. The all-day program included a statewide motorboat review, boat safety demonstration, equipment displays, and an aquatic show. Just in case Mother Nature didn't cooperate, the alternate date was July 20. Apparently Evinrude and Leonard Gasoline were the sponsors.

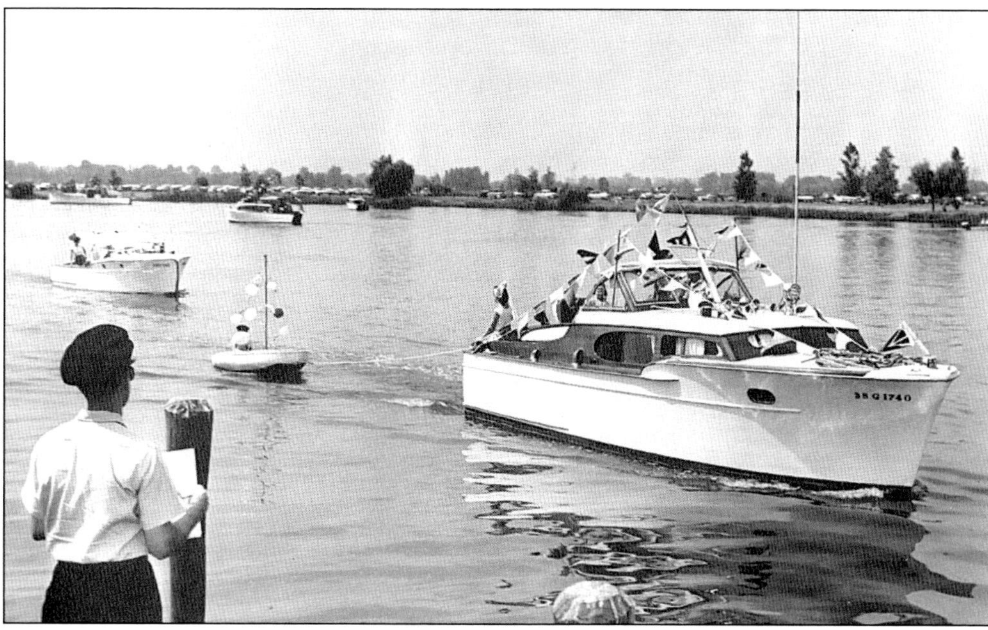

Bill Sherman, who later became the superintendent at Metro, is seen here surveying the entrants in the 1959 Fleet Review. During the annual event, boats cruised along the Black River and out into Lake St. Clair. It was, no doubt, an exciting event for participants, but was a far cry from the efforts and creativity put into today's Boat Town Parade of Lights.

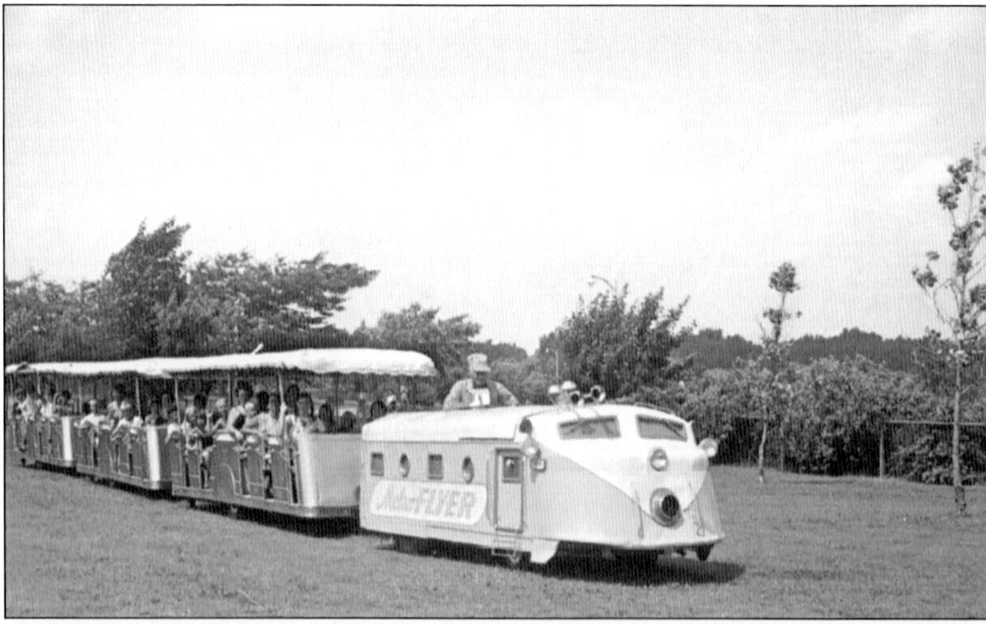

Picnicking, family and class reunions, and friends just getting together are common sights on the grassy areas of the beach. Pictured here in 1968, the first trackless train, the *Metro Flyer*, made lugging picnic baskets and blankets an easy task. The 1970 program listed the train stations as the parking area, roller rink, south marina, and Point Huron. The "Point" is pictured on page 126.

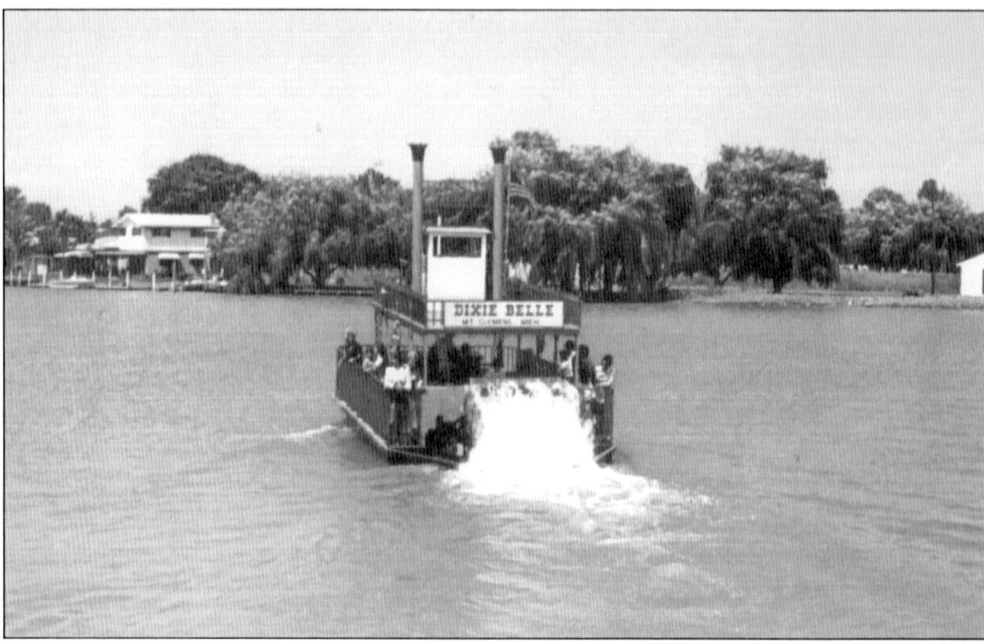

The *Dixie Belle* is just one of the boats that have taken visitors for trips on the Black River and out into the lake. The old-fashioned paddle wheeler also took its passengers back in time, but not as far back as the Voyageur Canoe. For those who would rather arrive by boat, the beach has offered an ever-expanding boat docking facility.

Eight

FUN AND GAMES

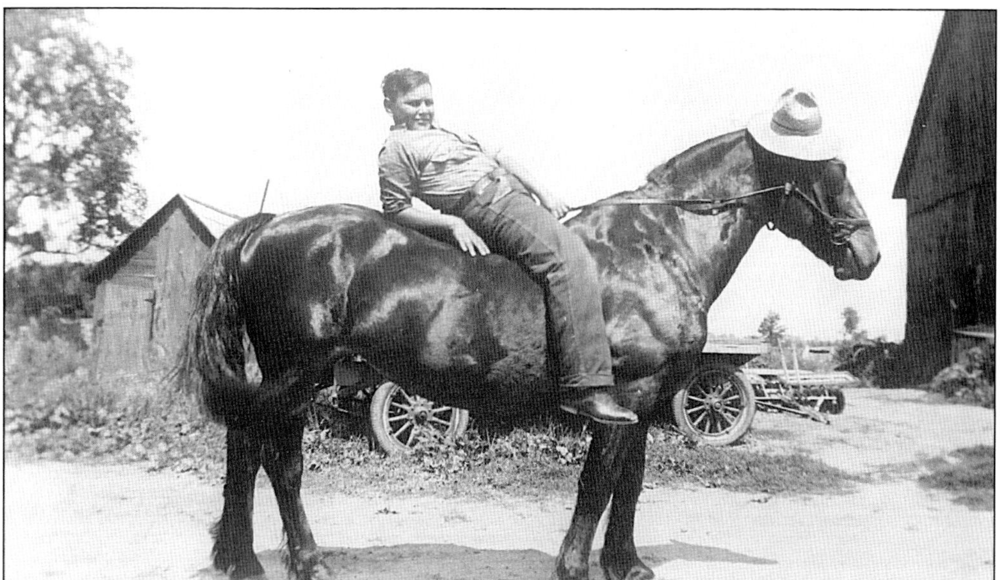

A farmer's life was never easy, but kids will be kids. Even the farm kids just had to have fun. Here Henry Callewaert enjoys a bareback jaunt on the horse normally used for cultivating. Luckily for Harrison Township, he grew up and switched from horses to fire trucks. Hank was the fire chief when he retired, but he never quite gave up farming.

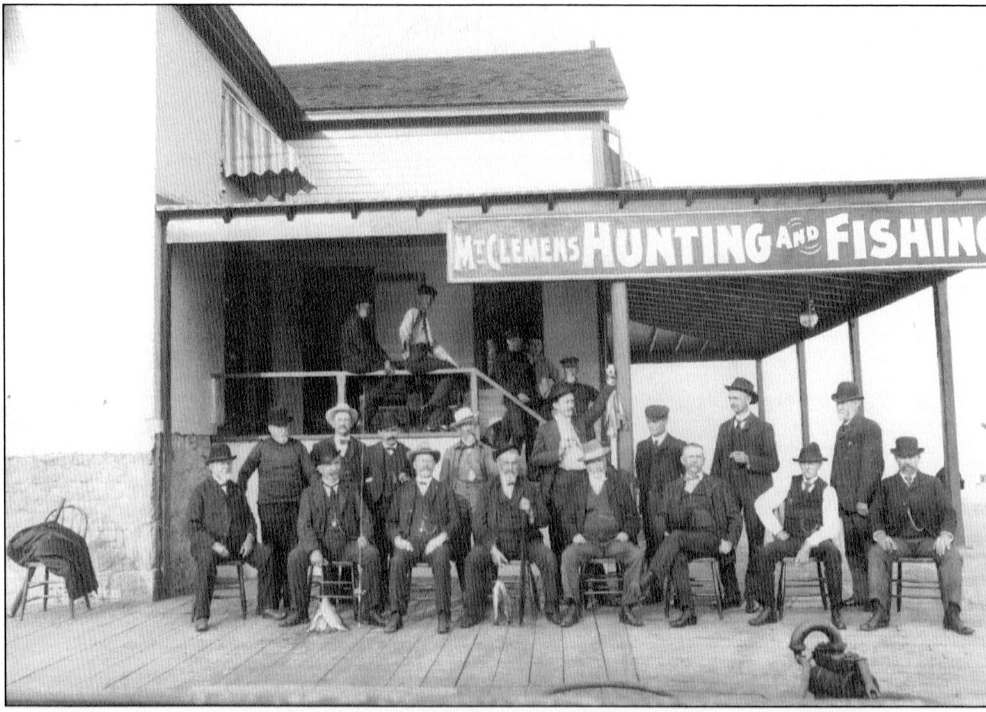

This 1903 photo of the Mount Clemens Hunting and Fishing Club shows how seriously some people took these sports. Actually, in those days, hunting and fishing were often a livelihood or a means of putting food on the table. The building was at the mouth of the river because it was originally the Belvidere Lighthouse keeper's home. The light structure rose from the middle of the building but was removed when the club took over.

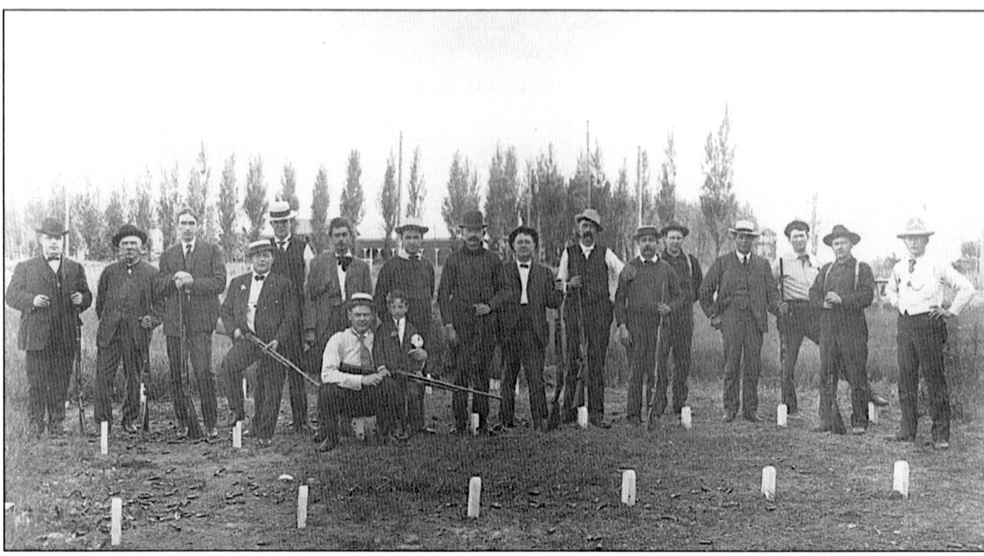

Frank Campau (sixth from the left) was not content to be a Harrison Township farmer. After establishing himself as the owner of the St. Clair House that he built on his land in Lakeside, he set out to provide for the interests and preferences of his guests. He created this early gun club and set up a shooting park on his property.

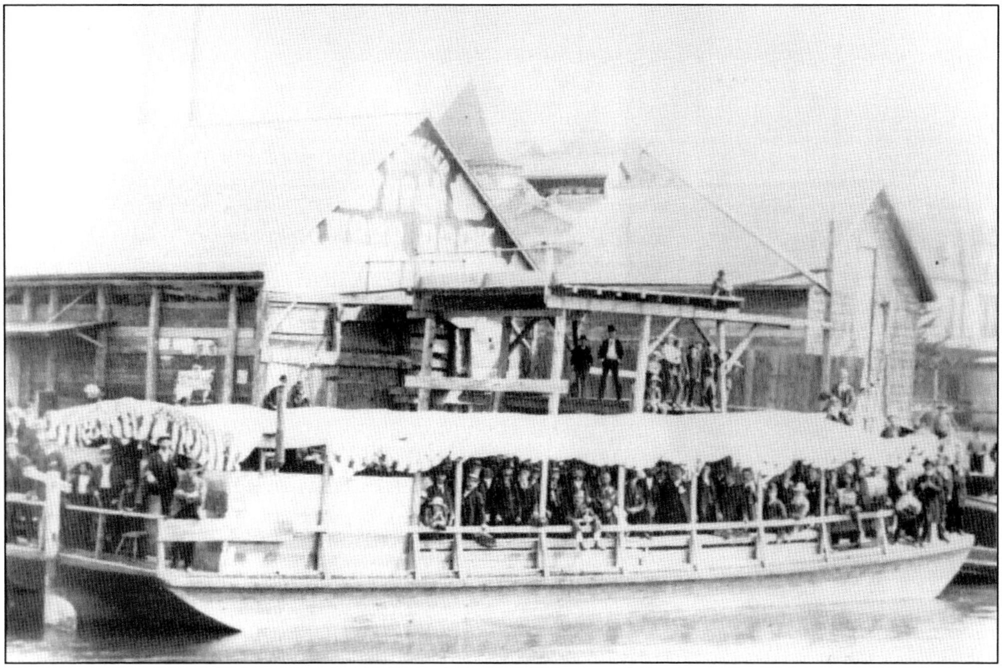

The roster reads like a "Who's Who of Macomb County." It is a select group that meets every year for the purpose of riding down the river for a day of fun and reminiscence. The Old Crowd is a tradition started in 1880. The Club has only two goals: to meet once a year for a "social re-union" and to keep women out. It isn't politically correct perhaps, but it is a tradition that has lasted for more than a century. Of course, women aren't the only ones who can't get included. Since membership is 240—no more, no less—many men have waited years or decades for the right opening. In the photo above, an early group of members waits at the Tucker Coal Dock. Below, the well-known Major Wilcox takes the Crowd on its annual outing.

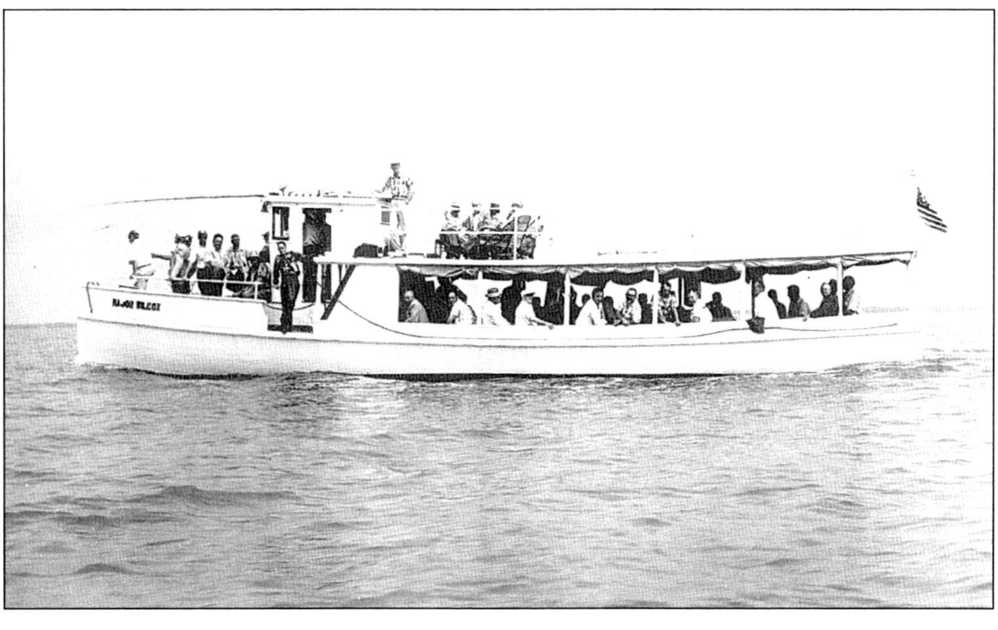

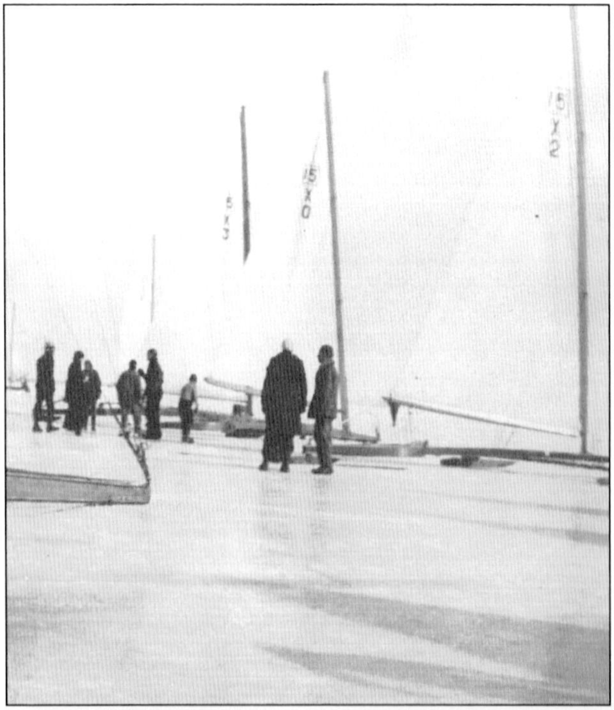

In the 1920s, the Mohawk Boat Club and ice boating brought national attention to the area. Races were held on the lake near Lakeside. In 1927, over 60 boats were entered in the annual regatta. The Lake St. Clair Ice Yachting Association was organized by local boaters. The Mohawk Club presented the "Dumb-bell trophy" to members who exhibited dumb-bell mentality while sailing or ice yachting. Today, police boats handle that task.

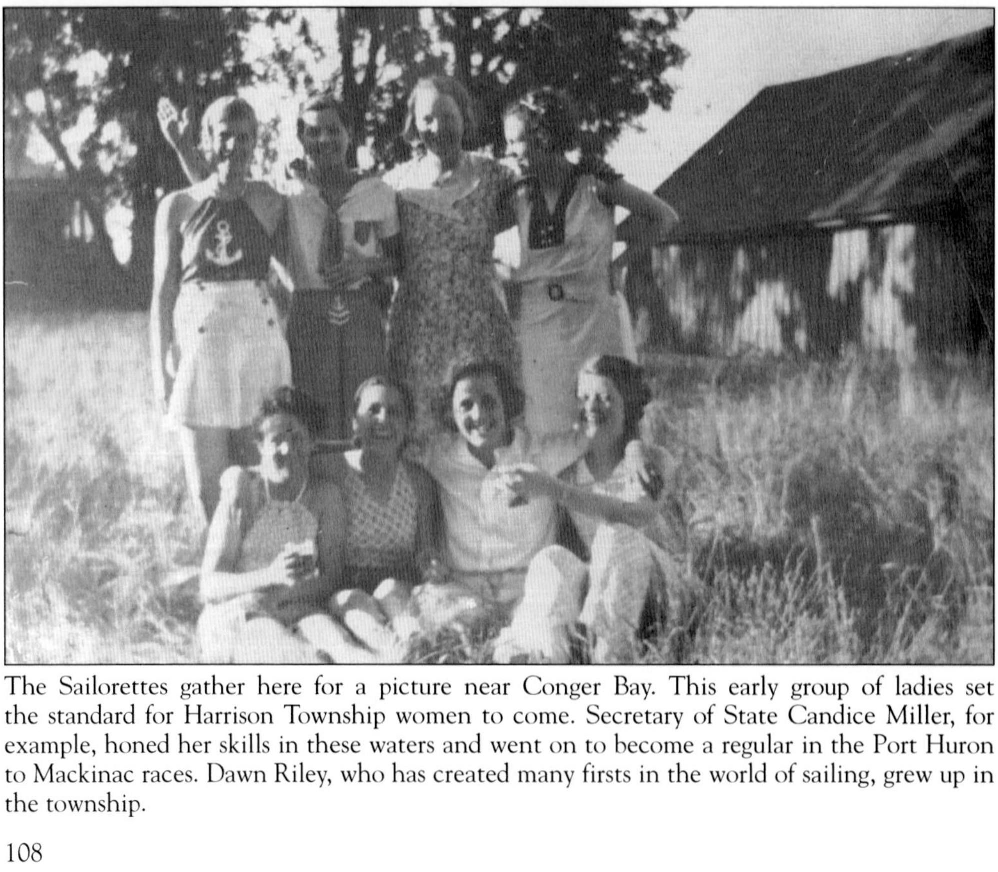

The Sailorettes gather here for a picture near Conger Bay. This early group of ladies set the standard for Harrison Township women to come. Secretary of State Candice Miller, for example, honed her skills in these waters and went on to become a regular in the Port Huron to Mackinac races. Dawn Riley, who has created many firsts in the world of sailing, grew up in the township.

1st " FESTIVAL OF LIGHTS "

4th of July Boat Parade

Bill Novak - Chairman

32575 So River Rd. Mt. Clemens, MI 48045

313 463-8627 463-2400

LIST OF WINNING ENTRIES

CATAGORY

1)MOST CREATIVE DECORATIONS
#104 John L., Doug & Marie McDougal
36 ft. Pacemaker
Sponsored by the Advertiser Journal Newspaper
Mr. Peter VanderVordt

2) BEST POWERBOAT UNDER 27'
#107 Dean Camphous
17' Boston Whaler

3) BEST POWERBOAT OVER 27' Belle Maer Harbor/Harbor Yacht Sales
#119 Mr. Jim Krause & Mark Howard
40' Tollycraft

4) BEST SAILBOAT UNDER 27'
#111 American Marine Survey
Bill & MaryAnn Novak
25' Northstar 500

5) BEST SAILBOAT OVER 27'
#117 Bob Slagle/Bill Netter
New Image Video
30' Hunter

6) BEST TUG
Sindbad
Sindbad's Restaurant

7) BEST USE OF LIGHTS
#119 Belle Maer/ Harbour Yacht Sales

8) BEST COSTUMES #113 Burr Sailboats
24' Seaward
Mr. Hugh Rugeroni

The Annual Festival of Lights Parade is a Boat Town USA charity event. The non-profit organization of local merchants and residents was formed in 1995 to promote Mount Clemens and Harrison Township businesses. An emphasis on water ecology and safety is important to both communities who share the Clinton River. The Festival of Lights, begun in 1985 by the group previously known as Boat Town, Inc., encourages residents with riverfront homes and boat owners to decorate and celebrate a different theme each year. The event is expected to draw in excess of 100,000 people to the banks of the river and Metropolitan Beach each year. The boats parade down the river out into the lake to Metropolitan Beach. Anyone on this list of the first winners knows why the festival was changed from a Fourth of July event during fish fly season to the first Saturday in August.

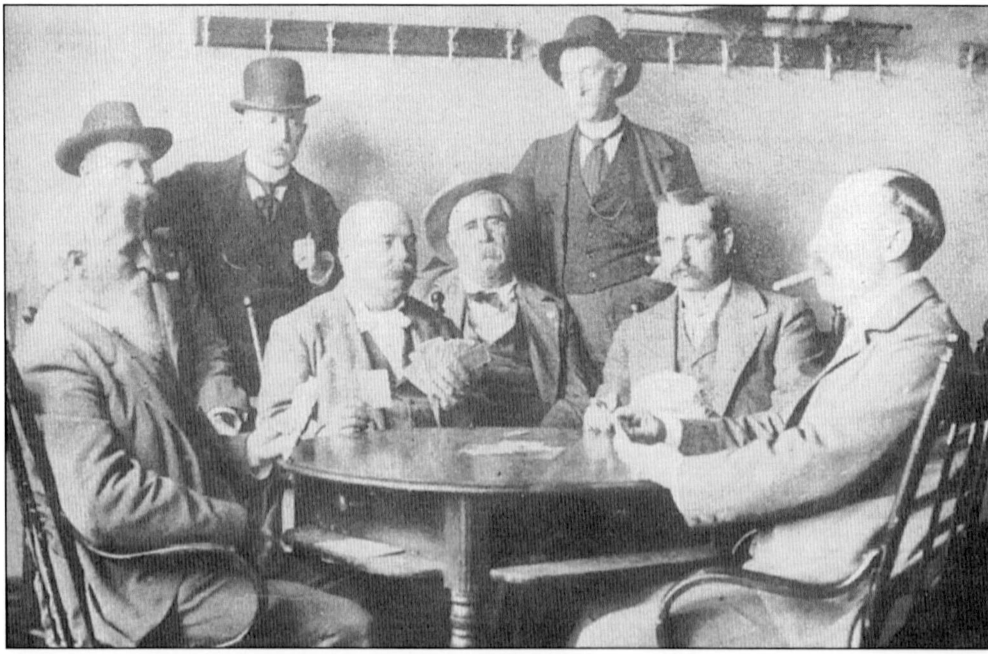

The photo above might just show a group of gentlemen out for a friendly evening of cards. Perhaps, but then again, during Prohibition, Harrison Township was known for its not so legal establishments. The Denmarsh, Sweet's Hotel, and the Kopper Kettle were a few of the local businesses that catered to those who refused to give up their "vices." The tunnels under the Kopper Kettle were handy for more than storage.

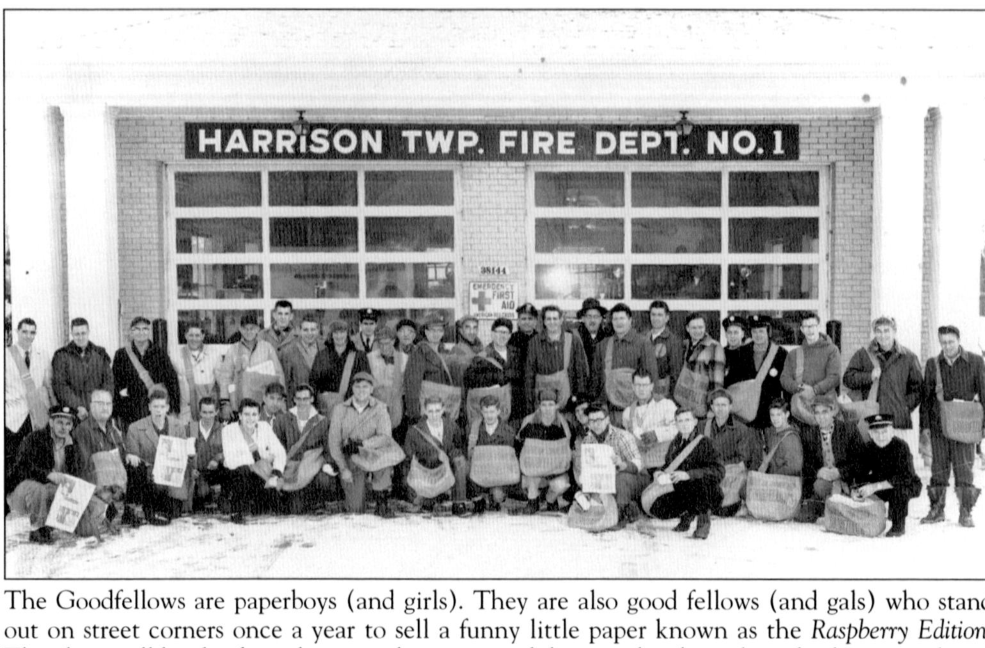

The Goodfellows are paperboys (and girls). They are also good fellows (and gals) who stand out on street corners once a year to sell a funny little paper known as the *Raspberry Edition*. They brave all kinds of weather, speeding cars, and drivers who show their displeasure at being inconvenienced. But they come right back next year. That is dedication to a cause, dedication to doing good deeds for others and for the community.

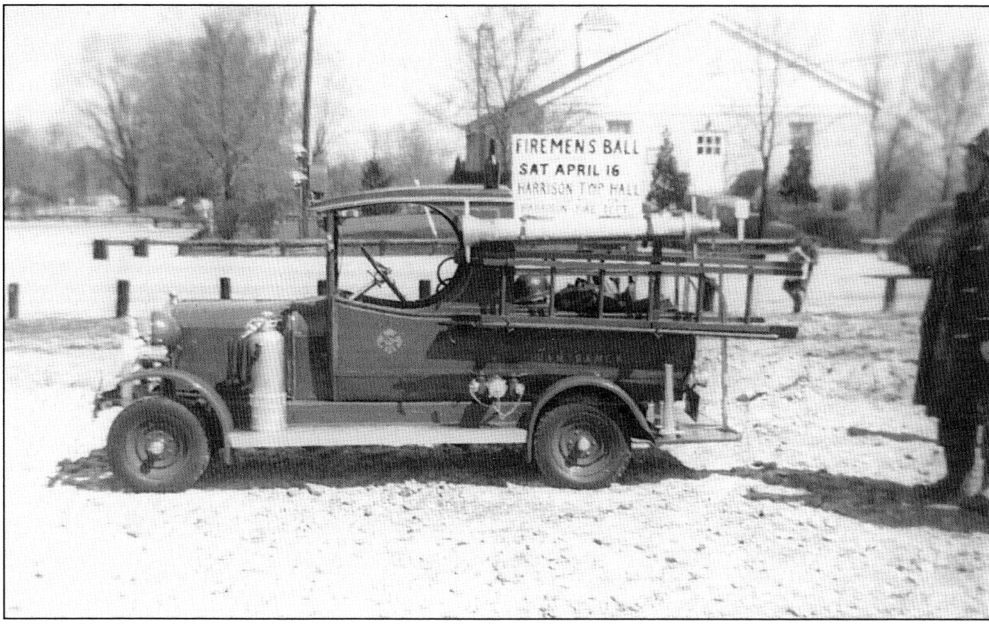

The first Annual Firemen's Ball was held on April 16, 1949 at the Harrison Township Hall. Sponsored by the Harrison Township Fire Department, the dance was semi-formal with an admission price of $1.00, tax included. The township fire department has a long-standing record of raising money for local residents and groups in need. From fundraising events like car washes to passing the boot, they work hard to benefit the community.

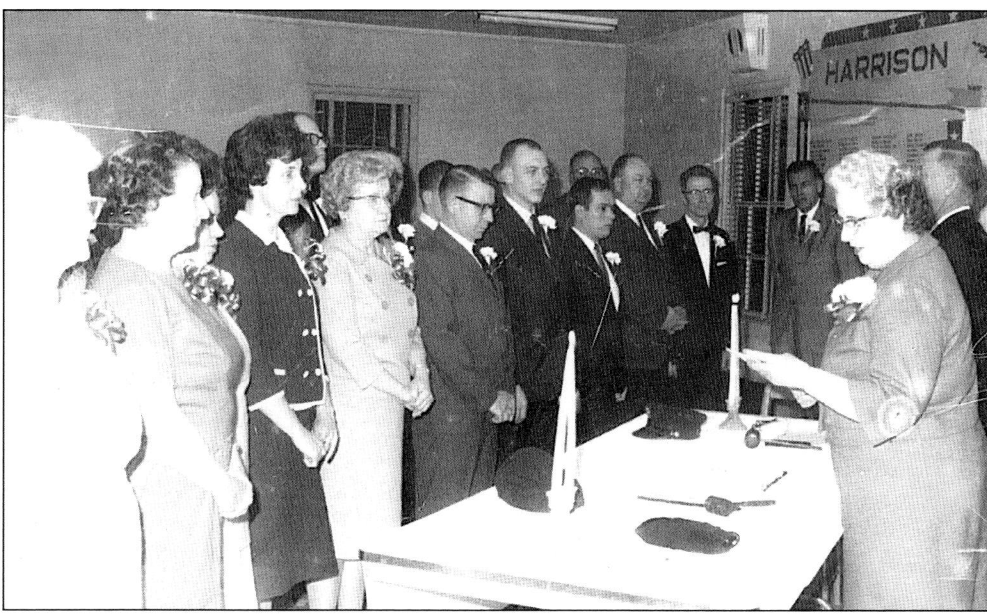

The Metropolitan Club, made up of local firemen, policemen, and postal workers, and the Ladies' Auxiliary were a moving force in the township in the mid-1900s. The officers shown here led the group in raising funds for such charities as the United Fund, Muscular Dystrophy, Red Cross, March of Dimes, Cancer Fund, and Heart Fund. They also supported organizations like the Goodfellows and Boy Scouts.

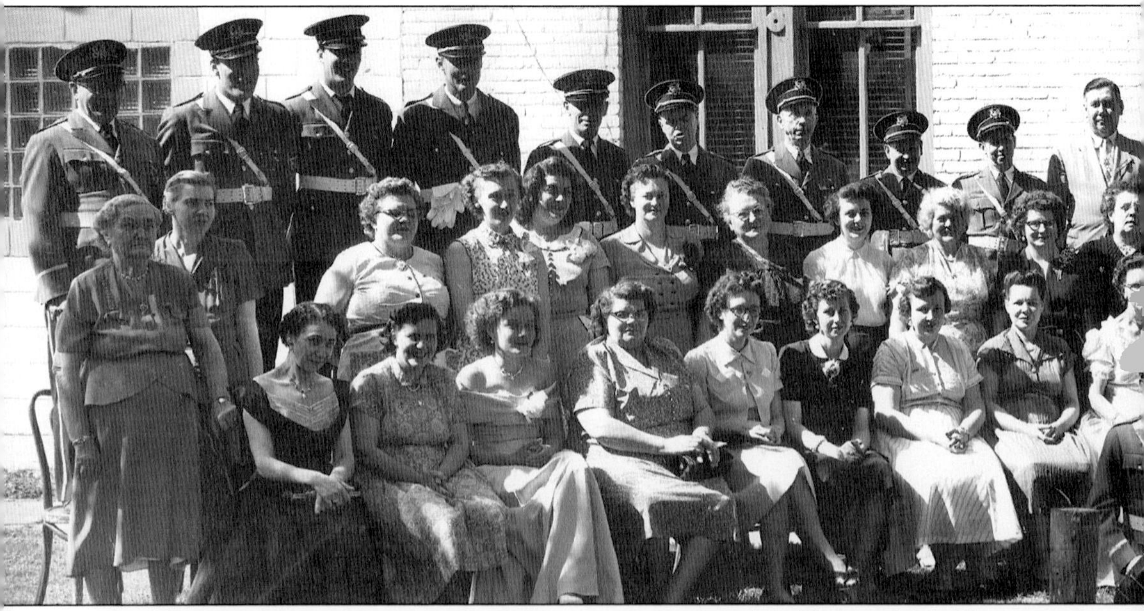

The Fraternal Order of Eagles has been happy since 1947 in the old Reimold farmhouse at the corner of South River and L'Anse Creuse. The non-profit, charitable organization, including the Ladies' Auxiliary, has 1,500 members. Although they added on to the clubhouse in 1950, if all the members show up at the same time, it will be standing room only. The Eagles are devoted to helping people and having fun while they do it. They hold fundraisers and are well known

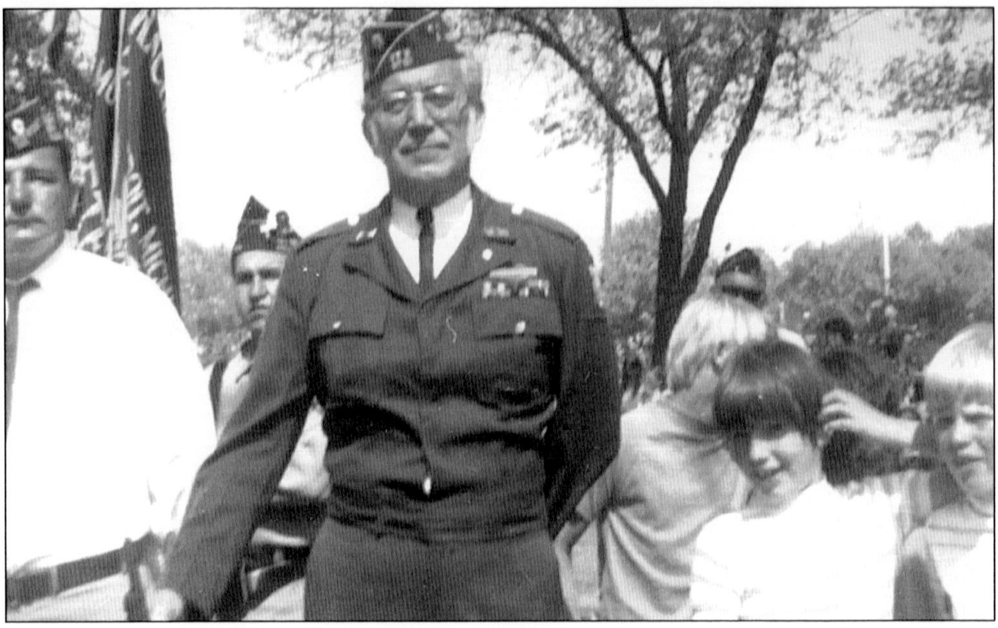

In the 1960s and '70s the population was smaller, and residents tended to get together to celebrate events like Memorial Day. The Harrison Township Veterans of War 3791 Memorial Day Parade was an anxiously anticipated chance to show community spirit. Here, VFW Commander Harold Cowan stands at attention during the 1971 parade, no matter what the distractions. After the parade, a reception was held in the basement of Rosso Memorial Hall.

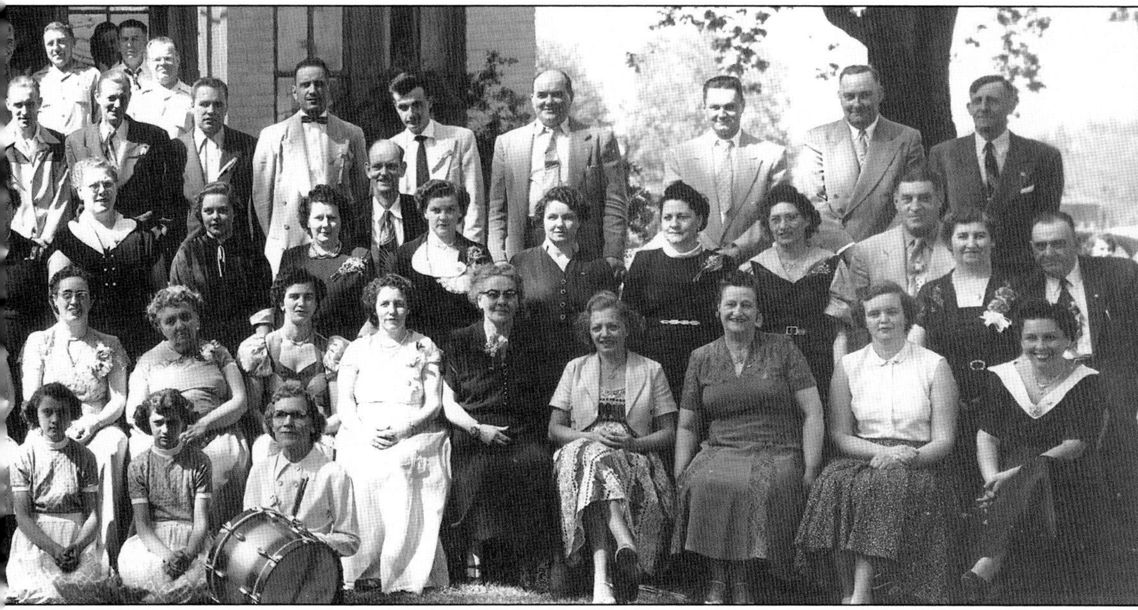

for their breakfasts, dinners, dances, and parties. They raise funds for local, county, and national charities, providing money for the activities of the Salvation Army, Care House, Turning Point, the township's Parks and Recreation Department, L'Anse Creuse High School band, Macomb County Sheriff's Department and many others.

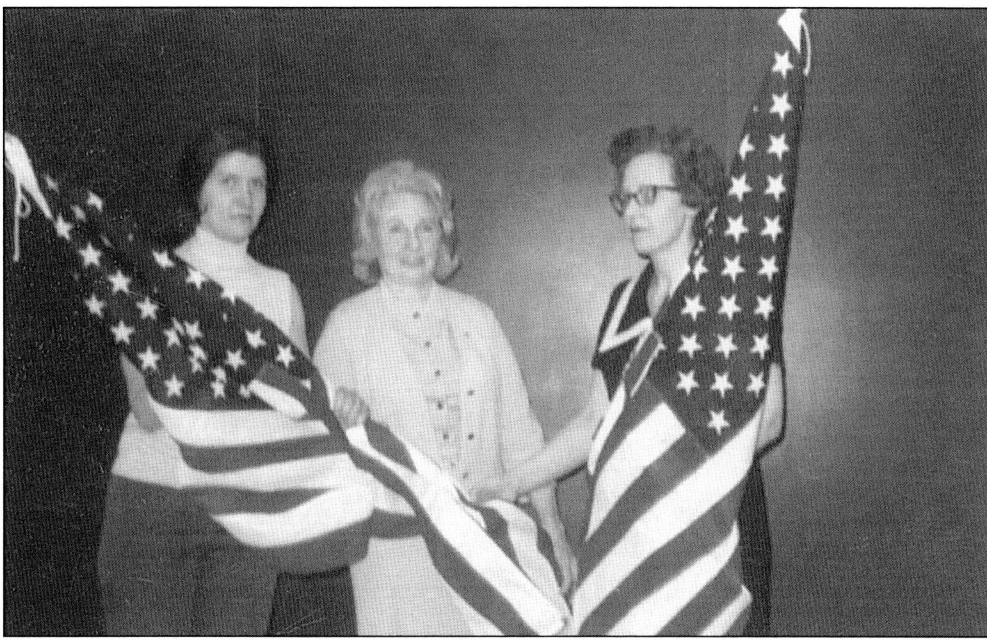

Members of the Veterans of Foreign Wars Ladies' Auxiliary Americana Chair, Virginia DeHate, and auxiliary president, Ruth Cowan, present two American flags to Girl Scout Leader Jean Holcomb for Girl Scout Troops 73 and 103 at Marie Graham School. Ruth Cowan was performing two roles since she was also a Girl Scout leader. The girls carried the new flags proudly in local parades.

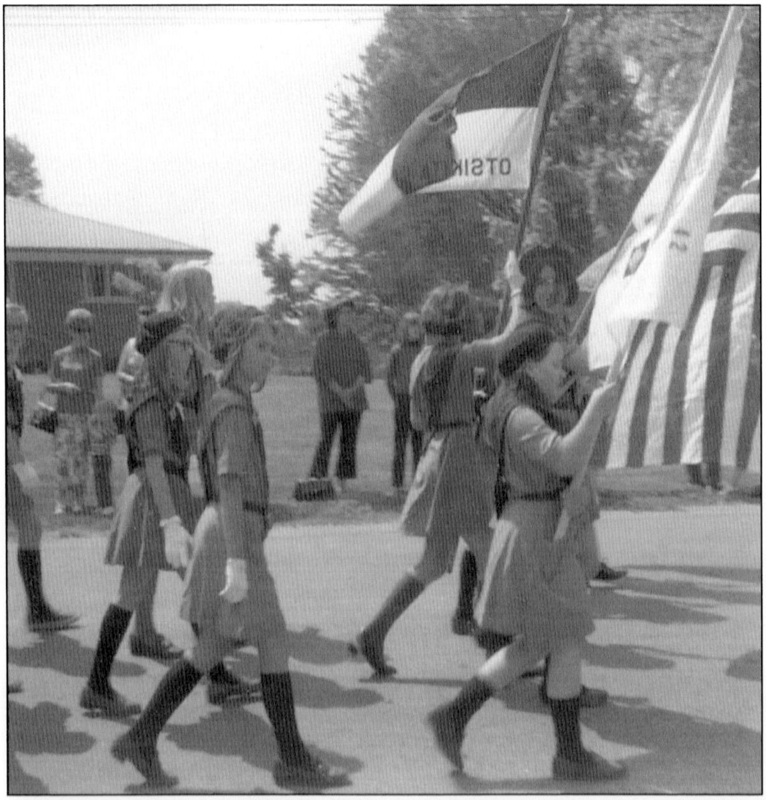

Scouting has changed in the last decades, but one concept remains the same. Girl Scout leaders work to prepare young women with the basics of living. Perhaps learning to build and cook over a campfire isn't quite as important as it once was, but telling a good, scary story is a useful skill. Citizenship and patriotism are never out of style. Creating something to be proud of can carry over into all aspects of life.

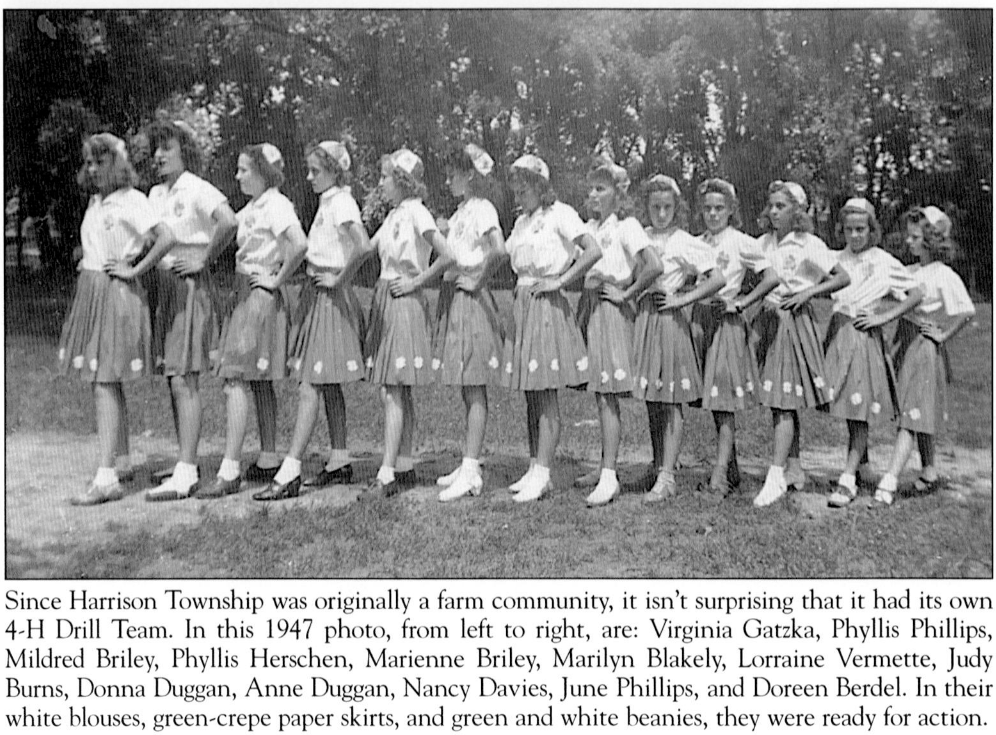

Since Harrison Township was originally a farm community, it isn't surprising that it had its own 4-H Drill Team. In this 1947 photo, from left to right, are: Virginia Gatzka, Phyllis Phillips, Mildred Briley, Phyllis Herschen, Marienne Briley, Marilyn Blakely, Lorraine Vermette, Judy Burns, Donna Duggan, Anne Duggan, Nancy Davies, June Phillips, and Doreen Berdel. In their white blouses, green-crepe paper skirts, and green and white beanies, they were ready for action.

Nine

Then and Now

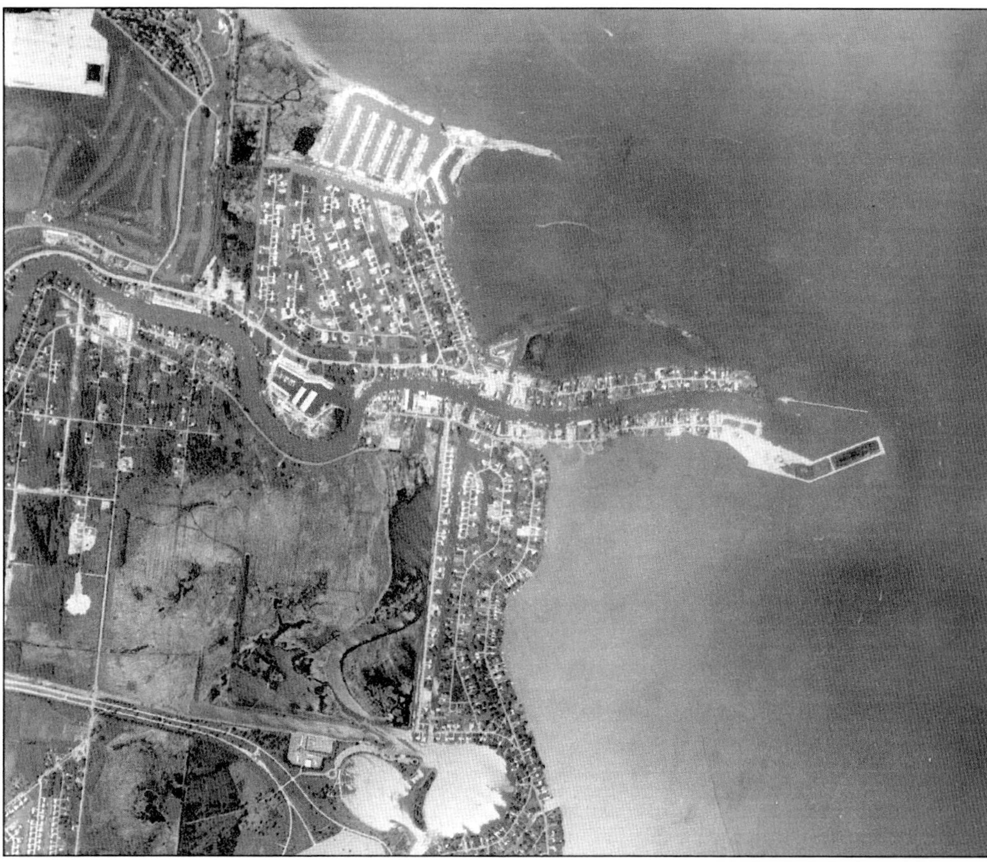

The township has changed greatly in the last three centuries. The Native Americans called the river that ran through their wilderness the Nottawasippee. Luckily, early settlers dubbed the river that flowed beside their farmlands the Huron. When the rivers called Huron in the area became confusing, the First Legislative Council of the Territory of Michigan officially renamed it the Clinton on July 17, 1824.

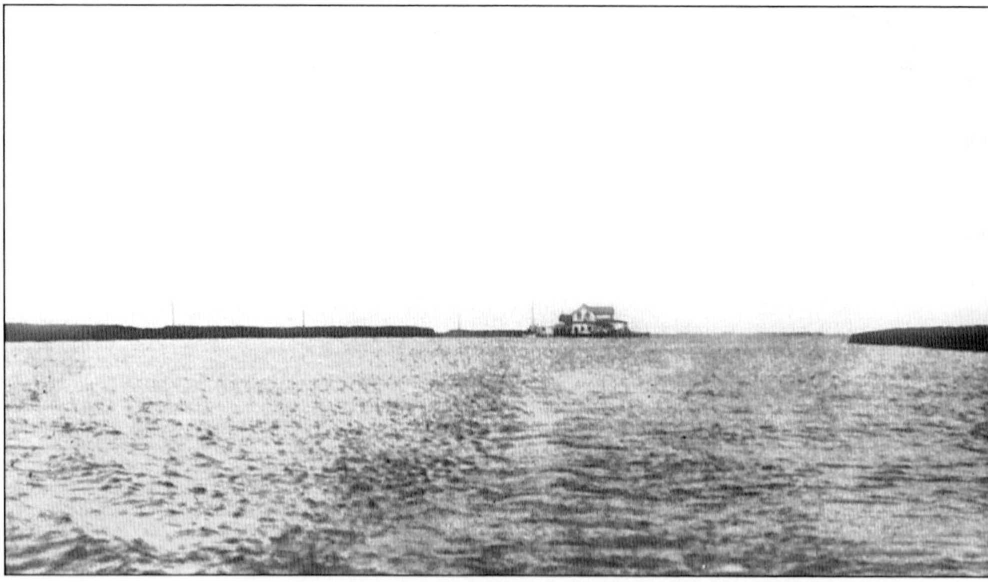

The mouth of the Clinton River has changed over the years. What was marsh is now dry land. The cement break wall has extended the north side farther into the lake. Above, the river in 1900 had only one building, and it was on stilts. The Mount Clemens Hunting and Fishing Club stood alone. While excursion boats brought passengers down the river, pleasure boats were hard to find. Even fishing boats were often towed out to the lake, four or five tied together, since motors were expensive. Today, the mouth of the river is an active place. Marinas crowd the south side, and the DNR launch site attracts small boats and fishermen. The north side is residential with only a few vacant lots. On a sunny, weekend day, pleasure boats clog the river, both coming and going.

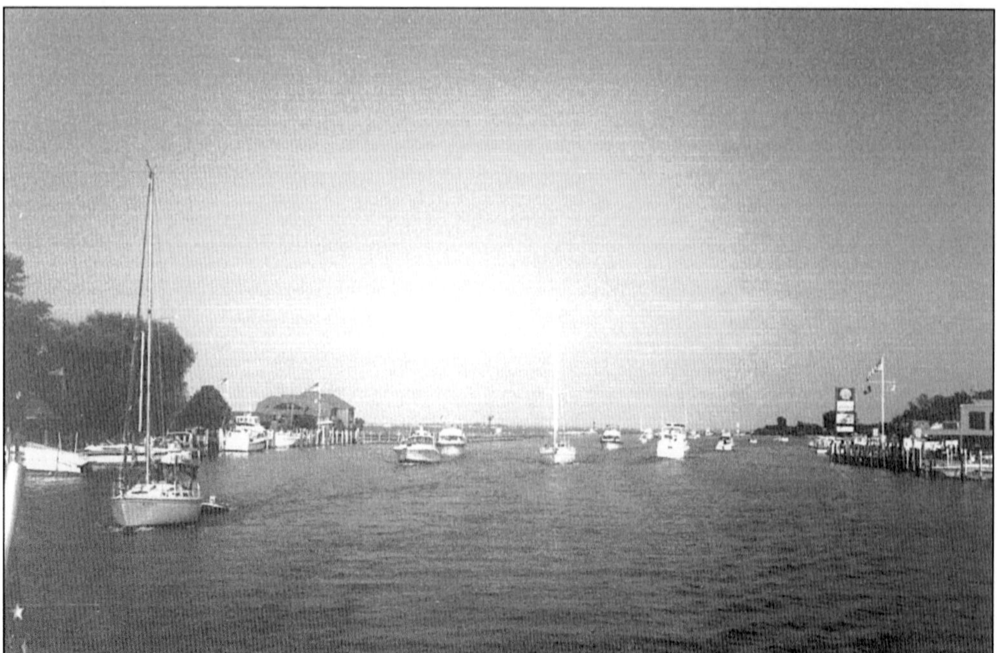

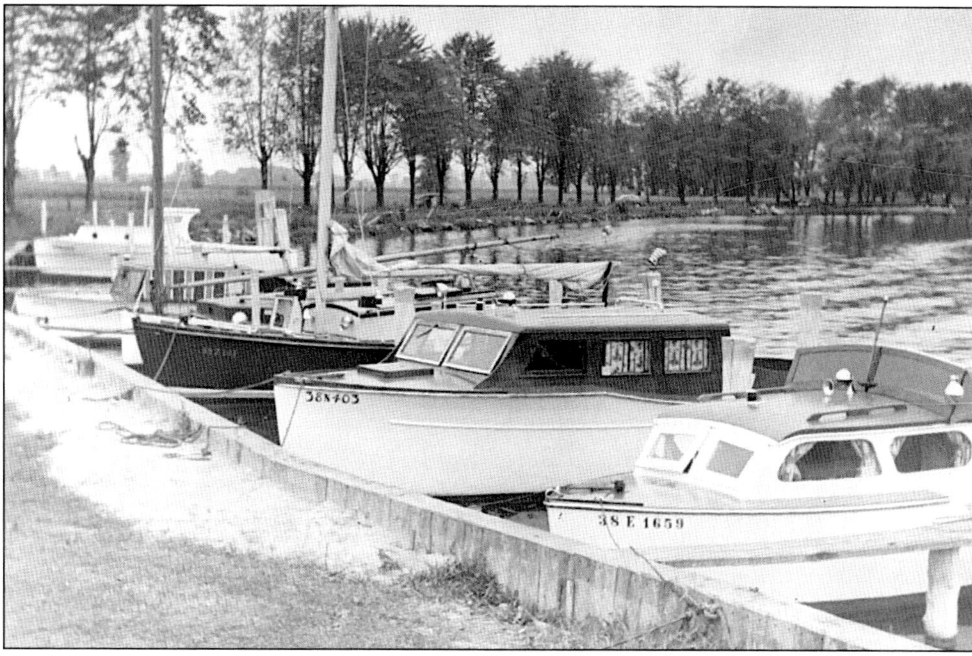

In the late 1700s, when Louis Campau squatted on 280 arpens of land on the Huron (Clinton) River, he could never have imagined that his action would result in several decades of legal battles between his descendants. His grandson, Joseph Campau, however, died in 1862, leaving nine children with complaints that involved, "mercenary ends, extreme and repeated cruelty, fraud and undue influence, and pretence" (mostly aimed at one brother-in-law) that would keep the property tied up for many years. By the end of the 1880s, the court cases were finally settled and restitution made. The property was divided and after several changes in ownership, 31631 South River Road was known as Turowski's Summer Docking, seen above. Today the cozy, little marina, below, is owned by Brian Wegner and called the Riverbend Marina.

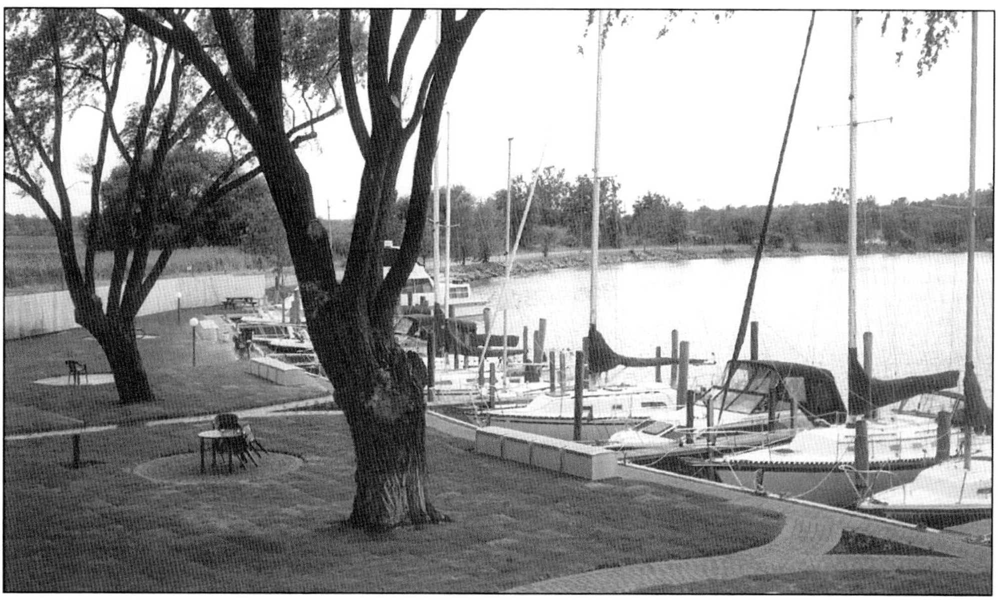

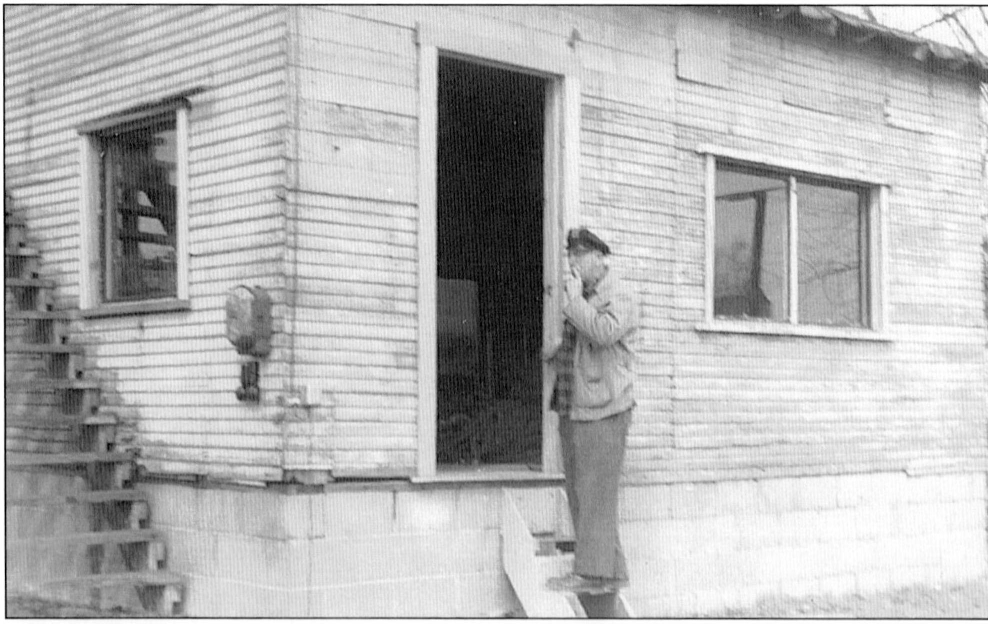

Today's new marinas are all glitz and amenities. In the 1940s and 1950s, however, they were simple and just provided a service, taking care of boats. The Clinton River Marina, above, started with an old carriage house with a chicken coop upstairs. George Aston, seen here, wasn't worried about swimming pools or tennis courts. He just converted old military towboats to pleasure boats. Later he added rental wells and began servicing the relatively few boats on the river. He must have been doing something right because the business passed down to his son, Jack, and now to his grandson, Steve. The photo below shows that the carriage house has stood the test of time. The marina recently suffered a setback, however, when only a quarter of the leased land it sits on was renewed. The location may be smaller, but the boaters in need will still find a smiling Aston ready to help.

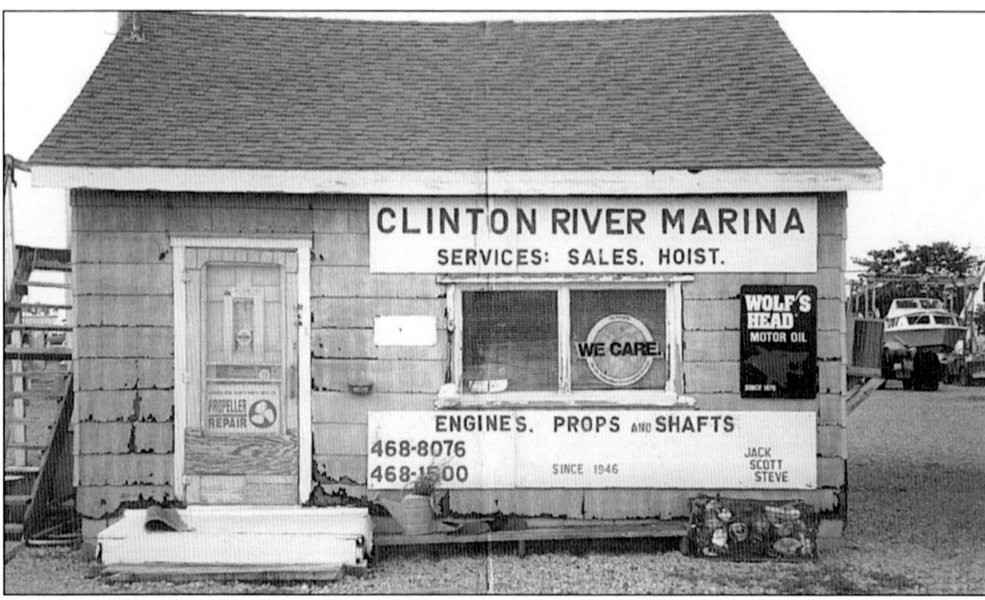

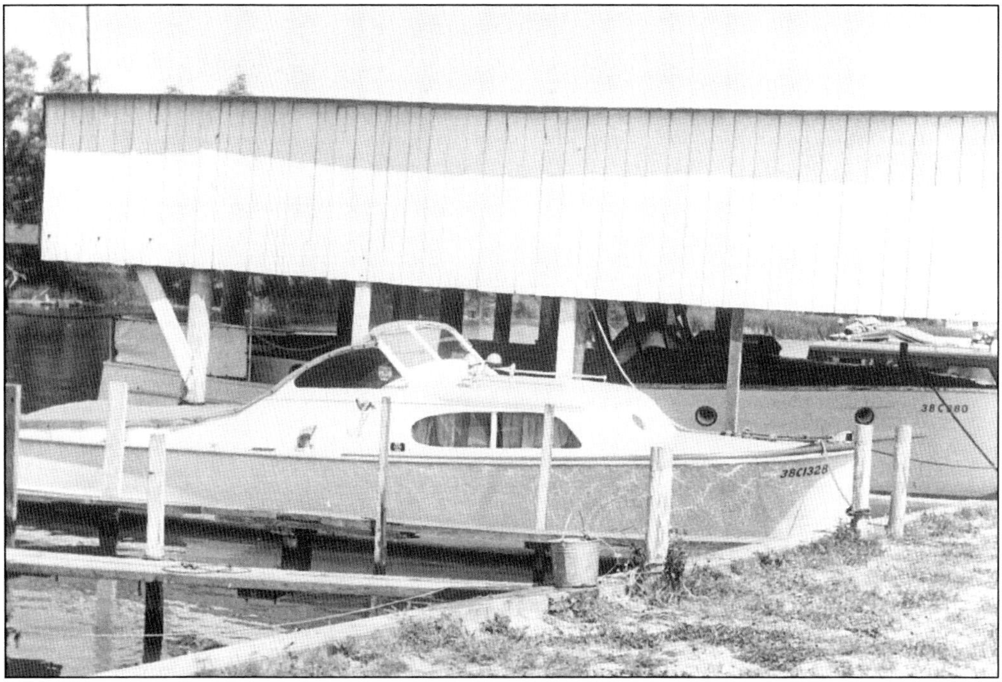

Where there are boats, there are bound to be boathouses. Most are just serviceable covers to keep the boats out of the elements. Some are built to cover hoists because boats on the lake need to be hauled up and out of the wave action. The boathouse above was on the Clinton River and was an adequate cover. Today, however, boathouses have become decorative. The boathouse below on the Black River is boat cover, sun awning, sunbathing platform, and patriotic statement. It's also a great place to watch the boats on their way to and from Metropolitan Beach and people watch the activities at the picnic and shore-fishing area.

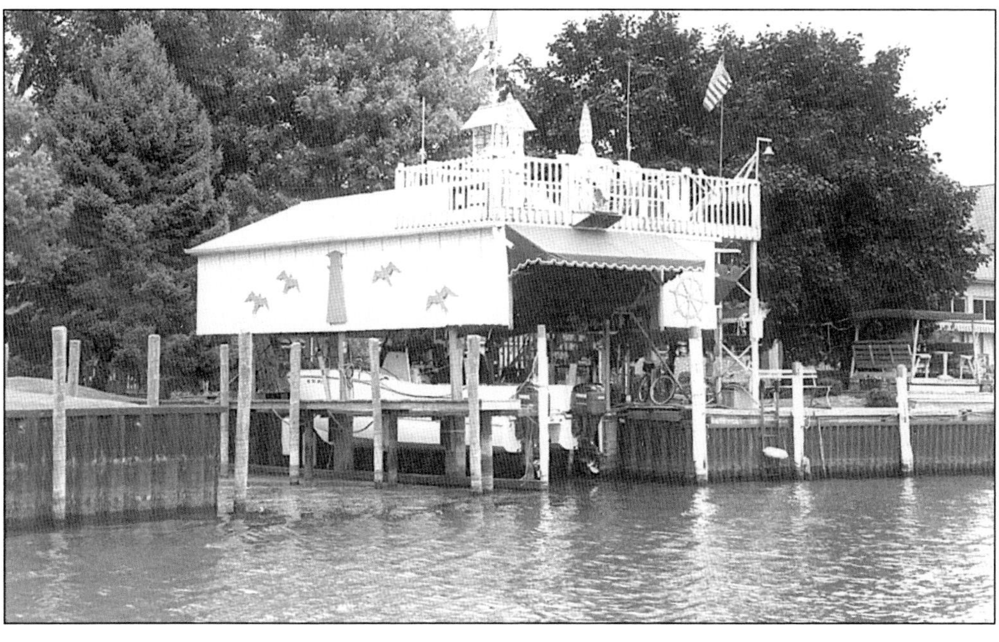

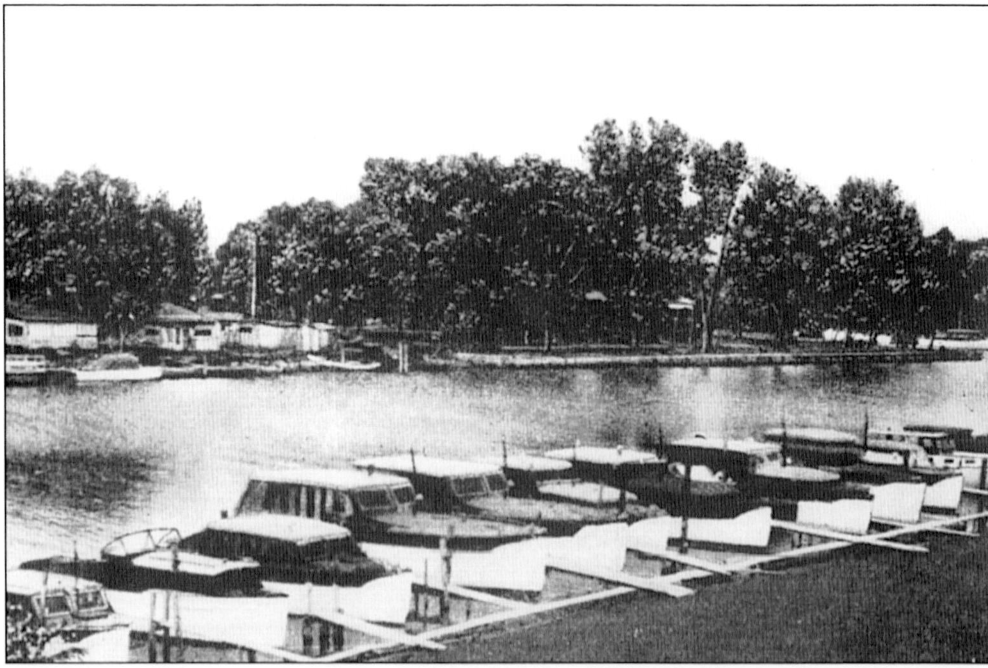

Early marinas were not too hard to build and maintain. Throw in a few pilings. Grab some boards for the walkways. Maybe even cut the grass now and then. As the years went by, pleasure boats became more prevalent, and marinas became more elaborate. A clubhouse, power and water outlets at every well, good lighting, a pool, a tennis court, a laundry—the list goes on. Boats have changed, and the time people spend on them has, too. In many cases the family boat is also the family cottage. Business transactions are formalized and finalized on boats. If people want to be on the water but can't afford a boat and its upkeep, they buy a personal watercraft. The lake on a beautiful day is often more crowded than the freeway at rush hour.

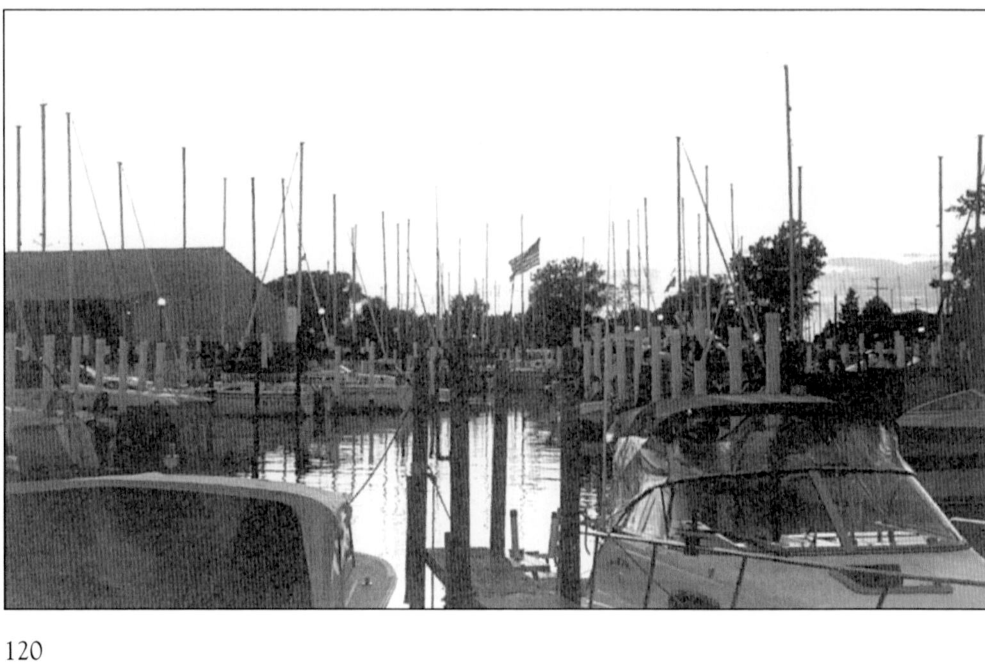

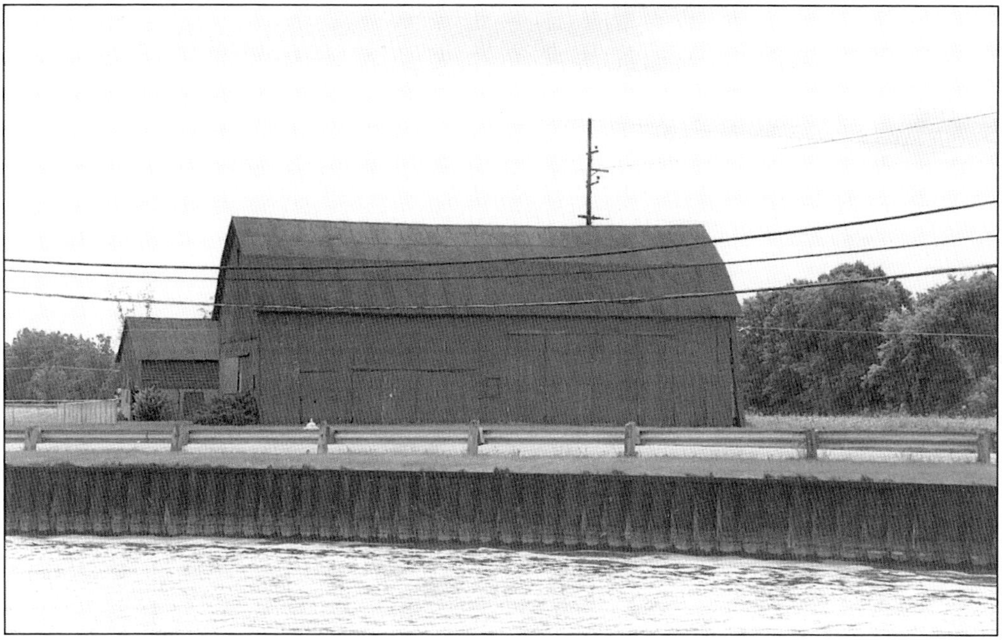

When the Harrison Township Historical Commission started sponsoring boat cruises on the river, the Blum barn seen above was a special feature of the historic narration. Believed to be the last existing barn in the township to be built with wooden pegs rather than nails, it was a symbol of a legacy that was all too quickly disappearing. Today the barn is gone and the River Bend Subdivision, pictured below, which replaced it is one of the many new developments that continue to draw new residents to the waterfront. It is a symbol of the changing face of the community and the diversity that comes with any kind of change.

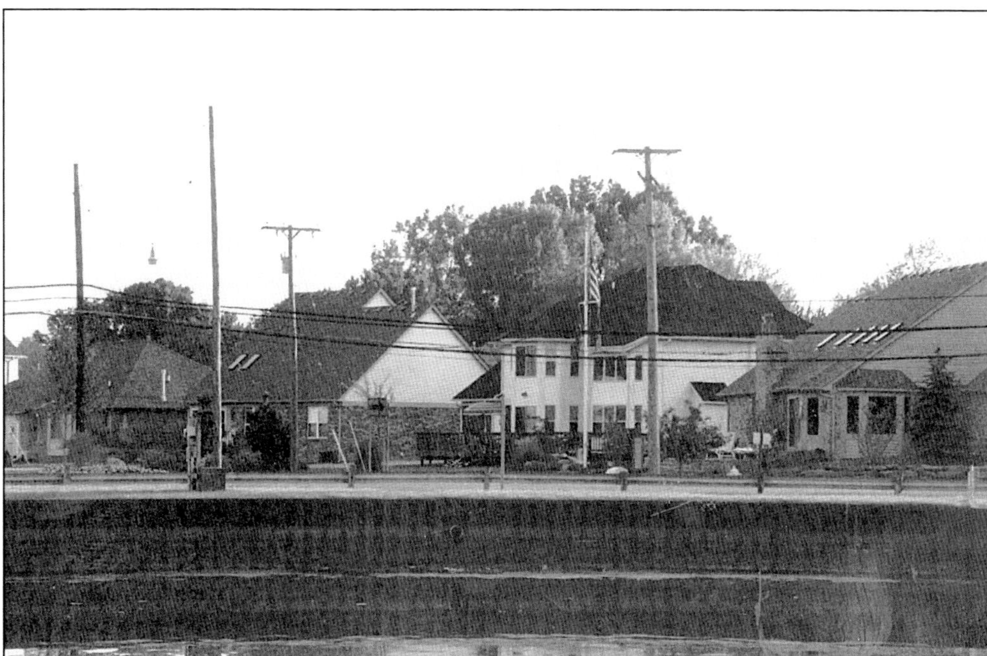

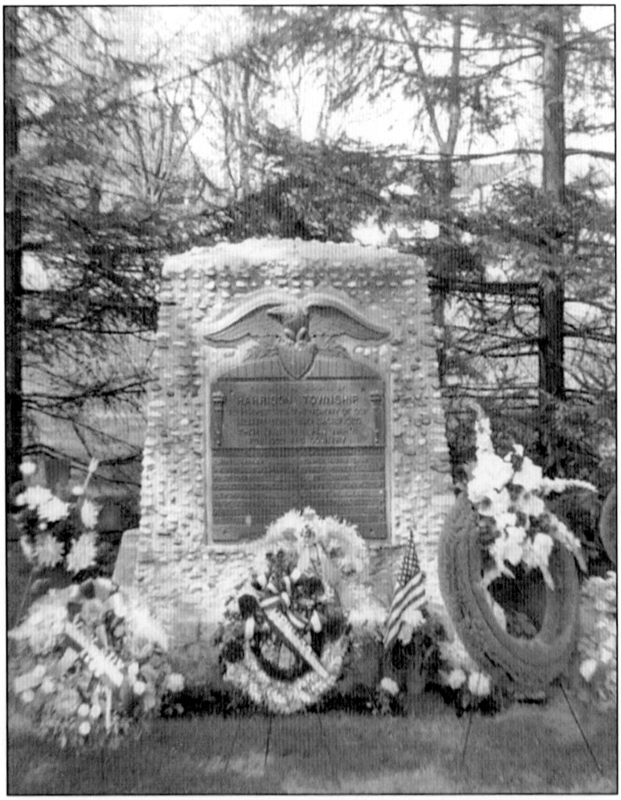

The original War Memorial, on the left, was donated to the township by the Snay-Beuschlein Post 3791. The inscription reads, "To honor the memory of the men from Harrison Township who served in the armed forces and gave their lives to preserve our freedom and way of life." There are 20 names on the marker. Today's monument to the men and women who have served in the military, below, has hundreds of names. The wall of honor was created by the Beautification Commission to pay tribute to the township's servicemen and women, living and dead. This book was created in September of 2001, when America is experiencing a time of heightened patriotism. Our military forces are facing a very real war against terrorism. The importance of these monuments and people goes beyond words.

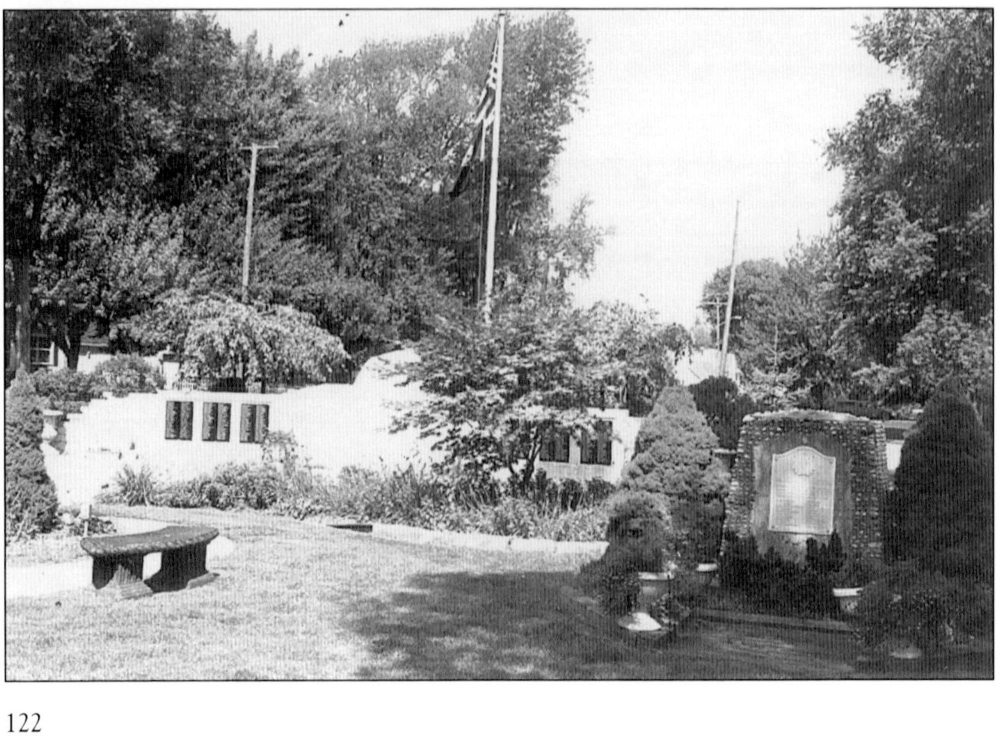

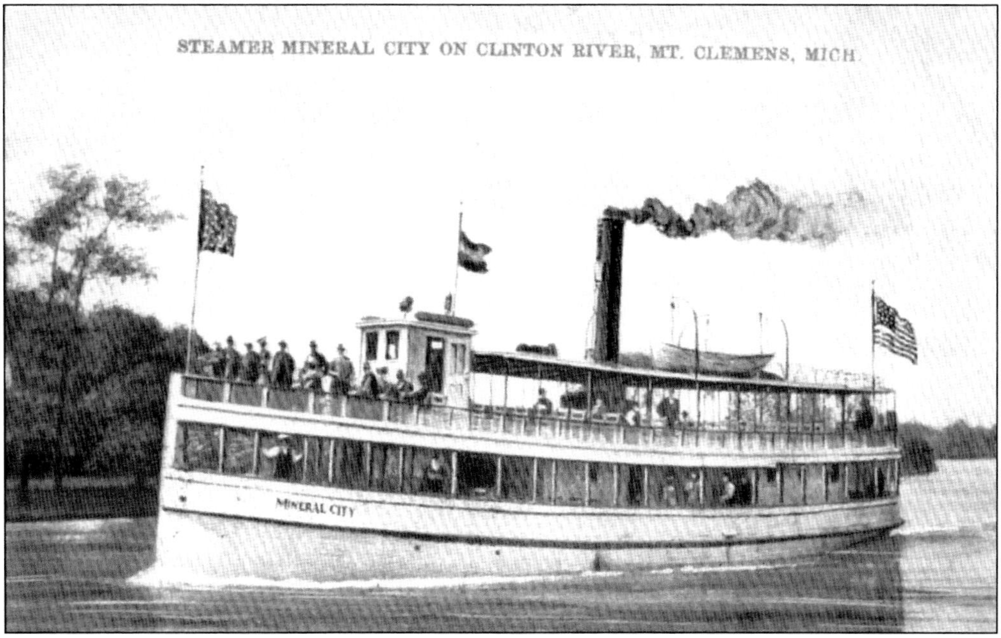

During the "Bath City Era" of Mount Clemens, excursion boats ran daily to take visitors to Walpole Island, Detroit, and the St. Clair Flats, to name only a few of the area's hot spots. The *Mineral City*, shown above, was one of many boats which held hundreds of passengers. Other ships to travel the Clinton were the *Roberta*, the *Bath City*, the *Mascotte*, the *Arrowana*, and the *Red Star*. Since 1990, the Clinton River again has an excursion boat. It is called the *Clinton*, and it carries 41 passengers. The Clinton River Cruise Line had so much success with the small boat that in 1994, they added the *Clinton Friendship*. The double-decker, seen below, carries 149 passengers and caters to groups for historical cruises, weddings, receptions, and organizational outings. The trip down the river can include lunch, dinner, and/or a live band.

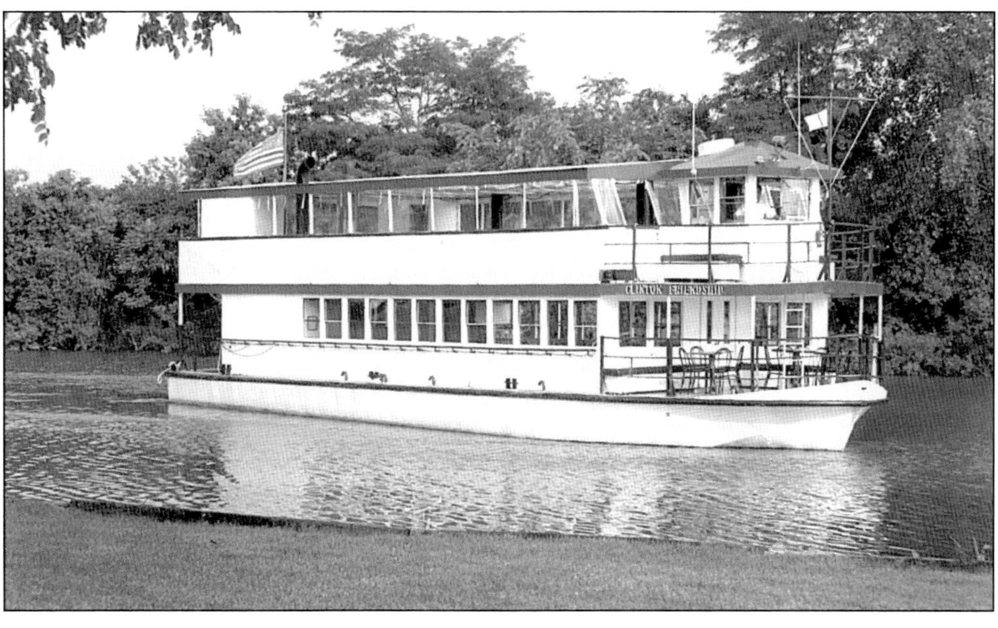

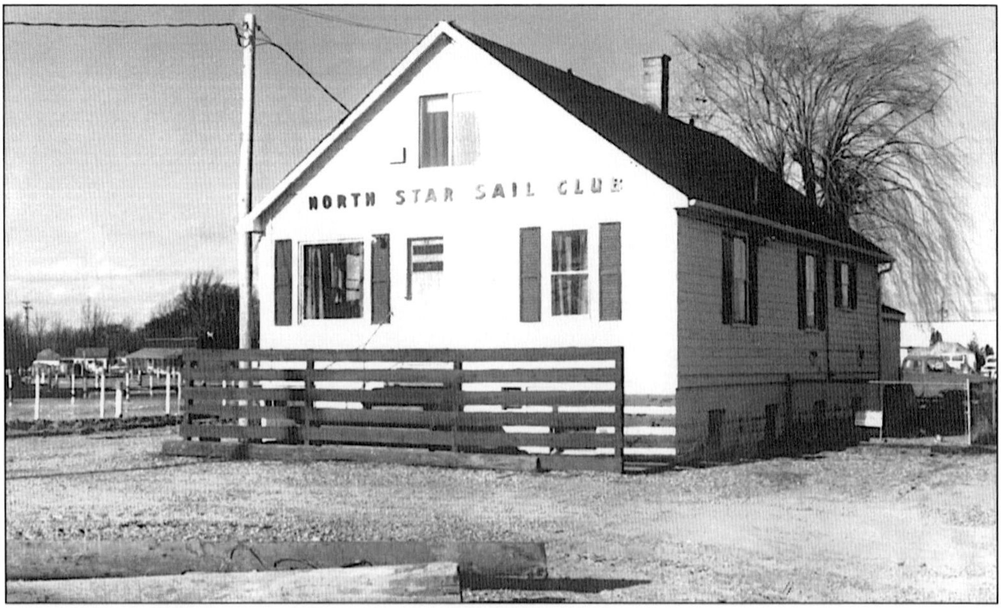

A decade of looking for a proper home led the North Star Sail Club to their current location on the south side of the Clinton River. After moving from location to location on the Detroit River, the group finally found their clubhouse in 1957. The photo above shows the original building after substantial work had been done to clean up the property. Although the move to this area created a drop in membership, interest soon grew, making it necessary to impose a limit of 150 members in 1967. In the 1970s, the cap was raised to 160, and planning for a new clubhouse began. The original "dream clubhouse" was designed and rejected as too costly. New plans were drawn up, and construction began. The photo below shows the club as it exists today.

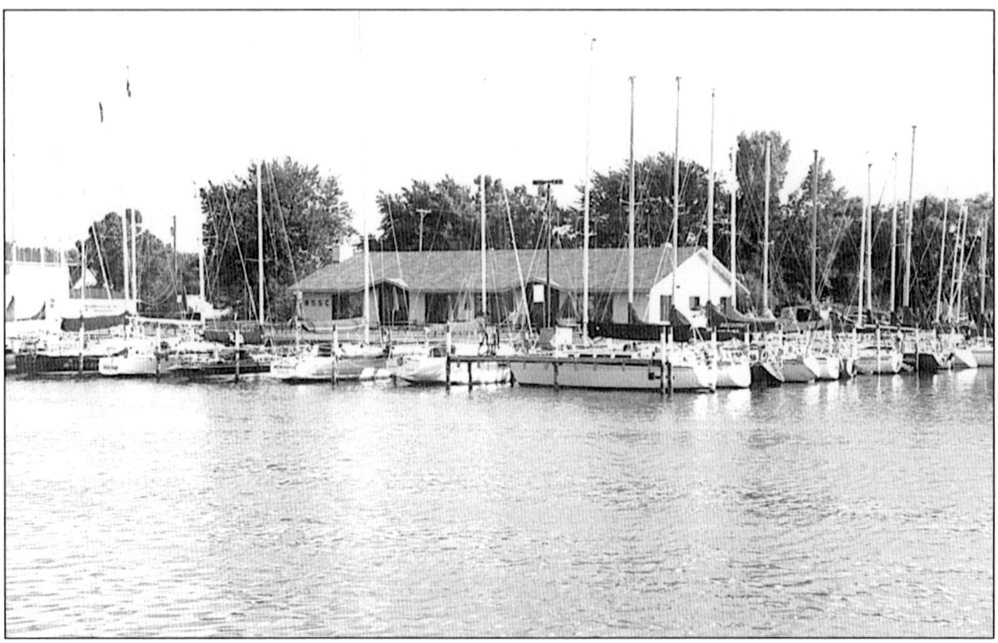

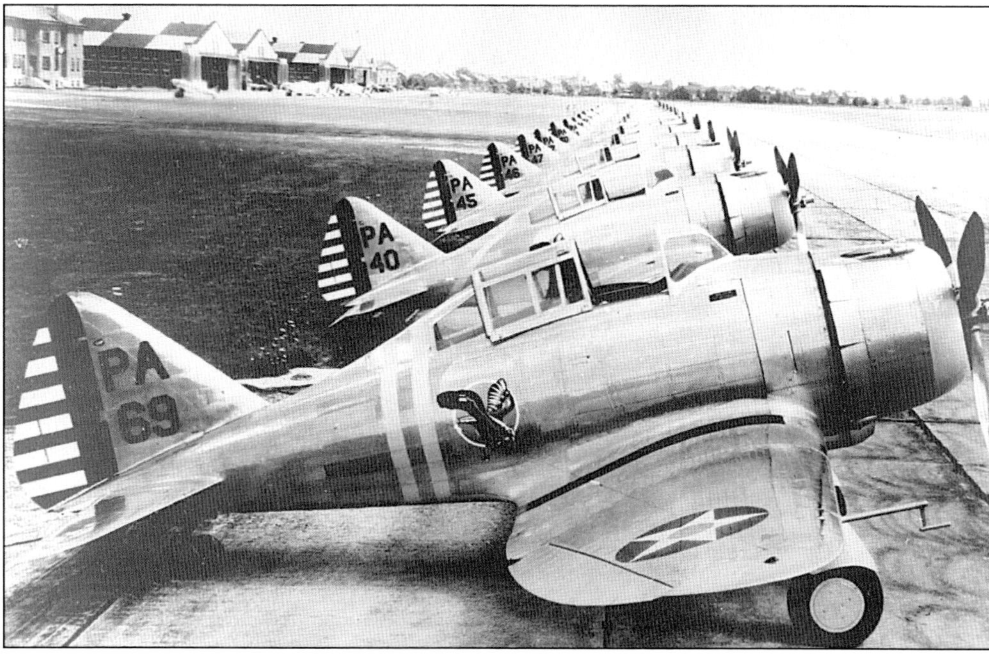

The airplane came a long way from Thomas Selfridge's fatal flight to the sleek Sevesky P-35, shown above, in 1937. It was considered quite a plane in the 1930s, but it still had to make regular fuel stops. The F-16 Fighting Falcon, pictured below, only needs a KC-135 Stratotanker in the area. Since the Stratotanker can fly at near supersonic speeds and refuel at altitudes in excess of 40,000 feet, the Falcon doesn't even have to slow down or descend to fuel-guzzling lower altitudes. No doubt, military capabilities have come farther than any of the early Selfridge residents could have imagined.

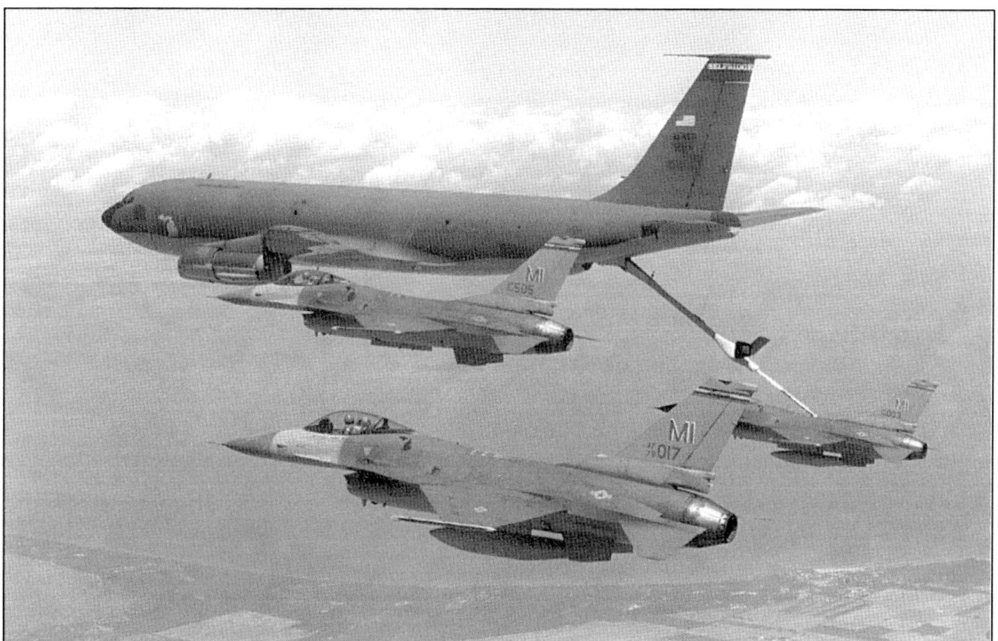

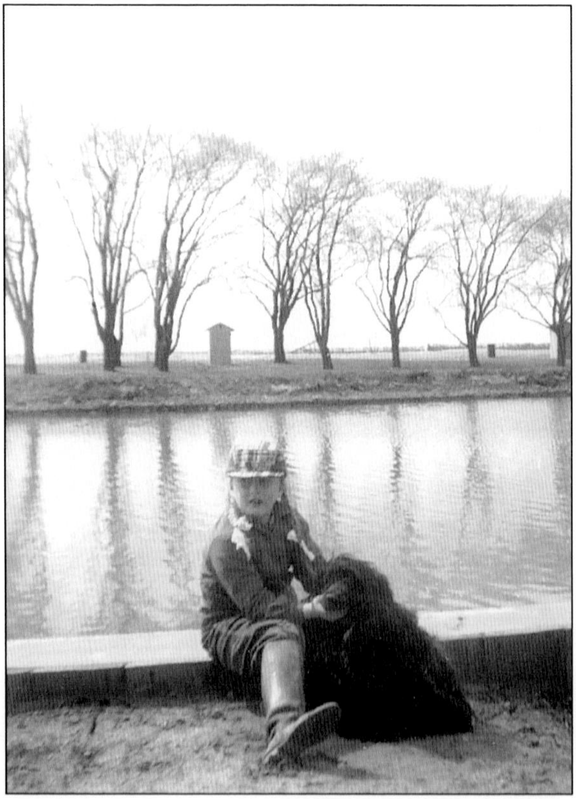

"The Huron-Clinton Metropolitan Authority was established in 1940 for the preservation of the scenic beauty and recreational opportunities inherent in the valleys of the Huron and Clinton rivers," according to an early park brochure. In a survey of the day, swimming was ranked second to picnicking in ratings of active and passive recreation. The plan called for the planting of thousands of trees to provide shaded picnic areas. One of those areas became known as "Huron Point." When Arlene Rood took her dog, Heli, to sit by the seawall in 1958, those trees were not providing much shade. The facilities were a little lacking as well. Originally known as a bird sanctuary, the Point, below, is now a great place for fishermen, picnickers, roller bladers, and bikers to enjoy the beauty of a natural setting.

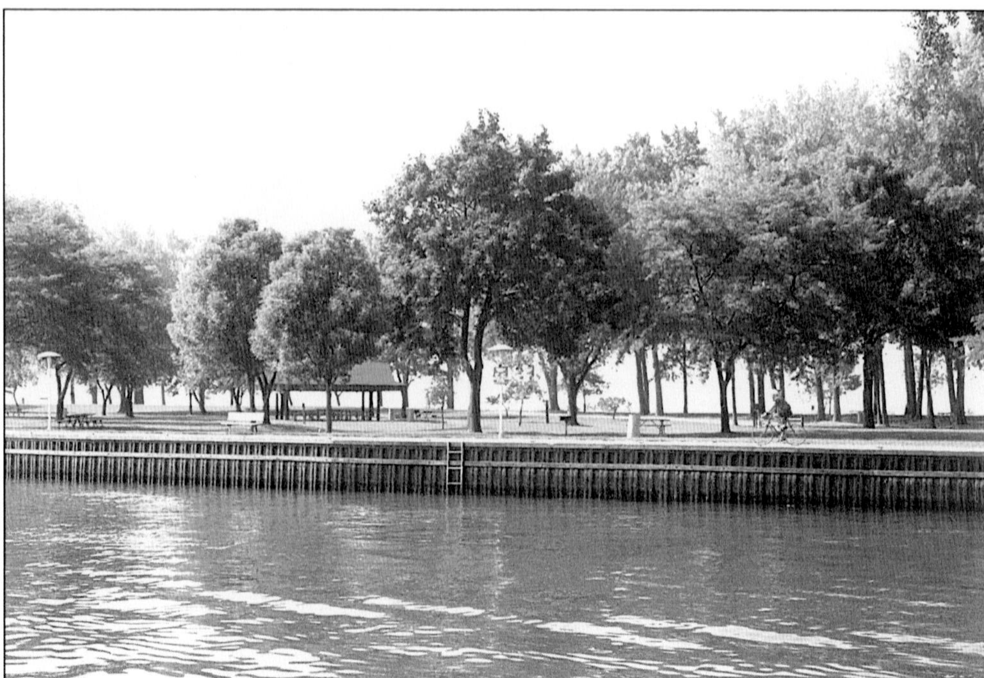

Index